How Anyone can make Money Trading Shares

The Naked Trader
2nd Edition

Robbie Burns

UNICORN BOOKS
BUSINESS

Publishers

UNICORN BOOKS

J-3/16, Daryaganj, New Delhi-110002

☎ 23275434, 23272783/84 • Fax: 011-23260518

E-mail: unicornbooks@vsnl.com • *Website:* www.unicornbooks.in

Distributors

Pustak Mahal®, Delhi

J-3/16, Daryaganj, New Delhi-110002

☎ 23276539, 23272783, 23272784 • *Fax:* 011-23260518

E-mail: info@pustakmahal.com • *Website:* www.pustakmahal.com

Sales Centres

■ 10-B, Netaji Subhash Marg, Daryaganj, New Delhi-110002

☎ 23268292, 23268293, 23279900 • *Fax:* 011-23280567

E-mail: salespmahal@airtelmail.in • *E-mail:* rapidexdelhi@indiatimes.com

■ **Hind Pustak Bhawan**

6686, Khari Baoli, Delhi-110006

☎ 23944314, 23911979

Branch Offices

Bengaluru: ☎ 22234025 • *Telefax:* 22240209

E-mail: pustak@airtelmail.in • pustak@sancharnet.in

Mumbai: ☎ 22010941

E-mail: rapidex@bom5.vsnl.net.in

Patna: ☎ 3294193 • *Telefax:* 0612-2302719

E-mail: rapidexptn@rediffmail.com

Hyderabad: *Telefax:* 040-24737290

E-mail: pustakmahalhyd@yahoo.co.in

First edition by the name The Naked Trader was published in Great Britain in 2005 by Harriman House. Revised edition printed in 2007 and reprinted in 2008.

Author photos by Jim Marks

Cartoons by Roy Mitchell

ISBN 978-81-7806-172-6

Edition: 2010

Printed at : Param Offsetters, Okhla, New Delhi

Contents

About The Author

Robbie Burns has been a journalist and writer since he graduated from Harlow Journalism College in 1981. After starting life as a reporter and editor for various local newspapers, from 1988-1992 he was editor of ITV and Channel 4's teletext services. He also wrote ITV's daily teletext soap opera "Park Avenue" for 5 years. He then went on to freelance for various newspapers including *The Independent* and *The Sun*, and also helped set up a financial news service for CNN. In 1997, he became editor for BSkyB's teletext services and set up their shares and finance service. While there he also set up various entertainment phone lines in conjunction with BSkyB including a "Buffy The Vampire Slayer" phoneline which made him nearly £250,000.

He left full-time work in 2001 to trade and run his own businesses, which included a café in London that he sold, doubling his money on the initial purchase. While at BSkyB, Robbie broadcast a diary of his share trades which became hugely popular. He transferred the diary to his website, www.nakedtrader.co.uk, which became one of the most read financial websites in the UK. Between 2002 and 2005, he wrote a column for *The Sunday Times*, 'My DIY Pension', featuring share buys and sells made for his pension fund which he runs himself in a SIPP. He managed to double the money in his pension fund from £40,000 to £80,000 in under three years as chronicled in the *Sunday Times*. By mid 2007 he doubled it again, reaching £165,000. Robbie now writes a weekly column for the leading financial website, ADVFN.com.

Robbie has made a tax free profit of well over £500,000 from trading shares since 1999, and has made a profit every year, even during the market downturn of 2000-2002. Public trades made for his website have made more than £400,000.

He lives in a riverside apartment on the Thames with his wife, Elizabeth, son Christopher and cat Diddle. His hobbies include chess, running, swimming, horse racing, and trading shares from his bedroom, erm... naked. After all, he wouldn't be seen dead in a thong...

Acknowledgements

Thanks to my wife Elizabeth for her support and putting up with me moaning constantly while I was writing the book. It's like putting together a giant jigsaw puzzle and often it drove me crackers. Thanks to Roy for the great cartoons. Also thanks to all the contributors to the success and failure stories. Thanks also to my editor, Stephen Eckett, for his always valuable contributions – and for making sure everything is as accurate as it can be. If there are any spelling misstakes they are his fault and not mine, OK?

Part 1
Introduction

"Money can't buy friends, but you can get a better class of enemy."

- *Spike Milligan*

Welcome To The Crazy World Of Shares

Ever wondered whether you could make money by buying and selling shares? And maybe eventually quitting that damn job to do it? Being able to tell the boss to stuff it?

I think you can – whatever your age, job, status or character defects!

I did it. And honestly I am not a planet-brain, not great at maths and pretty lazy! So if I did it you can too!

This book is going to be your best friend if you want to learn how to make money from shares. I'll reveal to you common sense stock market knowledge that's taken me years to learn. You can learn from the things I've got right – and learn even more from the things I've got wrong. And things other people have got right and wrong too.

Oh, and don't worry – I speak plain English, not the financial gobbledegook others hide behind.

I hope you'll gain from my experiences without having to trawl through a lot of boring old financial twaddle found in so many books about the market.

No need for wet towels

If you're standing in a bookshop flicking through finance books and wondering which one to get – what the hell are you waiting for? Buy this one! Have you no sense? This book is a bargain!

Just look at the others around you! Full of meaningless gobbledegook. Bollinger Bands, moving average divergences, graphic equalisers (or is that just my hi-fi system?)

Have a thumb through some of the other books. See what I mean? There is so much... STUFF in them! And you know what happens to people who believe all of it – their heads get so full of STUFF they lose money and soon quit the markets. In other words…they get stuffed.

I believe simplicity is the key to making money. Keep the head clear of stuff and concentrate on the important things. That's what I will teach you.

You'll be glad to know if you buy this book I promise you'll understand every word of it. You won't read a couple of pages, sigh, and go: "I'll read it tomorrow", then put it on a dusty shelf never to be seen again (unless you move or sell it on eBay).

Put simply: this book will teach you everything you need to know about how to make money from shares without giving you a headache. I've got a low concentration threshold myself. If I can write it, you can read it!

Umm…what the hell was I writing about again? Oh yes –

I hope this book teaches you simply how you can make money in the markets even if you have never bought a share before. And even if you have bought one or quite a few, but can't seem to make the money you want to.

And it doesn't matter whether you're 22 or 72, I can teach you how to make money without you needing to put a wet towel around your head. (But if that's what you're into, OK, I'm a liberal guy.)

So *welcome along* to…**Naked Trader 2**

Why a second edition?

I'm a tad surprised to be writing this. After all when I'd finished the original Naked Trader book I pronounced: "Writing a book is far too much like hard work and I'm buggered if I'm going to be doing that again!"

And I really did think that – so why a second book?

Pure vanity and ego is all I can think of. It's not the money, not at £1.67 a copy (or 50p if you've bought this at the bookstore). Think you'll get rich writing financial books – think again!

You see at parties I can boast:

> *"What do I do? Oh well, darling, I've written two books..."*

I can also boast at the playground to the other parents as well as boasting anywhere else I get the chance. (Holding a party? Invite me and see how good I am at it.)

Seriously though, thankfully the original Naked Trader book became a best-seller, but it was starting to get a little out of date. Also, since I wrote it things have changed and I've learned many new things. So this book contains lots of new strategies and ideas.

So if you bought the first book and enjoyed it I hope you will like this one as much. There are tons of new things for those who read the original.

And if you didn't buy the first book, it has all the info you need in it to get started in trading.

Jargon-free, common sense advice

If you've never traded a share before it doesn't matter, as I'll guide you every step of the way. And if you have traded for a while and have made losses, I am confident I can put you on the road to long-term stock market success by getting rid of your bad habits.

If you have traded shares for a while but you're struggling to make money, I hope you'll find some of my strategies useful.

You won't find any inexplicable stock market jargon in this book – I write in plain English. You will not have to start scratching your head and think "what is he on about?" or "what the hell is a head and shoulders formation?" I'm going to explain how to buy and sell shares the easy way, and guide you to the winners. I'll be taking you through every step and explaining all the silly jargon.

The fact is stock market investment is easier than you think.

Brokers and tipsters love to spout the jargon because it makes them look clever, and to persuade you to part with your hard-earned money as a result of their 'advice'. But I'll guide you through all that nonsense so that *you* can make your own decisions and do your own research.

This is not a get rich quick book (sorry!)

One thing I certainly can't do is promise that £10,000 you have spare is going to become £100,000 overnight as a result of reading this book. You know those ads:

> *'Make £400 a day from the markets...'*

> *'Become a stock market millionaire with our software...'*

Come on, you know in your heart that when it sounds too good to be true – it is!

This book is about building your wealth slowly and surely – with realistic targets and time frames. Using discipline, good stock picking techniques and avoiding the mistakes new investors nearly always make, I believe I can make you richer. But you just aren't going to become a millionaire overnight.

Trading shares is an exciting roller coaster ride with plenty of thrills and spills. I really hope that excitement comes over in *Naked Trader 2.*

If you have never bought or sold a share before, I hope I'll arm you with the information you'll need to start trading. This includes everything from how to buy a share to getting real-time prices. Then I'll tell you everything I've learned over ten active years of trading. You'll learn what makes shares move and what to watch for before pressing that buy button. I can also reveal how to make money by backing shares to go *down.* And I hope to provide you with tons of useful info you just won't find anywhere else.

Whether you have a small amount to trade, or you've inherited a hundred thousand, I hope after reading *Naked Trader 2* you will be well armed to enter the fray.

So, get a cup of tea, put your feet up and welcome to the crazy world of shares. Oh, and don't forget the toast.

Escaping The Rat Race

My story

I quit the rat race in 2001 and have never looked back. I love my lifestyle. No moody bosses or targets. Just me! Of course there are no office politics – but I can live without them!

I can now sit in my office at home overlooking the Thames with my feet up putting on a trade here and there and relaxing. My wealth continues to build in the markets over time.

Lucky for me I realised working for someone else – unless you absolutely *love* what you do – is a mug's game. You're just there to pay the mortgage every month.

So while I worked for BSkyB I also worked for myself. I had a shiny Reuters machine on my desk (after the cleaner had been) and I learned everything about the markets through practice.

I quickly realised I could make a lot more money trading than in my full time job and so I could easily quit my job in 2001 to trade more or less full time. I decided to find ways of making money outside the full time job.

The delectable Buffy

So while at full time work I started to develop other income streams which, bizarrely, included a "Buffy The Vampire Slayer" information line which made me £250,000 over 4 years!

That involved me reading out the latest "Buffy" news on my phone at home – and eager viewers would call the line and I made money out of each call. Sadly the series ended in 2000, and so with it the line.

I started it for a bit of a laugh...but on its first day the guy who owned the phone company called me and said: "Bugger me, it's just taken £400!"

Happiness is...residual income

And I sold mobile phones and cut price phone calls and energy for a company called Telecom Plus. And still do now actually from time to time via my website. I got – and still get – a cut of every phone call made or energy used by customers – it's called residual income and it pays all my bills even now. So I still earn from customers I sold to in 1999! For more info on Telecom Plus and how to earn new income, press the "Escape" button on my website. If you fancy making some money yourself after you read the piece about residual income, just email me and I'll fill you in on how to do it.

Armed, therefore, with a huge pile of cash, I quit my job and decided to trade full time.

Waiter, there's a fish in my fish pie

However, I did want a bit of a fallback in case I wasn't such a great trader. So I bought a café near a tube station in Fulham. That proved a lot of fun and I made quite a bit of money (my wife and I changed it so it made £1,000 a day instead of £300) and it got very successful.

So successful that it actually became a pain in the neck. More customers, that led to more staff, that led to more problems. Classic growing pains.

Sometimes staff didn't turn up and I found myself making coffees at 7am! It involved all kinds of problems: Firing staff; talking to customers complaining there was fish in their fish pie; and dealing with all the mess a café brings.

The worst time I remember was when all the staff were sick and I was on my own behind the counter trying to deal with a large queue of people.

So I shouted out to the café: "I need help! Anyone want a short-term job?£10 an hour." And one of the customers came to my rescue and started serving. There was a lovely community spirit and I met a lot of great people.

But with my son arriving on the scene it became too much effort to run it and enough was enough.

I had originally intended it to be the start of a chain and I nearly bought a second café but decided in the end I didn't want to be a retail mogul. Too much effort – I'd rather have less money and enjoy relaxing.

So I sold the café for roughly double what I paid for it. Interestingly running the café helped my trading because a café business is quite complex and learning the accounts helped me evaluate stock market businesses in a much easier way.

A lazy life

So now I just trade and run my website www.nakedtrader.co.uk.

I also hold 5-6 seminars a year where I show readers my techniques using live markets on a large screen. I really enjoy them and it gets me out of the house too. It's also good fun to meet readers and have a drink with them. If you want to come to one, see the info on the seminars at the end of the book. Maybe we'll have a drink together sometime!

The markets have certainly made me very happy. There are plenty of other people like me around who have managed to quit their office jobs and trade. And they, like me, are nothing special. All it takes is some discipline, determination, and I'm afraid some trading capital. I can help you sort out the discipline and determination, you have to come up with some capital.

I hope *Naked Trader 2* will put you on the first rung of the escape ladder.

Trading stock markets really is much simpler than you might imagine once you see past the jargon. And I promise you won't find any of that here. I hope you will find everything easy to understand.

What sort of trader am I?

I suppose I am more of a medium-term investor/frequent trader than a day trader. I expect you imagine a *trader* to be someone sitting at a desk all day feverishly buying and selling shares all day long.

Well, that's not me at all. I don't want to be like that. I want to be, oohhh…drinking tea and eating toast. Having a snooze. Going to the gym. Watching the racing. Sitting in the garden with a good book (or a bad one – I always fall asleep, whatever the book is like). And I enjoy playing with my son. And OK, basically I'm probably a bit lazy (is it time for a nap yet?)

What I hope you'll learn is that **you don't need to spend 40 hours a week in front of a screen watching every move the market makes.** And you can still have a full-time job and make money from the markets, as long as you have access to the internet.

It is possible to trade or invest if you have a full-time job as long as you can get some peace and quiet on the internet at work at some point during the day.

In fact that is the best way to start trading. Begin by making some extra money while you're working and learn the tricks of the trade.

Instead of spending all day emailing your friends (sorry, I mean working hard) spend a bit of time at work learning how to trade.

Keep this book handy

I suggest you keep me handy even when you think you've sussed out how to make money. Because even if you've read the book once or twice, you may need me again if you fall into bad ways – and believe me you will be tempted. And I will always be here for you to skim through...

> You don't need to spend 40 hours a week in front of a screen watching every move the market makes.

Anyway, I really hope you enjoy the book. You don't need to read it all in one hit. Read it in bits and let it sink in. Take it on holiday and read it on the beach. Keep it handy when you're going through a bad trading patch. Don't take it on a date though. There just isn't room for the three of us in the relationship.

Part 2
Getting Started

"The safest way to double your money is to fold it over once and put it in your pocket."

- Kin Hubbard

Is Trading Right For You?

Who are you?

First, the warning

I'm always in two minds as to whether to bother with warnings or horror stories. After all, I'm not a fan of the nanny state and I don't want to be your nanny. I promise you, you'd hate it!

Chances are you're a bit of a gambler at heart. OK, I can hear you say, "No I'm not!"

Look, I don't want to argue with you right at the beginning of the book. We'll save that for later, eh? And after all it would be good if we could get off on the right foot.

Obviously, you want to make money. Perhaps one day you see yourself in my position – in bed with your laptop, trading shares and not having to go to work. But those little warnings in italics you see in many financial ads are spot on.

There are plenty of sad stories on the financial bulletin boards: how some traders have hidden huge losses from their wives and how it affected their lives.

> You have to be careful – one bloke in a horror story later in the book lost his house playing the markets.

There have been various times in the markets when shares have slumped taking people's money with it. Like 2000-2002. May/June 2006 was pretty bad. As was August 2007. The point is shares just don't go up – they can go down a lot too.

Don't think you'll get rich quick, it probably won't happen. But if you take things easy, be careful with the amount of money you put in and learn from your mistakes, then I am happy to encourage you.

(If you do get rich quick then do email me with the subject line "Nurrrhhhh" – and please send me some cash, preferably used 20s.)

If you're going to sell your house to raise money to trade shares, with the idea of becoming a millionaire in double quick time, please forget it.

> Get yourself rich over years and not weeks whatever the gung-ho merchants say.

Can you afford to trade shares?

Before you buy a single share, I do urge you to look at your finances carefully and honestly. Ask yourself:

1. Where is the money coming from that I am going to use to trade?
2. Can I honestly and realistically afford to lose a lot of it?
3. Where the hell is the remote control?[1]

It's unlikely you will lose the lot – if you are careful and follow the rules laid out in this book – but it's not impossible. It is quite possible that you could lose 20-30%, if the market runs against you for a while.

Maybe you have £10,000 spare sitting in a building society account not earning much interest. Will you feel OK about it if you end up with £6,000 after six months of trading?

- If the answer is "yes" to the above question, then go for it!
- If the loss of the money would devastate you, keep it in the nice safe account and maybe trade when you can afford to.

[1] Under the second to left cushion on the sofa.

Perhaps you've suddenly come into money unexpectedly – say £50,000! Great – as you weren't expecting it and, presuming your financial status is OK, then no reason why you shouldn't invest £15,000 of it.

Are you a compulsive gambler?

Let's presume you have the money to play with. One final thing to check: are you a compulsive gambler?

- Do you bet on the horses, buy scratch cards, go to the casino, play online betting games on a regular basis? And does that give you a feeling of excitement?
- Do you feel unable to stop doing these things because they are really enjoyable, even if you are losing?
- Do you hide your bets from your partner? (Under the sofa's a good place.)

If the answers to any of the above are yes, then give this book to someone else (or chuck it so they have to buy a new one), because you would be enabling your current addiction, and losses on the markets can be difficult to control.

Your temperament would also not be right for trading. You need to be cold and unemotional to trade, but you will feel the same rush when buying a share as you would do backing a horse. So as an *EastEnders*' scriptwriter might say, "Leave it out!"

So don't trade if:

- You can't afford to lose some of the money.
- You are likely to get emotionally involved.
- You have, or could have, a gambling problem.

However if you feel you are sensible, level-headed, have a few quid spare and want to give it a go, then go for it!

Types Of Traders/Investors

From years of getting emails and looking at bulletin boards, I think I've identified a few different types of market player.

This is more fun than anything but you should recognize these types from the bulletin boards. It is worth looking at the weak points of these different types of traders and learn to avoid.

Mr Day Trader

Thinks he's going to make a mint from being a *day trader*. Anyway it sounds cool doesn't it? Imagine at parties! "What do you do?" "I'm a day trader!" Wicked! Day traders were common in the markets in 1998-1999 and many gave up their jobs to day trade.

Day trading means buying shares and holding them for not very long, taking lots of small profits. Trouble is most people lose at day trading and that's a fact. It takes an awful lot of effort and it's very stressful too. With commissions and spreads it's very hard to make enough each day to live off. Mr DT may easily get into denial and think he's making money when he's not.

Chances of success: 0.5/10

Q. HOW COME THE CONGA LINE KEPT BREAKING UP AT THE DAYTRADER'S PARTY?

A. NOT MANY OF THEM WERE WILLING TO GO LONG.

Mr Chart Guy

Has decided his charts are the True Answer and will only trade shares from looking at a chart.

He examines things like Fibonacci ratios and Bollinger Bands (personally I like Bollinger but can leave the bands). He also looks at things like moving averages and MACD divergencies and likes to draw pretty lines all over the charts to prove something is a buy or a sell.

Now don't get me wrong – there *is* the odd person out there who does manage to make money from charts alone, but I think they are few and far between. My view is those going for just charts are missing out on the whole picture.

Chances of success: 3/10

Mr Safe And Steady

He'll only buy something he considers safe. So companies like utilities ("people always need power") or Tesco ("people always need to eat"). He probably does OK in the long run, and he may end up making more money than leaving it in the building society. The thing is he won't lose very much. But then again you do need to take some risk to make money.

Chances of success: 6/10 Long-Term 9/10

Mr System Addict

Now here's the chap that just loves to buy trading systems. He'll be clicking on all the ads that offer to turn £2,000 into £75,000. He can't think of anything better than plugging in his amazing system that tells him when to buy or sell a share.

He just can't believe it when his system signalled a buy and yet the share went down! What is wrong with the share?! The system says it was going up! Especially as it was all meant to be so easy. The people that sold him the system said so. And they know what they are talking about don't they? I'm afraid the truth is you have to do a bit of work to make money in the markets.

Chances of success: 2/10

Mrs Long-Term Investor

Notice the Mrs here – more women than not are longer-term investors because they don't take as many gambles as the men.

Mrs LTI doesn't buy that often and is quite cautious. But she will do her research and will probably hold for long enough to make good profits. And you know what? Mrs LTI should do well. Her problem may be eventually holding on for too long and she needs to learn to take profits sometime.

Chances of success: 8/10

Mr Medium-Term Investor

Buys and holds shares for anything between 3 months and 2 years. Does some careful research. Sticks to stop losses. Takes profits when it's sensible to do so. Keeps an eye on his shares but doesn't necessarily wet-nurse them all day. Prefers smaller companies (with growth prospects) to the FTSE 100 ones. Sounds a bit like me!

Chances of success: 8.5/10

Mr Analyser

Take the first four letters of his name and you know what I mean. This trader tries way too hard and analyses everything way too much. So much so that he'll end up not buying shares that could go up quite a lot because he has over-analysed and got too worried.

Chances of success: 2.5/10

Mr Accountant

Loves poring over every detail of a company's accounts and takes great joy in PEG ratios and acid tests and all that. Thing is, he's misses the point of the market which largely ignores all that. If you look at all the ratios and the small things, you'd never buy a single share. Missed loads of good opportunities.

Chances of success: 4/10

Mr Short

Mr Short thinks the market is always too high and everything is too expensive, so he would rather bet on shares to go down. He shorts all the time rather than buying and enjoys being a bit of a maverick. One thing he's forgotten: over time shares go up more than they go down. So he's asking for trouble. Bull markets last way longer than bear ones and he is likely to make big losses during a long-term bull market. Shorting is fine in the right circumstances but not all the time.

Chances of success: 1/10

Mr Quick In And Out

As well as fairly obviously being useless in bed, Mr Quick In And Out may have trouble making much money in the markets. This character looks for something that's going up, and hopes to hop on board and get out quick if it starts to go down. But the problem is he is trying to find shares that have dropped a lot that are on their way back up – and he could end up holding some real shockers. For every one or two small successes, he is going to have the odd awful stinker that will bring his whole portfolio down.

Chances of success: 1/10

Mr Bottom Picker

Yes, I know what you're thinking, that title sounds a bit gruesome. But if you're into such things, then good for you, not really my cup of tea to be honest but I have an open mind.

Mr BP just *loves* shares that have suddenly plummeted, preferably on a profits warning. He'll get up in the morning and the first thing he'll do (well maybe after a wee) is scan the list of the worst performing shares and get stuck in. The reasoning is: "it's oversold."

He'll buy in and then start to worry a bit when it doesn't immediately start going up. It dips a little more the next day, but, "hey, it was nearly double the price the day before yesterday so it'll go back up and I'll make loadsamoney". Except it often doesn't, and what was meant as a short-term trade becomes a "long-term investment".

Chances of success: 3/10

Mr Scaredy Cat

This type of trader sells the moment the market starts to go down a bit. They are scared of the slightest drop in the market. They sell everything the moment the market goes down and buy it all back again when it goes back up.

Trouble is, once all the costs of commission and spreads are taken into account, profits are never going to be huge, although losses won't be that big either.

Chances of success: 3/10

Mr Bulletin Board

Mr BB spends his life on the bulletin boards – you wonder how he gets the time to do anything else. He reckons himself as a bit of a guru. He's everywhere telling people what he's bought. The buy is usually backed up with a pretty chart. He boasts about how well he's doing.

The funny thing is, if one of his buys tanks amazingly it's forgotten about. If he buys something that goes up, he will continue to remind the other people on the bulletin boards. The winners remembered, the losers forgotten. Whatever you do don't follow Mr BB's tips. Do your own research!

Chances of success: No idea!

Mr Penny Share

Loves his low-priced shares! Prefers to buy shares under 20p because they could double, treble or become ten baggers. More likely they will go bust than double! I'm afraid "look after the pennies and the pounds will take care of themselves" doesn't apply here.

Chances of success: 0.5/10.

Mr Footsie Player

Doesn't bother much with shares and prefers to play the indices. Usually reckons to have found some kind of super system which tells him when to buy and sell. Will be on the bulletin boards making predictions, most of which are wrong but somehow he persuades himself he is always right. Most people lose playing indices. If Mr Footsie Player tells you he's winning, take the boasts with a pinch of salt.

Chances of success: 1/10

Why did I write about these characters? Well, they all have flaws just as much as I or you – do. I think it's worth thinking about them though to decide the type of investor you arem or want to be. You may find you switch from one character type to another, but you have to decide what works for you.

What Do You Want From Your Trading?

Develop a money strategy/income streams

Before you launch yourself into the crazy world of shares, you need to ask yourself why you're doing it.

- What sort of return are you after?
- Are you a high risk, high return hotshot or just want a few extra quid?
- Are you looking to build wealth over a long period?
- Just want a bit of fun?
- Make a bit extra to buy a new car?
- Hoping it will help pay school fees for your kids?
- Provide a better retirement?
- Or do you want to become a "full-time trader"?

> Think about what you want from the market, because what you want (and how much you want it) will affect how you trade.

Make more money by not relying on the markets

I believe it is easier to make money on the markets if it is *not* your main source (or hopeful source) of income.

If you're currently in a full-time job you should do what I did and think about new income streams. I did a "Buffy" phoneline and became a distributor for

Telecom Plus selling telephony and energy in my spare time. Think about things you could do, or find to do, to make extra as well as the trading.

Is there anything extra you could do at work to make money for yourself? Any contacts who might give you freelance work? See if you can find yourself some new income. It's one of the ways to eventually quit work.

> The reason I suggest more than one source of income is that you will be more relaxed when trading. If you are trying to make trading your only source of income you will be much more stressed, therefore likely to snatch at profits, not cut losers and not make enough money.

Age matters

Much depends on how old you are and what sort of commitments you have. Here are some age groupings – yes, I know they are a bit stereotyped, but I guess you see what I'm driving at...

Age	Investment profile
20s	You have a well-paid job and plenty of disposable income. You might say: I want to get 50% back on my money and I don't care if I lose it; I have no commitments yet and I'd rather try and use money to make money than buy a flash car. And that's fine. Go for some risk and it might pay off! Just don't kid yourself that you can afford to lose the money easily if you can't.
30s	You have a wife and kids, a mortgage and commitments, but a little disposable income. You may decide you want to take a few risks, after all you're on a good wage. However, you may want to keep a good proportion of your money in lower-risk stocks.
40s-50s	Your income may begin to fall and you have more commitments. So a low-risk growth strategy might be best.
Over 60s	Dividend and high-yielding shares may be of more interest now. Low risk is a priority as you may not be able to afford to lose any capital.

New investors

There are various types of new investors. For example, you may suddenly find you have £10,000 spare and feel that now is the time to stick it in the market. You could be thinking: I want to double or nothing, stick the whole lot in a couple of risky shares in the hope they double. Judging by the internet bulletin boards, that's what a lot of people do – and probably end up with £4,000!

So have a good think about your current status, and decide, at the very least, a general strategy.

My advice

You may wonder what I think you should do, but this is difficult to answer unless I know your individual circumstances very well.

However, as a start, my favourite strategy would be to kick off with a £7,000 self-select ISA and try and grow it by more than you'd get in a building society – you might surprise yourself and grow it by a lot more!

The Trader's Toolkit

Introduction

Good news!

I give you full permission to skip the next few pages if you have already traded lots of shares via the internet and know how to do it. Or if you read my first book and have already traded. However if you do skim, it won't do you any harm and I've revised and re-written the 'how to get started' part of the book for this edition.

But I will allow you to get yourself some tea and toast and move directly to page 57 if you know how to look up a real-time share price, have bought shares, have an online broker account and know a little bit about the markets.

If though, you have never, or hardly ever, bought shares over the internet, then there is *no* escape. You need to read this chapter.

No skipping, right?

Promise you, it's not that boring. In fact, it's way easier than you might think to get started as a trader or investor. So you can start off by taking it easy. It really is quite straightforward.

Here's all you need to deal online:

- A computer, with internet access (I know that might come as a shock!)
- Execution-only broker(s) (easy)
- Access to share prices and market info
- A notebook and pen
- Lots of tea and toast

And that really is it – told you not to worry! I am sure you already have the computer.

The toolkit

We're going to look at five essential things in this section:

1. Computer and internet access
2. Online stock broker
3. Real-time prices
4. How to find the share price of a company
5. Notebook

Let's get started...

1. Computer with broadband

The computer's the easy bit. You've probably already got one, and it will almost certainly do. If you don't have a computer, then almost any new computer with broadband access will be sufficient. You don't need the latest, most powerful computer to trade shares. But if you really start to go for it and download lots of different trading systems, it *could* be that you may have to buy a bit more memory.

I find having an additional laptop quite handy so I can monitor share prices on one computer and trade on the other but it's not necessary, especially if you are just starting out.

2. Online stock broker

There are now countless ways to make money from trading without even having to open an account with an ordinary stock broker. There's spread betting, fixed-odds betting, CFDs, betting exchanges, binary betting, options and futures, and direct market access. It's never been easier to play the markets. However, even with all these exciting-sounding ways of trading, I still believe new investors should start with a basic online stock broking account.

All the new ways of trading shares can be pretty dangerous if you don't know what you're doing and so I think the best way to start is via one or two online execution-only stockbrokers.

Why?

Because it's straightforward. And you can only lose whatever you put in.

With a conventional online broker account you can easily get used to investing or trading the markets for a while before getting into anything more complicated.

Other accounts, such as spread betting, can be added fairly quickly once you've gained enough experience.

I will get to the other methods later in the book, but for now don't worry about it.

So which kind of broker should you go for?

Types of stock broker

There are two types of stock broker:

1. *Advisory brokers*
   These brokers will give you advice on what stocks to buy and sell, and even, if you want, will trade on your behalf (this latter type are called Discretionary brokers). **My view: some of them are absolute rubbish.**

2. *Execution-only brokers*
   As the name suggests, no advice is given at all. You're on your own. (But they will execute you if you lose more than 50% – joke!)

My view is forget about the advisory ones – they take loads of money from you and often make big mistakes.

This book is about how to trade for yourself so you should be looking for an execution-only one. I'm sure the reason you bought this book was to make your own decisions. So, from now on, when talking of brokers, I am writing about execution-only ones. Which is good as they're cheap.

Selecting a broker

It's difficult to recommend specific brokers as their services and charges are changing all the time These days though the top ones are really much of a muchness.

Generally speaking they will all provide a similar service. Which is quite simply: you buy or sell something over the internet and they do the trade for you. Your trade is usually recorded on your account which you can access anytime. And that's it.

Occasionally, brokers' internet services freeze or don't work. In my experience it happens to them all at some point.

So in the end it comes down to the price you're charged per trade.

It ranges from £6.50 to £12.50 per trade. Often this depends how much you trade. Those who trade a lot get the better prices.

Just go through a few brokers' sites (listed opposite) and check their price lists.

Watch the small print. Some charge an "inactivity fee" if you don't trade much.

Quite honestly, I have three accounts (being a completely greedy sod) and I don't find an awful lot of difference between them. They're all easy to use.

My accounts are with: Selftrade, Barclays, and E-Trade. I have no complaints about any of them and they get me the same prices. I hardly ever have to contact them.

As it doesn't cost anything to set up an account, I would initially open two accounts. I'll explain a bit later why this can be a good tactic.

> The best tip I can give you is to shop around, because as a new trader you hold the aces. In other words, they really want your business and you'll often find special deals around for "Newbies".

Many brokers offer new account deals like: "Your first 30 trades free" or "Trade free till [whenever]". So you may as well make the most of it and take up any special offers. If you like the broker, stick with them, if you don't, move elsewhere.

Broker checklist

A checklist when looking for a broker:

1. Check the **broker's website**
2. Trades should cost **no more than £12.50**
3. Watch out for **hidden charges**
4. Be a "tart" – **shop around for special deals** for newbies
5. Consider opening **multiple accounts** with two or more brokers and compare their services directly

Q. HOW MANY STOCKBROKERS DOES IT TAKE TO CHANGE A LIGHT BULB?

A. TWO. ONE TO TAKE OUT THE BULB AND DROP IT, AND THE OTHER TO TRY AND SELL IT BEFORE IT CRASHES.

Share certificates

Share certificates are a thing of the past – forget about them. Most online brokers use *nominee accounts*. This means you don't get a certificate, you are the electronic owner of the shares.

In fact getting certificates is next to impossible. So don't bother.

When you buy shares they simply go straight into your online account and when you sell them they leave your online account – wonderful! If you have any certificated shares you can transfer them into a nominee account with your broker. Call them for details.

Show me the money

You need to put some money in!

Sorry, but...well, you need to put some money in your account or else you won't be able to buy any shares. Doh!

The best and quickest way is simply to fund your account with a debit card, or you can send them a cheque. But sending cheques takes some time so a debit card is best. Because of the new money laundering rules (why people want to clean their cash is beyond me), some brokers may ask you to send proof of who you are, so you may need to send in a copy of a driving licence or passport. Don't get annoyed with them. Blame the government or the money launderers – take your pick as they're both thieves!

Brokers do pay some interest on cash in your account, but not a lot. You generally should be using the money for trading.

You can usually sign up online.

You've gotta have an ISA (or two)

Consider putting your money under an ISA (Individual Savings Account) umbrella. Especially if it's raining. Basically you can trade the money inside self-select ISAs without any liability to capital gains tax.

I know, you've seen ISAs advertised in papers, and hardly anyone has any idea what the point of them is. Well, thanks to recent government action most of the tax benefits of ISAs have been wiped away (they've robbed us right, left and centre), but the big benefit is that there is no capital gains tax to be paid.

You might well say: what's the point, you can only put a small amount in so surely capital gains tax will never be a problem?

Wrong!

I have saved thousands upon thousands of pounds in taxes, that I would otherwise have had to pay if I hadn't put all my share money into ISAs (and PEPs as they used to be called).

As the years go on, and you build your portfolios, the ISA tax advantage becomes more and more apparent.

> I have saved thousands upon thousands of pounds in taxes.

Let's say you have a few good years and build up £150,000 of capital inside your ISAs. All tax free. Now say you have a very good year and turn that £150,000 into £250,000. That's a profit of £100,000. Outside an ISA that profit could cost a huge £36,800 in capital gains tax.

Say you put in £7,000, and you strike lucky – you bought a penny share that trebled. You sell and you now have £21,000 – a profit of £14,000. Inside the ISA – no tax. Outside, your profit will be taxed at £2,400. (Assuming you're a 40% taxpayer.)

That's because as I write you can only make £9,200 profit a year on shares – after that you get taxed! Sad but true!

It is worth checking to see if they make any standing charges to look after your ISA. Most do, expect to pay around £15 a quarter.

There is no maximum amount you can build in your ISA. One chap who writes for the *Financial Times* has managed to build his ISA fund to over **£1 million!**

Withdrawals from ISAs can be made anytime, but once cash is taken out, it cannot be replaced except within your annual allowance. But the great thing is there is *no limit* to profits you can make.

- If you have more than 7k to stick in, you could set up an ISA account and a normal trading account and run them both through the same broker.
- If you have a few shares still in certificate form you should be able to send them in and they will transfer them into your electronic account.
- Oh, and if you have a partner use their ISAs if they'll let you. Although of course they could run off with your money if you have a massive row and split. But, hey, you're in love so that shouldn't happen!

- And finally, it's dead easy to trade inside an ISA – you trade as normal. To trade under an ISA when you sign up via an online broker, press the ISA sign up button.

Right – you have a computer, you have an online broker. We've talked ISAs... Now you need...

3. Real-time prices and some extra stuff

If you're going to invest or trade you will need to know the current buy price and sell price on the shares you're interested in or you own. Even if you only dip in once or twice a day.

Plus you need to know some other stuff too:

- How to keep an eye on news about shares and what companies are announcing
- The dividend they pay
- When their next results are announced
- A chart of how the share price has been behaving
- What the company's worth
- How much profit it makes

It's known as *research* and something a lot of people can't be bothered with. But please be (bothered).

Because really you ought to keep yourself informed, especially once you are the proud owner of a few shares and so you can idly mention to your mates:

> *"I have a portfolio..."*

(*Portfolio* means a basket of shares.)

On the other hand, maybe best not to mention it as they may suddenly expect you to buy all the drinks.

Now, onto the sexy bit...

Real-time prices

Where do you find real-time prices and other stuff like news about shares?

Well, there are quite a few websites and the good news is most of the stuff you need is free.

So you can look up real-time prices for nothing, though the "real-time" service itself may only last a minute or so. If you want 'always on' access to real-time prices you usually have to pay (not that much). Hey, the web sites have to make some money!

I personally use a site called ADVFN.com. However, there are a number of similar sites you could use instead if you wanted to.

For the purposes of the book, I'm going to use ADVFN as the basic information supplier. They've not paid me a bean to do this by the way. It just makes it far easier for me to describe how to look for things if I use the one site.

Once you've understood where to find what you need on ADVFN, you could move to another site if you wanted once you know what you need.

ADVFN is not the only source for real-time prices and research tools, below are the main ones. It may be worth opening accounts with two or three real-time price companies in the event of your favourite breaking down and having to spend an hour with a shrink. All these sites offer free services, once you've settled on the one you like most for whatever reason you could add other services which you may have to pay a bit for.

- ADVFN – www.ADVFN.com
- Interactive Investor – www.iii.co.uk
- MoneyAM – www.moneyam.com
- Proquote – www.proquote.net
- Hemscott – www.hemscott.net
- Digital Look – www.digitallook.com

Right – wakey up – you beginners!

Unless you've switched off, missed stuff or been sneaking looks at *Heat* or *Nuts* instead of paying attention…here's a summary so far:

1. Get some online broking accounts set up
2. Think about sticking some of your money in an ISA to avoid tax
3. Find a place where you can access real-time prices and other info

Now, what other info do you need before you get cracking?

4. Finding information on share prices

How do you find the share price of a company, or monitor the share prices of a bunch of companies? It's easy! Let's dive in properly now to the ADVFN web site...

How to use ADVFN (and other similar sites)

Best place to start? I guess it's the home page. You'll need to register (it's free with ADVFN).

Obviously you may be reading this book on the train, or even on the loo. But for the next bit it may be worthwhile you reading it while you're by a computer or laptop.

ADVFN home page

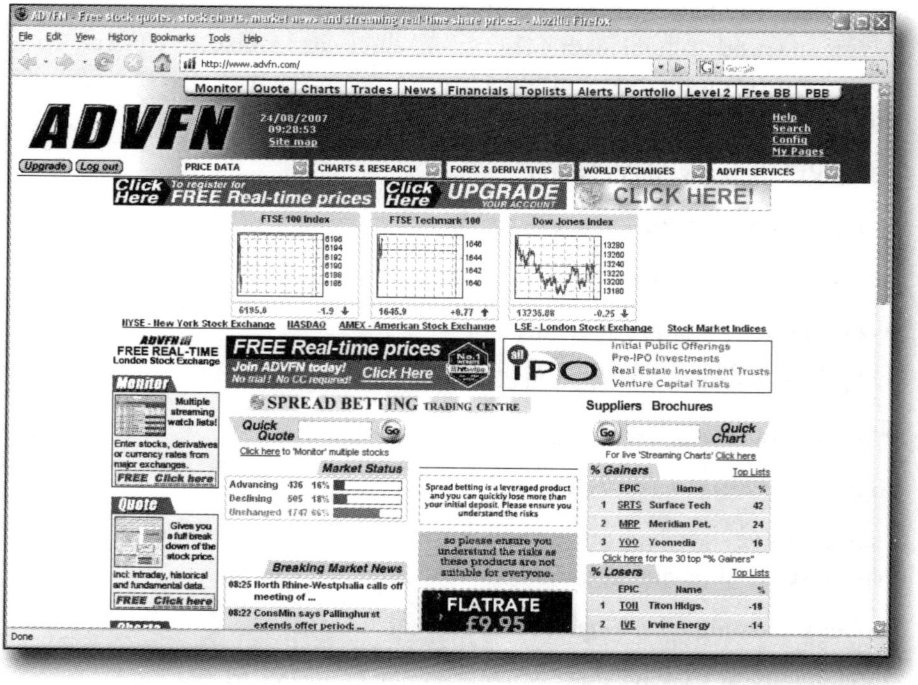

The main thing you need to focus on is the navigation menu near the top of the page (see the screenshot above). I'll go through the sections you need to be interested in initially.

1. *Monitor*: this is the most useful page! This is the basic list of shares that you are interested in and may want to follow on a day-to-day basis.
2. *Quote*: gets you a quote on the current price for any share.
3. *Trades*: data on buys and sells that have taken place in the share of your choice.
4. *News*: obvious…it's, er, financial news!
5. *Financials*: very important, has lots of info to help you research a share.
6. *Free BB and Premium BB*: these are the bulletin boards that investors use to gossip.
7. *Toplists*: one of my favourite pages. Contains rankings of stocks by all sorts of criteria, such as top movers of the day. Basically, a great place to find out where the action is happening.

The other buttons you'll want to use in time, but these should get you going.

Let's look at the information you get when you ask for a quote on a share.

Stock codes

You'll quickly realise that everything on the ADVFN website (as with most other stock market websites) revolves around something called *stock symbols*. These are short (three or four character) symbols used to represent shares.

For example, the following table lists the symbols for the ten largest companies on the London Stock Exchange.

Top ten largest companies on the London Stock Exchange

Company	Code
BP	BP.
HSBC Holdings	HSBA
Vodafone	VOD
GlaxoSmithKline	GSK
Royal Bank Of Scotland	RBS
AstraZeneca	AZN
Shell Transport and Trading	SHEL
Barclays	BARC
HBOS	HBOS
Lloyds TSB	LLOY

Note: Be careful, the code for BP is 'BP.' – including the stop.

These symbols are also – rather confusingly – sometimes called EPIC, or TIDM or RIC, codes. Or *tickers*. It doesn't really matter, throughout this book I'll refer to them as codes. (I hope you're not falling asleep at the back there – this is important stuff!)

If you don't know the symbol of the company you are interested in, you need to find out what it is. The best way to explain this is by way of an example.

Finding the stock code for a company

You've come across mention of a company called Harvey Nash in the paper, and you want to find its current share price and start doing some research on the stock.

On the ADVFN website click the 'Quote' button in the top menu bar.

If you knew the stock's symbol already, you could at this point simply input it into the box (to the right of where it says 'Symbol:'), click the OK button, and you'd be off. However, if you don't know the symbol, then type "Harvey Nash" in the box, and then click the Search button.

A page should come up with, on the right hand side, a table with a title 'Search results'. Just one stock should be listed, which is the one you want. From here we can see that the symbol for Harvey Nash is HVN.

At this point you can return to the main Quote page and input 'HVN' as the symbol (or ADVFN make it easy for us, as clicking on the symbol itself jumps straight to the relevant Quote page).

Alternatively you can use the A-Z search for stock codes.

You'll see that there's quite a bit happening on the ADVFN Quote page. It's worth spending some time finding your way around this page.

So let's have a look at the quote for HVN. Perhaps when you're next at your computer press 'quote' on ADVFN and see the latest.

ADVFN quote for Harvey Nash

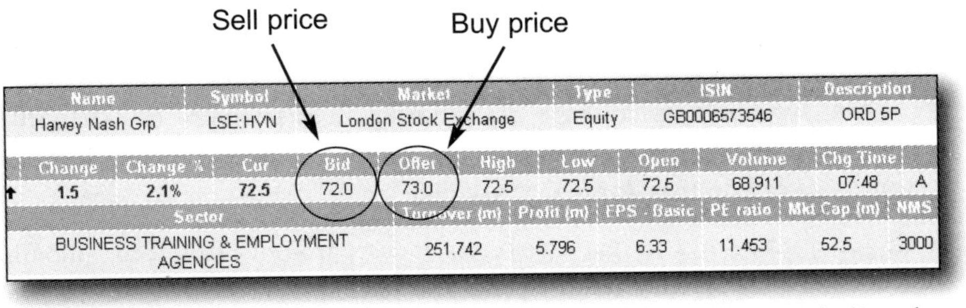

On this particular quote, you can see there's price information including the current sell price 72p, and buy price 73p (jargon is: *bid* and *offer*), the high and low prices for the day and the volume of shares bought or sold.

There's also some summary financial data. (You can see at a glance the company makes nearly £6 million in profit a year and the market values it at £52m (market cap). The NMS (Normal Market Size) is 3,000 so you can easily buy or sell 3,000 shares. The PE ratio is 11.5 and Earnings Per Share 6.33p – more on this later!

The rest of the page shows you the latest news stories and the chart.

Now click on 'Financials' if you want a range of other data including what the dividend is and when it's paid.

'News' stories is where you can begin research, which I will show you later.

Using the ADVFN Monitor

You may decide you want to start watching Harvey Nash regularly, so you should add it to your 'Monitor'. You'll be able to track its real-time buy and sell prices, amounts traded, highs and lows of the day and whether there are any new news stories.

To start your monitor or 'watchlist' of shares, just click the 'Add Stock' button (near the top of the page).

You can add as many shares as you like to the Monitor. Remember, first find the code, then just add it to your Monitor.

You can have loads of different monitors. For example, you might want to track different types of shares. You could call one monitor 'FTSE 100' to keep an eye on the FTSE, and call another 'Small companies' to track the smaller sector.

I use ten or so monitors for different areas of the market.

ADVFN also has cracking research facilities too. I'll show you later how to use these to your best advantage.

Real-time prices

- When you look up a share price during market hours (0800-1630), ADVFN will quote you a real-time price for a few seconds before it times out. You can do that as often as you like.
- If you want always on real-time prices, it costs around £10 to £15 a month via most sites. Money worth spending I reckon. It's usually given to you for free if you pay for Level 2.

5. Notebook

So computer sorted? Broker account on the way? Access to real-time prices set up? Vaguely understand that quote page? Still awake?

Good, we're nearly there. Final thing, I also recommend keeping a notebook handy. It's always good to jot down ideas, share prices and bits of info. It's also obviously handy for jotting down phone numbers and losing them.

Try and be disciplined and keep a trading diary: write down everything you've bought and sold, the prices transacted and the reasons for buying or selling. This will come in handy later on when you analyse why you made money, or lost it.

It's also worth buying a punchbag and some boxing gloves from eBay or your local leisure shop. Then, when you've lost money you have something on which to take out your frustration!

Your trading environment

Stay clutter free!

Keeping a clear head is very important when it comes to share trading – it's just not possible if you're surrounded by clutter. I think it can seriously affect trading decisions if you're surrounded by hundreds of old fag butts, empty bags of crisps, loads of bits of paper, newspapers and empty beer cans. Clutter will subconsciously put you under more pressure when making trading decisions.

Therefore, keep a clear desk and a tidy office and your head will feel clear too. And this will help your trading. Tea and toast is also vitally important to good trading. (Oh bugger, just spilled crumbs all over the desk. Fine example I set.)

KISS – Keep It Simple Stupid

Don't make trading too difficult for yourself. What I mean is: don't overburden yourself with dozens of trading screens plus a bank of TV screens in every corner of the room.

That's just to impress the girlfriend/wife/friends, right?

Keep it simple. You don't need to start buying chart systems and complicated software to start trading. All you need is access to news stories, fundamentals, charts and real-time prices. You can get this from free web sites, or you might need to pay a small amount to access them. That's fine.

But don't go buying multi-thousand pound systems if you're starting out. All they will do is confuse things. You need to keep that mind free to concentrate on just one thing: is that share a good buy or not? I promise you your expensive systems are just dumb computers. Stay with the simple stuff.

Anytime you catch yourself drooling over a glossy ad for a trading system promising to make you millions, walk away and just think of Baloo Bear from *The Jungle Book* – it's all about the bear necessities!

One day, when you've made your first million, by all means fill your office with impressive, flashing machines. But not for starters.

Important Things To Know About Trading Or Investing

Hallo those of you who have traded one or two shares and already knew about monitors, share codes and stuff. This is the point which I hope is a good place for you to start *Naked Trader 2.* Even those of you who have invested or traded for a while may pick up a thing or two. I hope so. If you don't, you only blew £12.99...what's that? Four grande lattes at Starbucks?

So why don't I start with...

The most important lesson I can teach you about trading or investing...

Which is, bizarrely:

Make money by making losses!

You heard what I said. Don't pretend you didn't.

Before you start trading I want you to bear this in mind – taking lots of losses will make you a lot of money.

Sounds crazy right? But really, taking losses will make you a lot of money.

In fact I should say it in capitals for emphasis. Why don't I?

TAKING LOTS OF LOSSES WILL MAKE YOU A LOT OF MONEY!

And I have honestly not just knocked back six pints and am writing this three sheets to the wind trying to wind you up. It really is true.

Let me expand on that a little. I should add the word "small" – taking lots of *small* losses will make you a lot of money.

And further to this I must add: take lots of small losses and one or two big gains and you will make a lot of money.

What I look for is to take losses of no more than 10%-ish when a share turns bad but hold on tight to the really good ones and look for 30% and upwards.

So a really good trader's banked losses and profits could look something like this:

Last ten closed trades
-7%
-5%
+25%
-10%
-3%
+40%
-7%
-6%
-9%
+32%

This trader looks like he's losing money at first glance. He's taken a lot of losses. The trader has taken 7 losses and only had 3 winners, *but* has made a lot of money.

In fact, if each trade had been £5,000 of shares, the trader would be up by £2,500.

So **it's really a percentages game and not the number of wins or losses that matters.**

If the trader above had taken his profits too quickly, despite cutting his losses he wouldn't have made much because he may have been tempted to take profits at just 10% instead of the 25%, 40% and 32%.

I've just taken a look at one of my ISA portfolios – I've turned roughly £21,000 into £150,000 using this method.

> You need the courage to sell losers fast and hold winners for a while.

Right now, I have 4 losers and 7 winners. The losers are -9% -4% -8% and -5%.

But the winners are +36% +277% +7% +344% +86% +2% +53%

If the losers start to head much above 10% losses they will be cut immediately. But I have run the winners. The biggest percentages among the winners have been held for a couple of years. And I think they still have further to go. The 8% and 9% losers in this ISA are now on a yellow card and if they lose much more will be axed without emotion. (Call me Mr Spock…)

But joking aside this is why this portfolio has grown so nicely.

Of course I have picked some decent shares. However, I have also picked my fair share of losers but cut them before they started to eat away at the profits.

It is one of the hardest concepts in share trading – to sell at a loss. And blokes are really bad at it. Just as hard a concept as resisting taking profits too early.

Some traders find taking losses next to impossible. So you have to steel yourself into thinking that taking a loss is a *good* thing.

It's all down to our human emotions. If you can conquer those when you're trading you'll be a winner. You need strength and courage to sell those losers and hold onto the winners.

Emotions

So let's talk more about emotions shall we with your agony uncle: Dear Robbie.

> *To Thine Own Self Be True*
>
> **Shakespeare**

Well, OK I just put that quote in to make me look intelligent. Gives me some feelgood emotions and shows how cultured I am. (Don't believe it, never read Shakespeare since school. Where's my copy of *Nuts!* gone?)

But you do have to get to know yourself and your own emotional strengths and weaknesses.

> Emotions, quite simply, get in the way of making good investment decisions.

Because **however cool you think you are, your buy and sell decisions will end up being affected by your emotions.** And, being humans, we are very emotional animals. We let emotions rule various aspects of our lives (which often can be fun); and it's just the same with investing (which is usually disastrous).

So, imagine you're Mr Spock...Be logical!

Emotions lead to taking quick profits...

We all want to feel good about ourselves, and selling for a quick profit makes us feel *very* good. The trouble is, our feelgood emotions harm long-term investment gains because it stops us sticking with the winners.

Many investors even take profits if a share has only gone up 2 or 3 per cent. That's because they can proudly boast to themselves and others: "I banked a profit."

... and hanging onto losers

Emotion is also the main reason for hanging on to losers for far too long.

We hate feelings of regret, and selling a losing share makes us regret and maybe feel a bit mad at ourselves. We want to avoid that. So we'd rather watch the shares continue to decline, than take the loss and feel bad about it. It's stupid really, because eventually, when we sell even lower we feel even worse!

I've met people who have bought shares at something like a tenner and watched them sink all the way to 20p – *without selling them*!

Arrrrgggh!

It's almost unbelievable. Once a share has gone down so far, it appears investors can't bear to take a loss. Another reason to take the loss early.

I met a trader once at my café. He said:

"I bought Tadpole Technology at 60p and I've still got it."

"But it's 5p now," I gasped in horror.

"Yeah, but it could go back up now, couldn't it?" he argued.

I didn't have the heart to tell him to ditch the sodding share and move on. Something he should have done at 50p. Plus all that time he's probably spent watching it go down over the years. All that waste of energy and money.

Revenge on the market

> Our inability to sell something at a loss is mainly due to ego.

There's another psychological problem when it comes to selling at a loss: feelings of revenge! We want to get our money back and that causes us to be emotional and start taking too many risks. If we've lost half our money we might be tempted to go for a small stock we think might double to get the money back – or some other dodgy trading behaviour.

This is where the unemotional stop loss (discussed shortly) comes into its own and will ensure we sell shares before we lose too much. That way a stock is sold without bringing in the emotions of regret and getting even. And that means you are less likely to make an overly-risky next trade.

On man and egos

Our inability to sell something at a loss is mainly due to ego. Taking a loss is very difficult to do. I used to find it difficult too – now I love it. Mmmmm, taking a loss...delicious!

Taking a loss means accepting you have got it wrong. If we just stick with the share, we believe it'll go back up, we might even make a profit and – hey presto – we were right all along. But usually the opposite is the case – the share keeps sinking and we lose more money. And absolutely every investor has done this and you will do it too!

I did this a few times in my early trading career. The worst I remember was Hartstone, where I bought at 450p and allowed it to sink all the way to 250p before bailing out.

Another good example is when I bought Coffee Republic. When I bought the shares for 28p, if I had set a stop loss of 22p, and acted on it, I would have sold without emotion at 22p and lost only £500. As it was, with no stop loss, I eventually lost around £7,000.

Let's look at an example.

You want to buy a new share but you have to sell a current one to raise the cash. The choice for selling is between two shares:

1. Stock A is showing a loss of 20%
2. Stock B is showing a gain of 20%

Which share should be sold?

I would bet that, nine times out of ten, the investor would sell the stock that has gone up 20%, rather than sell the loser.

That's because selling the winner shows what a good decision it was to buy it and validates that decision. There's also an element of pride involved and it feels good to lock in the profit. It affects all of us. Personally, I feel pretty good when I lock in a profit and extremely irritated when I have to take a loss!

You can also tell your best friend: "I just made 20% profit" – while you keep the loser to yourself! Bad move, buster, guess who's going to have to buy all the drinks tonight!

You really have to learn not to postpone the feelings of regret. Avoidance of regret is one of the main reasons investors lose money.

> So you have to love to take losses and hate to take gains.

To a beginner investor, that will sound odd and counter-intuitive; and until you understand that saying, you will remain a beginner investor.

Overtrading

As well as not taking losses, another mistake made is quite simply, overtrading.

People simply press the buy and sell button too often – they feel like they should be making a trade every day – or most days. And this is quite common with new traders starting out. They get the bug and want to chase every stock that moves.

This is OK if you're a really hot day trader, but sadly there are hardly any of these around. I've had it said to me time and time again (especially from people I've met who work for spread betting firms):

> *Our losing accounts make too many trades*

they say (once I have got them drunk enough to tell me).

The desire to overtrade probably again stems from our emotions.

We want to make money quickly and we think if we keep trading, the money will come pouring in. Wrong! It's more likely to go out.

> The more trades you have running the more time you have to spend monitoring them. The more stress you'll feel, the poorer your decisions.

So don't go bananas and have a whole raft of open trades everywhere. Stick to a sensible number that you can keep control of.

Gambling or investing?

For a couple of years in the 1990s, I was a professional gambler on the horses. I even owned a couple so had a bit of inside info. But even with that info I didn't make a lot of money – just about enough to get by but never big money.

It's next to impossible to make a living on the horses. However, the stock market is different because if you stay disciplined and calm you can definitely make big money.

But you have to invest and not gamble to become a stock market winner making real regular money.

What's the difference between a stock market gambler who loses and a market investor who wins?

Quite simple: a market gambler is itching to trade and press that exciting deal button. And gamblers make up 90% of spread betting accounts that lose.

- **Gambling** is putting money on shares that you know nothing about. Buying something for a punt – with no trading plan in place.
- **Investing** is buying into a company you've done your research on and trying to get your timing right.

I get so many emails starting:

> *I am going to have a punt on...*

Don't have "punts". Invest. Make money. If you have punts you will lose, maybe not right now but eventually. Punts are just lazy gambling.

So there – have I made myself clear?

Fear and greed

It's a stock market cliché, but fear and greed is prevalent in all traders and investors.

The fear as shares fall, and fall again, then the greed as they start to rise. We all want to be out when shares are falling and back in when they are rising – there's nothing worse than being frightened out of the market and then feeling irritated when you see it rise back up and you're missing out.

> The main thing you must consider is your capital – above all else that must be protected.

As a general rule:

- **Buy shares** trending upwards and breaking new highs.
- **Don't buy shares** trending downwards and breaking new lows.

This may sound obvious, but so many people make the mistake of doing it the wrong way round.

Down trends

When it comes to investing, the human reaction is generally to want to buy a share that is a bargain. In particular, investors are attracted to shares that have fallen – they think that's a bargain:

> *you see it's come down a long way so look at how far it could go up.*

Take a look at the following chart.

British Airways, 1997-2002

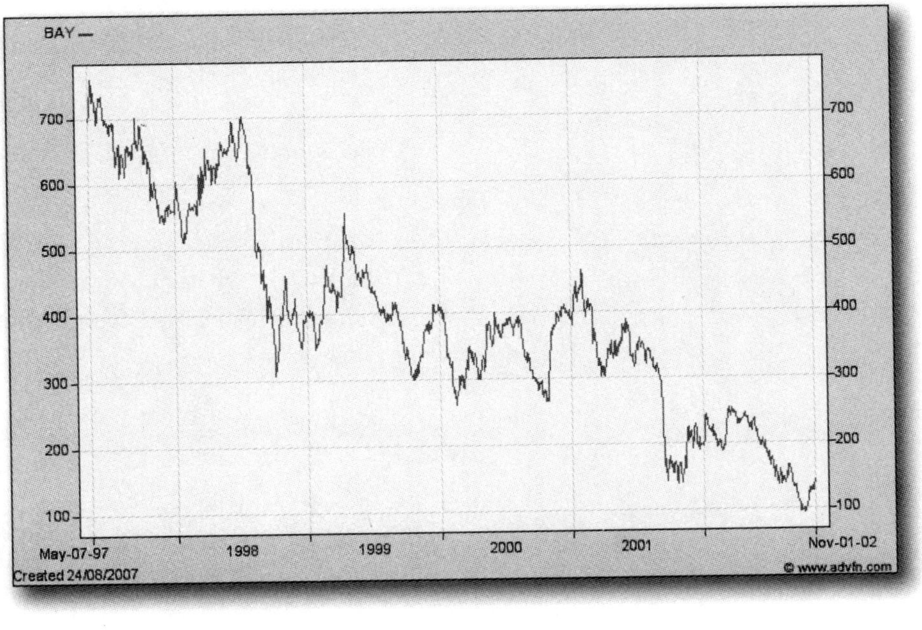

As can be seen, British Airways was in a well-established, 5-year down trend from 1997 to 2002. Have you ever wondered why share price charts don't simply move down in straight lines? Well, I'll tell you! Bottom pickers (not a nice topic, I know – but we have to face the truth). Look again at the chart: at multiple points throughout the 5 years, investors thought:

> *The share price is going to bounce off this support level, and I'm going to make a packet in double quick time – easy money...*

and then a little later when the downward trend has reasserted itself:

> *Ooh-err, whoops.*

The share price then falls some more until another would-be "support level" is hit, and the cycle repeats itself. All the way to the bottom. Over the 5 years, British Airways fell over 85%, and investors would have been buying it all the way down, thinking at each point it was "cheap". By mid 2007, the shares still hadn't recovered their 1997 high of 760.

And because this point is so important...take a look at the following chart.

Mystery share!

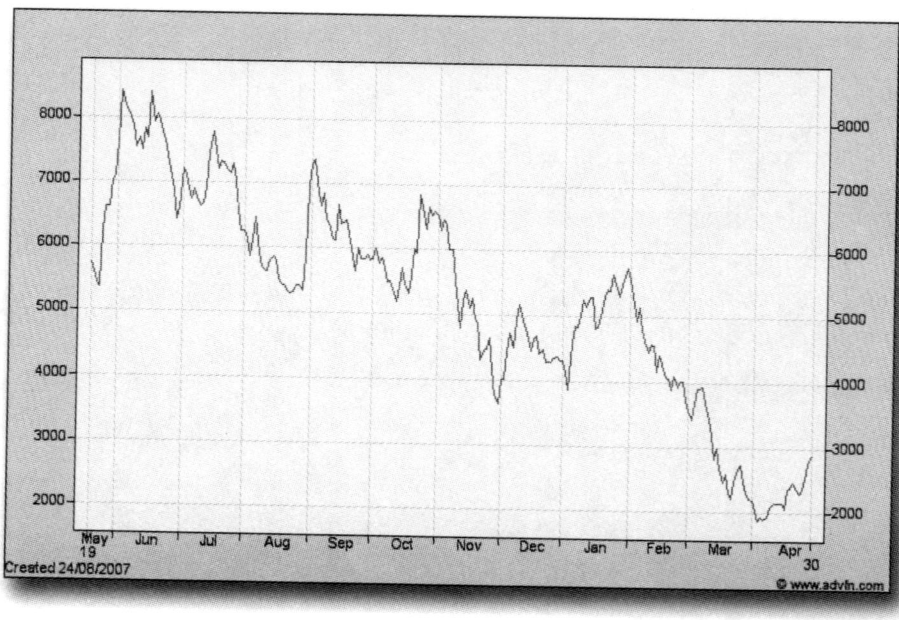

(By the way, I've blanked out the name of the company – sneaky, aren't I?)

The chart looks tempting doesn't it? The shares have fallen 75% from their high, and the price has recently bounced off the key support level of 2000. Frankly, the price looks like it could double in a few months. Perhaps treble or quadruple. *Easy money.*

So, would you be a buyer? Be honest now.

The following chart shows what happened to the share price.

Colt Telecom (2000-2002)

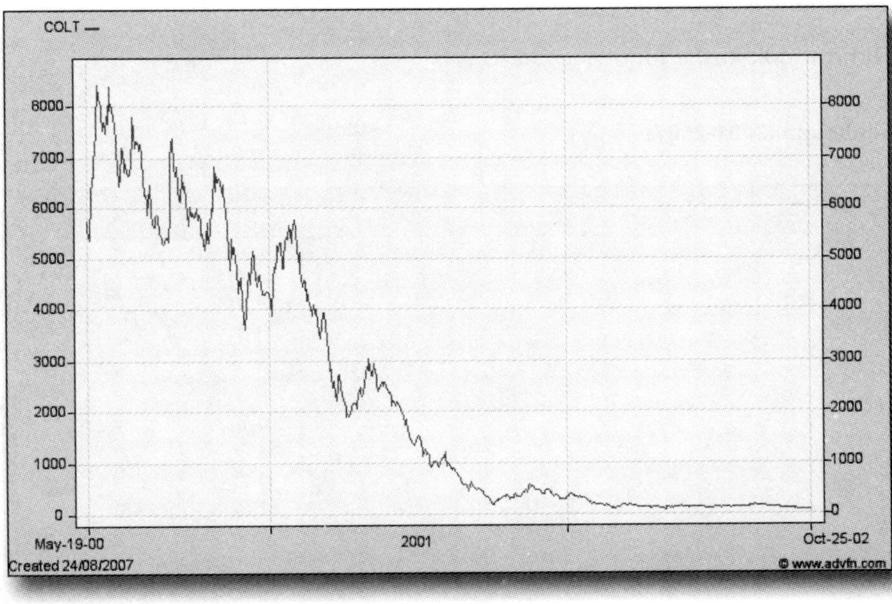

The company is COLT Telecom, and in the 5 months following where the first chart left off the price fell 80% – and hasn't recovered since.

But *it was in a down trend* – duh, what did you expect!

The moral is:

> *Don't try to bottom pick – it's a nasty habit, stop it!*

Up trends

Conversely, investors can be terrified of buying shares that have gone up a lot. Their reaction is:

> *"That share's gone up a long way ... it'll never go up any more and ooh it could easily go back down again... woah a bit dangerous...!"*

This is what I used to think when I first started trading. I did what a lot of newer investors do: look for the shares that have fallen and are showing signs of imminent recovery.

Take a look at the following chart.

Inchcape (2001-2007)

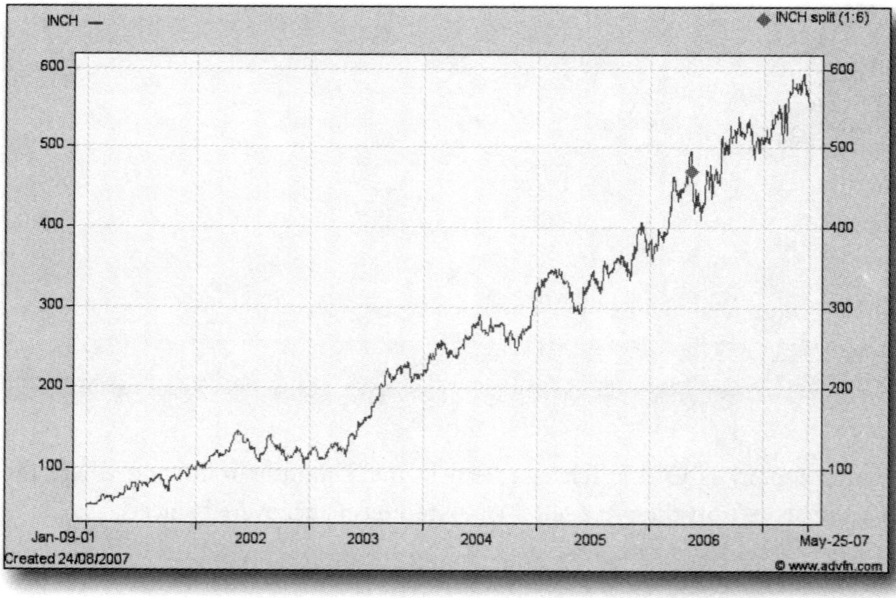

In the 6 years from 2001 to 2007, Inchcape was in a steady up trend. Again, the share price is not a straight line, but this time the cause was not due to bottom pickers but Chicken Littles. At every stage the Chicken Littles were crying:

> *Ooooh, help, it's too high, it's going to fall.*

Then the share would go up another 50%, and the Chicken Littles would shout louder:

Ooooh, help, it's too high, it's going to fall.

Repeat, *ad nauseam.*

Confidence and handling pressure

If you're going to win at trading I'm afraid you are going to need some confidence and you'll have to be able to manage a little pressure (I know, I know, it sounds like a job interview: *where do you see yourself in five years' time*, etc.)

But you really have to stay cool when the markets aren't doing what you expect or your money will start to disappear. Of course some anxiety will always be present as it is in me. In fact I'm feeling scared right now. I think I'm out of choc bars.

You have to cope with it somehow (the pressure, not the lack of chocs). The fact is you *will* make losses on some trades and that's inevitable, but it isn't the end of the world. The first company I bought into went bust! You either give up or plough on. And those who have the guts and determination to plough on through adversity often become the big winners.

Remember the Chumbawumba song:

I get knocked down but I get up again...

> You really have to stay cool when the markets aren't doing what you expect or your money will start to disappear.

You don't? [Nope – Ed.] Look, those were the lyrics. You *are* going to get knocked down. But you just need that confidence to get up again and have the resilience to keep going.

There have been many times in my trading career when the market was going down and I thought: do I need this stress? Shall I just jack it all in? No! I got up and fought on, and every time I'm glad I did. Learn from the pressure.

Mark Douglas in his book, *Trading In The Zone* says:

> *Winning in any endeavour is mostly a function of attitude.*

And he's right. It's a question of staying positive. Keep a good attitude and you're much more likely to make money.

Tiredness

A quick note here. You should try not to make any, or too many, trading decisions when you're tired. If you've had a few drinks the night before and you wake up with a sore head, watch what you do. Or if you feel generally in a bad mood. If you don't have a clear head don't expect to stay unemotional and make good trades!

You don't have to trade

Finally, there's no one forcing you to have lots of positions open in the markets and sometimes you're better off not having any. So don't trade just because you're bored.

Summary

Well, I guess you realized – the last few paragraphs have been all about market psychology and it *is* important. What goes on in your mind will affect every trade you ever make.

OK, time to move on.

How do you research the company you're thinking of buying shares in?

Good question and next topic!

Get to know your area of expertise

There are so many shares out there, and so many different indices that you can trade. And you can trade them all in different ways. The whole array can be bewildering.

Where to start?

What you must do is learn to specialise – don't spread yourself too thin. You're not Marmite.

For example, I have a good record of picking shares, but for some reason I decided to have a go at trading indices. I suppose I wanted to try another area of the market to see if I could crack it. So I began to trade the FTSE 100 Index, up and down.

One day I thought:

> *Well the Footsie is down 30 point I can't see it going any lower today so I'll bet on it to go up.*

'Bet' being the operative word.

What I was really doing was a mix of gambling and boredom buying. I was just guessing, tossing a coin and hoping! This is no way to invest and I started losing money on this. I soon stopped!

Of course, it would be a different matter if playing indices was my area of expertise and if I used some kind of skill to do it. But I didn't.

So while I suggest you slowly look at every area of the market, do be careful about launching yourself into a new arena without doing the proper research or knowing what you are doing.

If you are going to look at a new area, paper trade it for as long as possible until you are sure you know what you're doing.

PRODUCTION The Naked Trader 2

Top Ten Movies For Share Traders

1. The Money Pit
2. City Slickers
3. Carry On Regardless
4. Carry On Screaming
5. Titanic
6. Rogue Trader
7. Trading Places
8. Look Back In Anger
9. Casino
10. Buy & Cell

DIRECTOR Robbie Burns

Part 3
The Knowledge

“Where large sums of money are concerned, it is advisable to trust nobody.”

- *Agatha Christie*

What You Need To Know To Start Trading

Beginners: things you need to know about shares!

Let's look at some of the things you really need to know about shares. They include:

1. Spreads
2. Trading costs
3. Normal market size
4. Trading hours
5. Why shares move up or down!
6. Market makers
7. Volumes

I'll accept that some of this may not be immediately fascinating, and having read the above list you may well yawn and decide to stop reading for the moment.

Well, thanks a lot! I'm sitting here working hard (while watching *Who Wants To Be A Millionaire*) and all you can do is get bored.

But these bits and pieces are essential to understand before making that first trade. This is because many new traders lose money in the market as they don't understand what's going on. So you've got to get your head around these things!

Spreads

If you're a girl reading this, when I say spreads I am *not* talking about those woolly things you buy to put over a sofa to hide the stains if someone is coming round. Us blokes don't really care if there are stains, heathens! I *am* talking about the difference between a sell price and a buy price, known as the *spread.*

Although you will often come across references to the 'share price', the idea of the price of a share is actually a little more complicated than it may seem, and people new to the market can get confused over this. First, we need to define some terms:

- *Bid price*: the price at which you can sell shares
- *Offer price*: the price at which you can buy shares
- *Spread*: the difference between sell and buy price (bid and offer)
- *Mid price*: the price halfway between the bid and offer prices

A key point we can see from the above is that, at any one time, the price for buying shares and selling shares is different.

Let's look at an example.

ADVFN quote for Harvey Nash

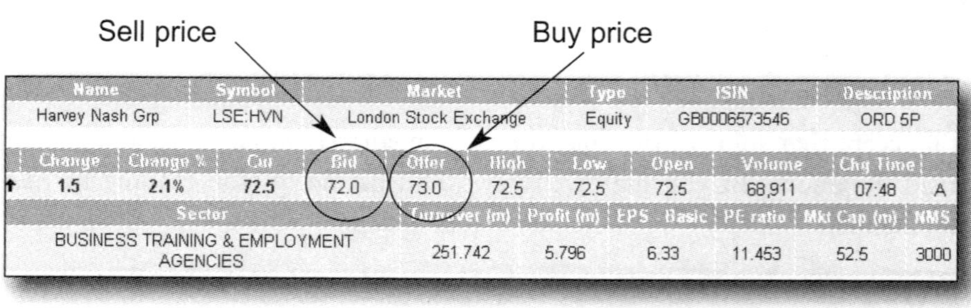

Name	Symbol	Market	Type	ISIN	Description
Harvey Nash Grp	LSE:HVN	London Stock Exchange	Equity	GB0006573546	ORD 5P

	Change	Change %	Cur	Bid	Offer	High	Low	Open	Volume	Chg Time	
↑	1.5	2.1%	72.5	72.0	73.0	72.5	72.5	72.5	68,911	07:48	A

Sector	Turnover (m)	Profit (m)	EPS Basic	PE ratio	Mkt Cap (m)	NMS
BUSINESS TRAINING & EMPLOYMENT AGENCIES	251.742	5.796	6.33	11.453	52.5	3000

In the above screenshot we can see that Harvey Nash has a bid price of 72p and an offer price of 73p. That means, if you want to sell the stock you'll get around 72p a share, and if you want to buy the stock you'll have to pay 73p.

Say you buy 10,000 shares at 73p, costing £7,300. If you changed your mind immediately after having bought the shares and wanted to sell them, you'd have to sell at 72p. That's £7,200, so you are down £100 (before even taking into account the commission cost and stamp duty).

The *spread* is the difference between the offer and bid price and, as can be seen in the above example, is a real and significant cost of trading. Why are spreads there? It's how the market makers (the people that allow you to buy or sell) make their cut.

Be aware of the importance of the spread, and realise that as soon as you buy a share, you're down on the deal.

Spread size

You'll soon find spreads can be wide or narrow.

Obviously the narrower the spread, the better for us. Spreads will be very narrow on heavily traded stocks, like those in the FTSE 100, and wider on the smaller stocks. On some stocks, especially in the junior AIM market, spreads can be ridiculously wide.

For example:

- Look at the bid-offer spread for a **large company** like Vodafone. The bid-offer prices quoted could be 130-130.1. That's a spread of next to nothing – it's tiny.
- But for a **small AIM stock** the bid-offer price could be 10-12. That's a spread of nearly 20%! If you bought at 12, the shares would have to go up 20% just to break even!

If I'm buying a smaller company, a spread of 3% is about as much as I'll allow. 4% max. If the spread is more than that, I would seriously have to consider not buying, even if I like the look of the company.

Always work out what the percentage of the spread is. If you're rubbish at percentages, ADVFN will tell you the percentage under 'Financials'.

Spread headlines – the news tonight is:

- Remember: you're losing money as soon as you buy a share
- Work out the percentage of the spread
- Be cautious about trading a share with a spread over 3%, and never over 5%
- The wider the spread, the bigger the risk

Trading costs

The costs of buying and selling shares can add up quickly, so here's a rough guide to possible costs.

There are generally three elements to share trading costs:

1. The **commission** charged by your broker *plus*
2. (Said through gritted teeth) a nasty and horrid tax on buying shares called **stamp duty** *plus*
3. **The spread.**

Stamp duty is set at 0.5%. So if you buy £5,000 worth of a share, the government will take £25. Of course this tax is outrageous. Why we should have to pay a tax to buy shares in companies I will never know. But there is no point bleating about it – we have to pay. Maybe not for much longer but for now.

Note: You only pay stamp duty on a buy, not when you sell a share.

Let's take an example of a buy and a sell and how much it costs.

Example – trading costs

You buy 1,000 shares in a company at 500p. Total value: £5,000.

Costs:

- Broker commission: £12.50 (average)
- Stamp duty: £25

Having bought the shares, you decide to sell them immediately, but because of the bid-offer spread, you may only be able to sell them at 495p. Total value: £4,950.

Costs:

- Broker commission: £12.50 (average)
- Stamp duty: £0 (only applies on buys)

So:

- Total direct costs (commission + stamp duty): £50
- Indirect cost (a result of the spread): £50

Beginner investors sometimes forget to factor in the cost of the spread, but this is a real cost. So, direct costs of £50 are bad enough. Factor in the spread, and total costs might be around £100! That's 2% of the trade value gone just in costs. Put another way, the share price has to rise 2% just to cover costs.

This is in the age of the internet, discount brokerages and efficient trading platforms. Imagine what it was like before, when broker commissions were a cool £50 or more!

As you see, the more you trade the more the costs will stack up. In the above example, trade 5 times, and you've knocked up total costs of £500. I probably pay around £3,000 a year to trade.

It means that if your mind is set on, say, becoming a day trader – that is buying and selling a share on the same day for a profit – you have to be really good to cover the costs, and that's one of the reasons 98% of would-be day traders fail. One lesson is don't overtrade because of all those wasted costs.

Normal market size

This is an important topic because you can rule out buying some shares you like the look of, just because of the shares' *normal market size*.

You may think you can buy as many shares as you like in any company, but it doesn't always work like that. It might be true for FTSE 100 stocks, but one has to be very careful when buying a smaller company.

Normal market size (usually abbreviated to NMS) is the number of shares market makers guarantee to sell or buy at quoted prices. If you want to buy or sell shares in a quantity above the NMS it can lead to problems.

Let's look at Harvey Nash again. The NMS is 3,000 shares. (Note: refer back to the screenshot of the ADVFN Quotes page for Harvey Nash – on page 76 included the information that the NMS for the company was 3,000 shares.)

That means that the sell-buy prices quoted (87-90), are valid only for trades up to 3,000 shares. If you wanted to buy, say, 8,000 shares, the market maker may quote a higher price (than 90). Conversely, if you wanted to sell 8,000 shares, the market maker may quote a lower price (than 87).

The NMS is set by the London Stock Exchange and is a minimum level market makers are bound by. In practice, however, I've found that you can pretty much deal in 3-4 times NMS without being charged extra.

But if the market suddenly tanked, the market makers can shut down and only offer you quotes strictly in NMS size.

The danger is that over time you might build up a sizeable position in one company's shares, say 15,000 shares. If a time then came when you wanted to sell all those shares quickly, you would have a problem if the NMS was below 5,000.

So bear this in mind before building up a holding too many shares in one company.

I am very careful and make sure the shares I buy have a decent NMS. I usually ensure the NMS is at least £2,000 worth of shares – though I prefer £4,000. To work out the NMS in pounds, simply multiply the NMS by the share price.

Summary

- Always check the NMS of a share before buying
- You may pay more to deal in quantities larger than the NMS
- Don't deal in shares with an NMS equivalent to less than £2,000

Trading hours

The London Stock Exchange opens for trading shares 08.00-16.30.

For a few minutes before the market opens and for a few minutes after it shuts there are auctions, but these are generally only for institutions. The opening auctions tend to decide the 8am opening price for most shares.

> Be careful of dealing in the bigger stocks between 8am and 9am - the spreads can be huge because there is no depth to the market and you could get caught out.

Why shares move up or down!

Before we go any further here's something you must get your head around:

What makes shares move up or down?

Not an unimportant question, no?

You might think that it would be an easy question to answer. But the factors affecting shares prices are quite complex. I get emails all the time from investors very puzzled by the movements of shares. They get very frustrated, for example, when shares move and they can't see the reason why.

A classic example is when a share price falls following the release of good news (perhaps strong annual results). What a perverse market, people wail. But the explanation, for this case, can be found in the old stock market maxim:

> *Buy on the rumour, sell on the news.*

By the time the news is actually announced, all the information has *already* been assimilated into the price, i.e. look at the share price behaviour in the short period leading up to the announcement. When the news is actually announced, the smart money (having bought previously in the run-up) is looking to sell and bank their profits.

There are many reasons why a share might move. I'll examine some of the reasons in greater depth later. But for now, and to show how difficult it can be to know why your shares are doing well or badly, here are some of the reasons:

- **Broker upgrade/downgrade**

  Brokers regularly put out recommendations to their clients – the share may temporarily be affected by a buy or sell recommendation. You'll usually find your news feed will reveal which broker and what that recommendation is.

- **General market move**

  The whole market may move up or down – for whatever reason – and your share will move in line with the market.

- **Sector move**

  Say your favourite stock is a telecoms share. A different telecoms company may have put out a profit warning, so your share could be dragged down along with all telecoms stocks.

- **Institution move**

  An institution has bought or sold stock. (Big trades – such as those made by large institutions – are usually notified on the news wires one or two days after the event.)

- **Director buying/selling**

  Directors have bought or sold shares in their own company. Investors often follow movements by directors so more stock might be bought or sold than normal, moving the price.

- **Results/news story**

  If the price is moving quickly, check the news wire for any story. It could be a price-moving statement from the company or other news story.

- **Dividend dates**

  The price will always move lower on 'ex-dividend' day. So if the dividend is 10p the share will move down around 10p.

- **Tipped**

  The share has been tipped by a newspaper, magazine or one of the many tipsters.

- **Bulletin board manipulation**

  A tiny stock could soar because a group have got together to make it sound irresistible on the BBs.

- **Market maker manipulation**

  Market makers are moving the price to encourage buyers or sellers to suit their own ends.

- **Tree Shake**

  Market makers push the price down quickly and drastically to encourage sellers, then move the price back up again.

- **Surprise events**

  Something major happens like a terrorist strike – all shares could be hit. Or some political drama unfolds somewhere.

- **Rights issue**

  A company decides to raise money by offering more shares at a lower price. This usually lowers the price.

- **Takeover/merger**

  Companies announce a takeover or merger.

- **Stake building**

  Someone is building a stake in the company.

> My brief summary above shows just how on the ball you must be. Always know why a share you might want to buy or sell is moving.

Market makers and the crowd

It's the job of the market makers to always provide sell and buy prices for some stocks. But, generally, not FTSE 100 stocks where sellers and buyers are matched electronically. Without them, trading could be difficult in some stocks.

Market makers are there to ensure that there is always a buyer, and a seller, for shares.

For example, you might want to sell some shares in a company, but what happens if at that time there are no other investors wanting to buy your shares? You'd be stuck with the shares, as you couldn't sell them. Market makers are there to ensure that there is always a buyer, and a seller, for shares. In technical terms, they help create what is called *liquidity*.

The way market makers operate and how prices move up and down have changed a lot quite recently (since the first edition of this book). And you have to try and get your head around these ways as it will help with timing your trades.

Market makers basically have less and less influence on share prices the larger the company is.

Company type	Price influences
Large	Prices move around constantly because it is basically "open outcry" with thousands of people inputting different prices direct onto the order book. These shares can move FAST! In jargon, these are *SETS stocks.*
Medium (roughly up to £950m)	The price is moved by market makers *and* those with direct market access. This includes spread betting firms, CFD traders. In fact, many different players. These shares jump around much quicker as there are lots of people trying to buy and sell at different prices. In jargon these shares are called *SETS/MM stocks.*
Small (roughly up to about £100m market cap)	The price will be moved by market makers only – during any normal day when there is no news on a stock the price may just move up and down very slowly. In jargon these shares are called *SEAQ stocks.*
AIM	These shares are, in the main, tiny tiddlers but there are also some big companies too. The smaller ones have market makers only and the bigger ones are *SETS/MM.*

Back for a moment to market makers.

A quick glance at bulletin boards will reveal that market makers are not popular with traders. According to some traders, they are masters of spin – up there with Tony Blair Esq.

Why is this?

The reason is mainly due to the way they make their money, which can put them in opposition to traders.

Remember, market makers make their money from a share's spread. The more that traders buy and sell, the more money market makers make. Therefore, it is in the interests of market makers to move their prices around a bit to encourage active buying and selling of shares.

So, the market makers may move a price up to encourage you to sell your shares, or move it down to encourage you to buy. Or even the other way round. The result is that share prices can move in odd ways, sometimes with little seeming relation to the actual situation of the company.

This can be very confusing to new traders who see a price moving, but can't understand why it's moving. It drives a lot of investors crackers – especially if it makes you sell your share at the wrong time.

Tree shaking

All sorts of 'tricks' are employed by the market makers. For example, when they drop a share for no reason, it's known by investors as a *tree shake.*

One morning you'll roll out of bed, switch on your computer and see your favourite share is down 2p, then 3p, 5p and 6p...! You'll start to scream, sweat, swear and probably panic – that's exactly what they want you to feel. In a panic, you'll sell immediately at any price because something terrible must be happening.

What's really happening is a tree shake.

It's designed to make you very afraid. Afraid enough to think the share's going down further so you should get out. Once you and a few others have sold out, the price will gradually start to go back up. This will also make you scream and sweat, and probably swear. At least the panic will have gone!

You've been shaken out!

So why do they try and shake you out?

It may be because the market makers have a big buy order to fill, and they need your shares to fill it. Or perhaps the company is doing well, results are due and they want to get some cheap shares into their 'bank'. It's more likely they will get your shares by dropping the price, especially by doing it one pence at a time.

> You'll start to scream, sweat, swear and probably panic – that's exactly what they want you feel.

Tree shake antidote

Instead of panicking and swearing, here's what you do:

Check to see if there is anything on the news wires regarding the share. Then check if there is any major selling showing up. If there is no obvious reason for the fall, it's 90% certain that it's a tree shake.

So instead of selling, go and make a cup of tea and some toast and relax. Later in the day you can pat yourself on the back – you weren't shaken!

A tree shake will also usually only last a few hours. If the share continues to go down over a day or two, it could be more than a shake. Watch volumes and see if there has been any serious selling.

A final point: If you do get shaken out of a share and it goes back up, sometimes it's best to swear a bit at the computer but then leave it alone. Otherwise you will go back in and immediately be emotionally involved with that share.

There is always another share, another day.

> The general point is, if you are happy with your share, there is no bad news about and it still looks cheap to you and the main market itself is not in meltdown, it's best to ride out the fall and sit tight.

Dividends

Dividends are cash that you receive, usually twice a year, from a company in which you've invested. Most decent shares pay dividends.

They may at first glance seem to be quite small amounts, but I can promise you over the years they can add up to an awful lot of money. Some companies payout more in payments than you'd get in a building society. So not only are you getting a capital gain (as the share price increases), but income too!

So how do you find out when the company is likely to send you some money, and how much will it be?

The best place to go is ADVFN, or one of the many other financial web sites.

Example – dividends

Let's take one company for example – Macro 4.

As usual, click for a quote (code: MAO). Click on 'Financials' – if you scroll down a little you'll see the actual dividend yield, which in this case is nearly 4%. This is what you'll pick up over a year holding the share. Not a bad percentage.

Now scroll down a little further and this is where it gets interesting.

Under 'Dividends', you can see all the dividends that have been paid out over the years.

Dividends paid by Macro 4

Date you get your money

Ex date

Amount paid

Dividends

Announcement Date	Type	Curr.	Dividend Amount	Period Start	Period End	Ex Date	Record Date	Payment Date	Total Dividend Amount
25 Feb 2007	Interim	GBP	**2.50**	01/07/2006	31/12/2006	21/03/2007	23/03/2007	11/05/2007	-
12 Sep 2006	Final	GBP	**5.00**	30/06/2005	30/06/2006	04/10/2006	06/10/2006	23/11/2006	**7.25**
21 Feb 2006	Interim	GBP	**2.25**	01/07/2005	31/12/2005	15/03/2006	17/03/2006	03/05/2006	-
16 Sep 2005	Final	GBP	**4.75**	30/06/2004	30/06/2005	21/09/2005	23/09/2005	07/11/2005	**7.00**
10 Feb 2005	Interim	GBP	**2.25**	31/12/2003	31/12/2004	30/03/2005	01/04/2005	03/05/2005	-
14 Sep 2004	Final	GBP	**4.50**	30/06/2003	30/06/2004	29/09/2004	01/10/2004	29/10/2004	**6.50**
17 Feb 2004	Interim	GBP	**2.00**	01/07/2003	31/12/2003	24/03/2004	26/03/2004	22/04/2004	-
04 Sep 2003	Final	GBP	**4.00**	30/06/2002	30/06/2003	24/09/2003	26/09/2003	11/11/2003	**6.00**
13 Feb 2003	Interim	GBP	**2.00**	01/07/2002	31/12/2002	19/03/2003	21/03/2003	22/04/2003	-
05 Sep 2002	Final	GBP	**4.00**	30/06/2001	30/06/2002	18/09/2002	20/09/2002	12/11/2002	**6.00**
14 Feb 2002	Interim	GBP	**2.00**	01/07/2001	31/12/2001	20/03/2002	22/03/2002	23/04/2002	-
04 Sep 2001	Final	GBP	**4.00**	30/06/2000	30/06/2001	19/09/2001	21/09/2001	13/11/2001	**6.00**
14 Feb 2001	Interim	GBP	**2.00**	01/07/2000	31/12/2000	21/03/2001	23/03/2001	25/04/2001	-
07 Sep 2000	Final	GBP	**5.00**	30/06/1999	30/06/2000	18/09/2000	22/09/2000	14/11/2000	**15.20**
15 Feb 2000	Interim	GBP	**10.20**	01/07/1999	31/12/1999	20/03/2000	24/03/2000	25/04/2000	-
31 Aug 1999	Final	GBP	**15.90**	30/06/1998	30/06/1999	06/09/1999	10/09/1999	01/11/1999	**26.10**
01 Sep 1998	Final	GBP	**15.90**	30/06/1997	30/06/1998	05/10/1998	09/10/1998	02/11/1998	**26.10**

Dividends generally get paid twice a year in varying amounts.

Ex-dates

Now a question that must be in the top ten questions I get asked about shares:

When do you have to be holding the share to get the dividend?

It's quite easy. It's called the 'ex-date'. In the Macro 4 example, the 'ex-date' is March 21st.

It means on March 21st the share is trading 'ex' or without the dividend. So if you held the share up to and including the close of play on March 20th, you are entitled to the dividend.

If you buy the shares on March 21st you are *not* entitled to it.

'Record date' is March 23rd – that's the date where they go through the share register and make a list of all holders entitled to the dividend. Just ignore this date, it doesn't really matter. The 'ex' date is the big one.

And when do you actually get the readies?

That's under 'Payment date' further along the line on ADVFN (which in this case was 11 May in 2007).

Now, often new investors say to themselves:

> Aha! I'll just buy Macro late on March 20th, and sell early on the 21st, and pick up the dividend. Say I bought 20,000 shares I'd end up with a nice cheque for £60 and only hold the shares for five minutes!

Nice try, clever dick! Don't you think the market has thought of this not-so-cunning ploy!

Well, it has – so there goes your nice little earner.

Sadly, what happens on 'ex' day is that the share price will usually start the day lower by the amount of dividend. So if you bought the day before 'ex', and sell the day after, what you make on the dividend payment, you'll lose on the fall in the share price.

Dividend payments are normally announced whenever a company makes its twice yearly results statement. You'll usually find a paragraph in the results which states the next ex and payout dates.

You should know the dates of ex-dividends for your shares.

For example, Macro would fall 2.5p on the day it goes ex-dividend. If you weren't aware that was ex day, you might panic and sell because you thought the share was being sold off, or it had dropped through your stop loss.

So pay attention to these dates.

My views on dividends?

I don't worry about them too much and consider the extra money coming in should pretty much pay for the costs of buying and selling the shares.

"Is it worth buying shares just for the dividends?"

It really depends on your market strategy:

- **Low risk investor**

  The answer is yes, if you are an older investor and are looking for very steady shares with good dividends. For example, utility companies pay big dividends, however their actual share prices don't move much, so you won't get quick capital growth. But say you're 60-years-old and want to grow a fund slowly but surely with minimum risk, you could just go for an income portfolio of high-yielding shares.

- **Medium risk investor**

  A medium risk investor might look on dividends as a bit of a bonus.

- **High risk investor**

  This investor doesn't care about dividends because he only wants big growth, and the kinds of shares he invests in generally don't pay dividends.

How do you buy and sell a share?

This might sound too bleedin' obvious but:

How do you buy a share online?

Dead easy! Each broker's web site is slightly different but generally they operate along similar lines.

On the web site look for: "Deal", "Invest", or "Dealing" – they usually use one of these words.

Then you type the code of the share you want to buy into the box (e.g. "VOD" for Vodafone). You usually get a choice of something like "at best" or "limit".

If you deal at best you are asking to take the best available price – a limit means you won't pay more than the price you want. Type the most you'll pay into the limit box. We'll talk about this a bit more later.

Then press the get quote or confirm button or "Next" and you should be presented with a price and a 15 second countdown box to accept the price. Once you press the accept button you are the owner of the shares! So don't press it unless you are sure you want the price. Don't worry about the 15 second countdown making you feel under pressure, you can always get it again!

All the above is also true when it comes to selling a share, except obviously you press "sell" not "buy". (Actually, in the heat of the moment, it's easy to make a mistake here – we've all done it. So, be careful!)

If you don't get a 15 second countdown it means the share you want can't be dealt with online in the amount you want and the deal will have to go through a dealer. So instead of a countdown your order goes through to a dealer. The site will shortly tell you if your buy or sell was successfully done.

If this happens you are not sure of the price you are going to get. So set a "limit" price before pressing "send order to dealer". A price you do not want to pay more than. Otherwise if the share is fast moving you could end up paying a silly price.

If you're a complete beginner, practise a lot before you press the accept button for real.

How Do I Find Shares Worth Looking At?

You want to know do you?

Oh, all right, if you insist. The best way to explain this is to tell you how I look for them. Usually I try the kitchen first, then the living room but I usually find them under the bed. [Robbie! Shares, shares – not keys. Concentrate please. Ed.]

There are many ways. A good summary, I think, would be that I am looking for shares where *something seems to be happening.*

And preferably the shares are rising.

My first stage is to simply try to find shares that *might* be of interest. I'm not saying I'll buy any of them right away – I'm on the hunt for shares I might buy soon, or I might buy next year.

Here's how I try to find shares at least worth adding to my daily watchlist.

Where I don't look for ideas

First, however, these are the places I *avoid* looking at to get ideas:

- Internet tipsters/tipsheets
- Bulletin boards
- Columns from gurus

Where I look for ideas

These are my favourite places I look for ideas:

1. National newspaper round-ups
2. Investment magazines
3. ADVFN news wire
4. ADVFN Toplists

Why do I use these particular sources?

Well, they have all served me well in the past and shares usually appear in these sources because there is a story to tell or the share is moving. Of course, if you read about a share rising in a paper or magazine it doesn't mean it'll carry on going up, it might well fall. But this is where I play detective and start my research.

Let's now look at these sources in more depth.

1. Newspapers

I usually get three national newspapers every day and have a good look at the financial pages. I'll look at any of the broadsheets including *The Times*, *The Daily Telegraph*, *The Guardian*, *The Independent*, and sometimes *The Daily Mail*.

The tabloids aren't much use when it comes to shares. In fact, one sign of the top of a bull market is when the tabloids start getting interested in the stock market. In other words, when the tabloids increase their coverage of the stock market, that's the time to get out of the market!

It might sound strange, but I don't bother with *The Financial Times* – I find it too dry and too heavy-going. It's more of an international, business-oriented paper. What I might buy is the weekend edition of the *FT*, which has some thoughtful coverage of shares.

Within the newspapers, I take a look at the daily stock market round-up – reporting on the shares that have gone up or down and why. I also have a scan of the news stories.

Once or twice a week I'll see something that looks interesting. I'll make a note of the share and why it might be one to buy.

It might sound strange, but I don't bother with *The Financial Times*.

2. Investment magazines

There are two main ones:

- **Investors Chronicle**

  Investors Chronicle is sober and has a large circulation – it's been around for a long time. It has some good analysis of company results, some good trading input and some interesting in-depth pullouts which are well worth reading.
  (Published: Fridays.)

- **Shares magazine**

  Appears to be aimed at the younger, more 'would like a punt' readership.
  (Published: Thursdays.)

I think both magazines do a reasonable job, so I do rate both magazines as worth a buy.

But I would never be tempted to buy into the tips of either magazine (especially as these would already have been marked up by market makers on the morning of publication). You should look at the comments made by the magazines as a guideline and not just buy something because a company is recommended.

Sometimes a story they've written about a company they write about might intrigue me, so I'll have a look at it. I especially like the round-up both mags do of recent company results statements. It's interesting to read their comments, they get some comments right and some wrong. Occasionally I'll notice a company I hadn't spotted before and pop it in my notebook to look at in detail.

A word of warning though: don't get fooled by the magazines which claim they produce winning tips. Some of their tips will turn out to be stinkers! Also, note that judging the performance of tips is not always straightforward:

- Was broker's commission and stamp duty taken into account?
- Was it actually possible to deal in the market at the prices used in the calculation?
- Often the aggregate tips performance will be heavily influenced by the stellar performance of one flukey share – if you'd missed buying that one share, the aggregate performance of the remaining tips might be nowhere near as good.

However, it is important to know which shares are being tipped (even if you don't buy them). This is because tipped shares will often increase in price before the market opens, and it's important to know why they rose (i.e. they were up on a tip). Otherwise you might buy them thinking there was more to the rise than just a tip!

> My tip is: by all means buy these good quality magazines, but use them for reference and as prompts for trading ideas, not as a source of sure-fire tips.

3. ADVFN Newswire

ADVFN has a streaming (i.e. it continually refreshes itself, without having to reload the page) newswire; I always keep it running in the background. It covers pretty much everything that's happening. It includes company statements, directors' dealings, market reports, all you need!

Most company reports are published between 7am and 8am, so I usually pay more attention to the newswire early on.

Again, sometimes I'll find a company worth looking at, especially if a company report looks very positive. I make a note of anything that catches my eye, from a company reporting to directors' buying – often waiting till the evening to check out the company concerned.

There are plenty of other newswires and web sites out there too, if you are interested in following the latest news.

However, I do find the majority of the most interesting stuff is released just after 7am. I read though what the various companies are reporting and take notes if there are things I like the look of.

But my favourite way to find shares worth looking at is...

4. ADVFN Toplists

These lists are a great way to look out for shares on the move. The lists are compiled by a computer which has been given certain criteria.

ADVFN Toplists menu screen shot

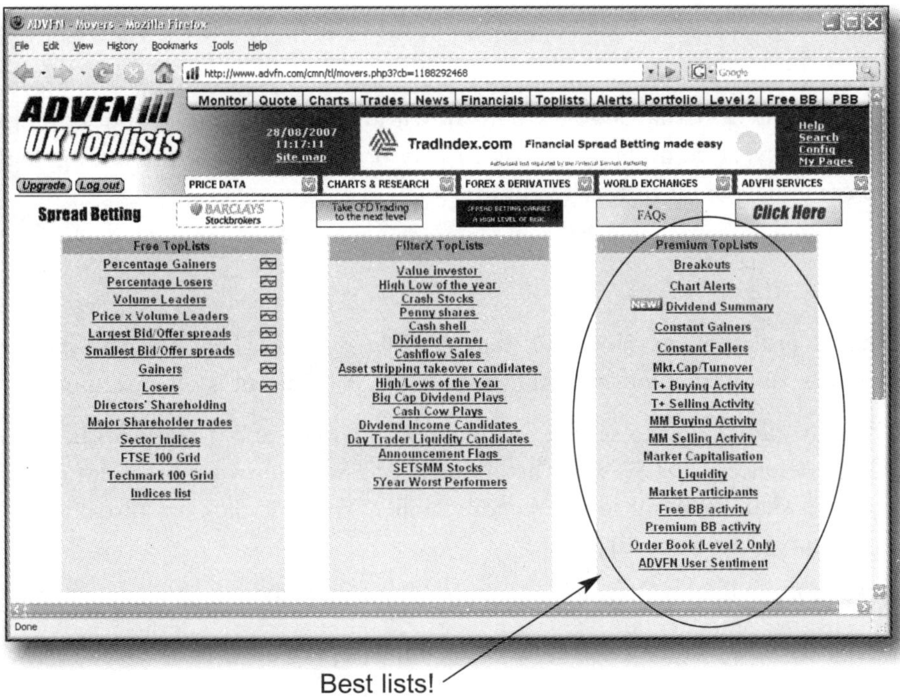

As you can see, on the left are the lists you can have for free and on the right premium lists that cost £60 a year to access. That's money well worth spending.

> I'm glad to say ADVFN offers *Naked Trader 2* readers access to the lists for just £40 for the first year, saving you a decent £20. It you want to take up the offer just email me at thenakedtrader@aol.com with "Cheap Bronze" in the subject line and I will mail you back with how to accept this good offer.

Bronze also gives you access to the premium bulletin board on ADVFN, where serious investors discuss shares and where my bulletin board is.

The lists I particularly like are:

Percentage gainers and losers

In other words: the biggest movers of the day. These lists give an excellent snapshot of what is moving.

To find out why the share is soaring up or plunging down, there is often an 'A' by the share. You click on that to find out why.

I'm interested in shares going both down and up, because the ones going down this year could be the recovery play of next year. And the ones going up could have a lot further to climb.

Breakouts

This is probably my favourite share finding method. This lists the shares breaking out of previously established ranges. A breakout is often significant.

ADVFN allows you to search for 52-week, 12-week and 4-week breakouts. My preference is for 52-week breakouts. A 52-week upward breakout often means a share is about to rise steadily higher. You just click on "Breakouts" on the premium lists, top right.

Why is looking at breakouts potentially so rewarding?

Because you are finding shares breaking out of a previously established range, and this often points out that something interesting is happening with the share. Probably more people are buying in. Volumes will be up, something good may be going on and there are fewer sellers around.

When you click on the breakout list you will often find 20-30 shares on there to have a look at. I do my usual screen and generally don't bother with AIM shares, illiquid shares, etc.

I tend to favour shares that have a market cap of between £50m and £900m because they have a lot more room for growth than, say, a FTSE 100 share.

So let's have a look at some breakouts which I spotted on the list, where the breakout happened.

Here's an example of a good 'un I found in this way.

Carclo

Carclo

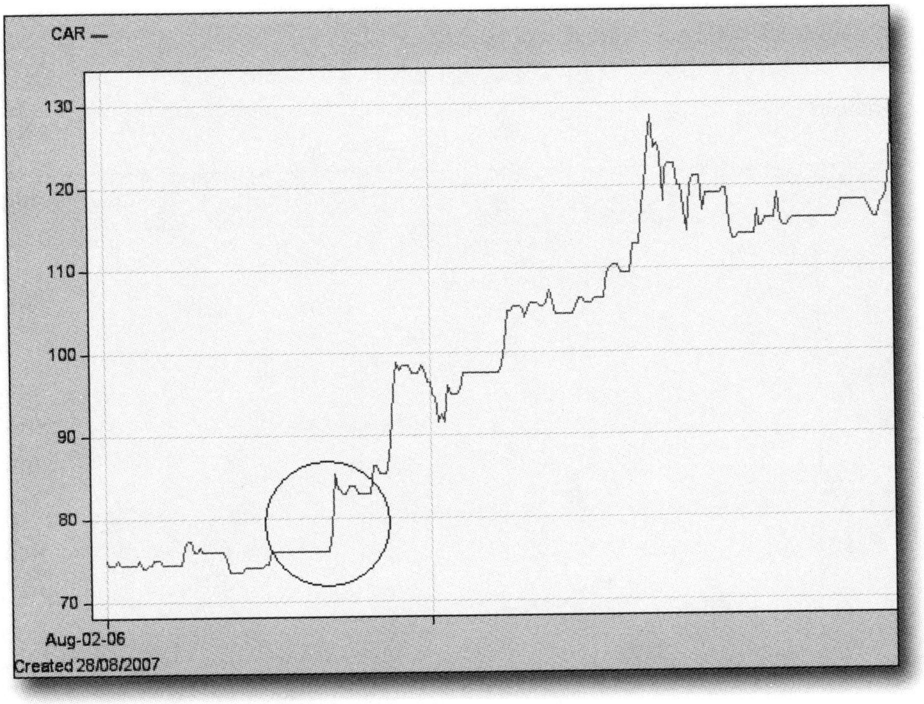

You can see ringed on the chart where the breakout occurred. It had been trading at around 76-78p for quite a while from July to November 2006, but notice where it suddenly breaks out of the range in November, going over 80p, which is when it went onto ADVFN's list and onto my radar as a buy.

I bought after doing my usual research, but I may not have come across it otherwise. You can see it went to 100p, and then started going down a bit. The next breakout you can see is when it broke through 100p and at that point it became a buy again for me – this time as a top-up on my original holding.

Let's look at another one...what the hell, let's live a little!

Renold

By October 2006, Renold had been trading flat for a long time. But as you can see it broke out suddenly as it headed up through 70 and went to 80. Then you can see it broke out again – after trading at 80 for a while, it broke through 80 before it headed straight up to 120.

Renold

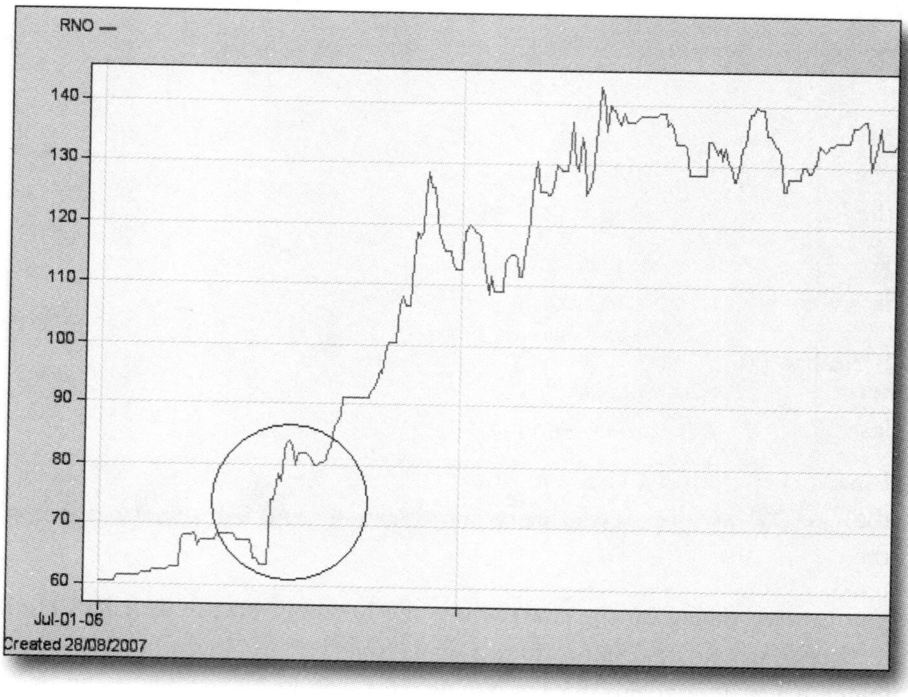

So, breakouts: very important!

Most of the ones you will find on ADVFN Premium Toplists will be similar. The computer is just telling you a share has gone up through an old resistance area.

Once you've found a share that's broken out, of course, the real work begins: it is then time to do the research.

Sometimes you will get what is termed a *false breakout*: the share breaks away for a short time and then goes back to where it was. So sometimes it is worth missing a point or two and checking it really is breaking out.

How To Select Shares

My research involves finding out everything I can about a company before I consider buying in. And so should yours. The lazier you are about research the less money you'll make. And really, it's not even that difficult.

For the moment I will assume you have already found a share you are interested in (more on how to find ones to look at follows later in the book).

I want *the whole story* about a share. *I want it* and *I want it now*! (Sorry – the last bit is a coded message to the Mrs.)

The lazier you are about research the less money you'll make.

I look at everything I can, and much of the research involves trying to pick out the negative things – I guess I'm trying to put myself off! I use every scrap of info I have to come to a decision – and so should you.

> Good research means if you reach a decision to buy you really are sure it is worth buying into.

Don't skip the research

It's only human nature to try and skip doing a lot of research. After all, it can be pretty boring, and it's more exciting to just press the buy button on a whim.

Much more fun to buy a penny share because a bulletin board punter has posted up some pretty charts and posted something about 'amazing news' on the way. Don't!

I urge you to get down and dirty: do your research. Don't skip it and be serious about it. Find out anything you can, however you can. This is your money you're playing with and if you really want to make a profit there's no such thing as enough research.

And whatever you do, don't see a share and think "I fancy that one" then do research only looking at the positive stuff and ignoring the negative – that's not research! In other words: don't pretend to research because you're going to buy the share anyway.

What's the story?

What I do is build up the "story" of a share.

Do I want to buy the story?

I want to share with you some of the questions that I try and answer in my research. And I don't buy a share until I have found the answers. What I'm trying to do is build a clear picture in my head about what this share is all about. Where's it been, what is it doing and does it hang around outside the fish and chip shop causing trouble?

First let me highlight one major point.

> I am looking for a share that has everything going for it with no question marks.

I am also trying to keep things simple. Perhaps what I'm trying to say is you need to cut through the bullshit. I'm looking for good things and trying to avoid shares with the bad – or with question marks.

Keep it simple

Let me give you an example.

You probably know and have seen TV shows with two no-nonsense people: Amstrad boss and rich guy Sir Alan Sugar, and millionaire chef Gordon Ramsay.

You haven't? Oh right you spend your time watching *EastEnders, Emmerdale* and *Neighbours*. I've got your number mate!

Well Sir Alan stars in a show *The Apprentice*, in which he searches for someone to give a job to. He's a no nonsense man. Now imagine what he'd want to know if he was going to buy a share in a company. He'd cut through the crap, which is exactly what I try to do. I can imagine him saying to the chairman in his gruff tones:

> Don't give me no bloody crap about Fibonacci Bollinger bands, resistance points, bleedin' double bottoms and moving averages.
>
> What I wanna know is: How much is your bleeding company worth, how much are the bloody profits, how much do you owe. Don't give me nothing else, don't need it.

And if he got the reply:

> But Sir Alan, the company has EBITDA of £5.3 million, our reorganisation is going well and we've hired some consultants...

Sugar would say:

> Right! I've bloody had enough. You talk and talk but don't give me no real answers – it's all complete rubbish, I can't make head or tail of it, so you're bloody fired!

So I try and be a bit Sir Alanish and cut through the crap. Keep it simple!

Similarly, chef Gordon Ramsay goes into failing restaurants and tries to rescue them for one of his TV shows. He generally finds out everything they do is too complicated. Which is why they are losing money. Their sauces are too complicated, they spend money on the wrong things. It's exactly the same with share traders who try and over-analyse situations. Simplicity is best.

I know just what he'd say if he visited a share trader losing money:

> F*** me!

Yeah, I know he says that about everything. (From now on I'll just put (f) when he talks to represent his favourite word.)

> Look at all those (f) screens on your desk. What have you got all those (f) chart packages for? (f) me you've got hundreds of stock analyser tools – no wonder you're losing (f) money, you haven't even got (f) time to buy a (f) share.

And I really believe both these successful people would approach share trading in the same way I have.

Sir A would be right. You just need to ask a few direct questions about a company and you should find all the answers on ADVFN or equivalent service. You don't need to get bogged down in too much detail.

There are so many traders out there with so many systems. Yet my simple methods have always worked and made me lots of money.

The questions

OK, best thing for me to do here is take you through some of the simple steps I use to build up my research.

As Sir Alan might say, the first two things I want to know are:

> *What's your bloody company worth and what your profits?*

But here is the list of questions I want to know the answers to when looking at a share.

These are the kind of questions you should be finding out the answers to as well. Write them down if you want and use them whenever you look at a share.

Questions to ask about a company
What is it worth? (Market cap)
What are its full year pre-tax profits?
Are profits rising?
Are dividends rising?
Is the outlook positive?
Are there any negative things happening?
What is the net debt?
What kind of dividend does it pay?
What does it do and what sector is it in?
Are its markets likely to improve or get worse?
When's the next statement due?
Is the share price on the way up?

All the answers to these questions can usually be found on web sites like ADVFN. I use the following pages:

1. Quote
2. Financials
3. News (to find recent report statements)

I want the answers to all these questions, and only when I'm satisfied with all my answers would I be tempted to buy – then it's down to timing which I'll discuss later (if I get my timing right).

(Some examples of shares I found and liked coming up a bit later in the book too.)

For now let's concentrate on getting some answers.

The answers

Perhaps a lazy, hazy mist is coming over you now and you're thinking:

> *Yeah, yeah, research, all a bit boring isn't it? Sod that, I know he's right but I can't be bothered and I'll take a chance and trust to luck.*

Well, not if you want to make good money and avoid losing it. It doesn't even take much time!

1. Market capitalisation

OK, market market capitalisation (cap) first. This is what the market thinks the company is worth. A quick guide:

- **Up to £50m:** is considered very small
- **£50m to £140m:** small-ish
- **£140m to £450m:** small-medium
- **Above £450m:** the company is in the top 350 in the UK
- **Above £2bn:** the company is probably in the FTSE 100 Index

As I mentioned the market cap is to the far right of the ADVFN Quote page.

I personally prefer to look for companies in the £50m to £950m size range – they often have better growth prospects than say FTSE 100 stocks. But I do buy FTSE stocks sometimes too.

2. Company report

The next thing I want to do is find out the health of the company. So, I click "News" and find the last company report – either full year or interim. To get into a company report on ADVFN, click on "News" and then scroll down till you get to the last results.

Two things in particular I'm after: finding out the negatives and looking for the positives.

How does that song go?

> *You've got to elim – in – ate the negatives and...accentuate the positive...*

What, you reckon was that a Beyoncé track? Sounds more like Westlife...

Reading company reports

Every few months, companies have to put out a financial report. These sometimes come in the form of a full report, which includes in-depth figures, sometimes it's a trading statement, which gives an indication of how things are going.

The statements are usually quite long and often complicated. And it doesn't seem to matter how badly the company concerned is doing – there will almost always be some kind of positive spin used on results. You really have to read through the positive spin and see if you can find the downside.

If you're like me, you won't want to trawl through a company report, it's pretty boring. Fortunately, there are one or two key things to watch out for when reading a report.

I came up with a system which would scan a company report in a few seconds and let me know whether it's worth getting into or not.

So let me present...

The Naked Trader Secret Traffic Lights System

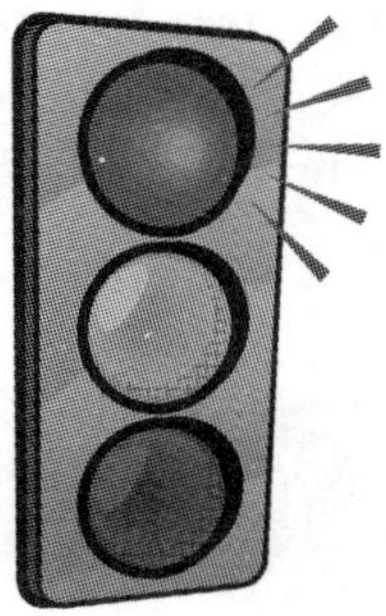

I call it my 'traffic lights' system: red for sell, amber for hold and green for buy!

I highlighted this in my first book but I've refined it a lot since then and there are quite a few additions – so readers of Book One take note!

What it's really done for me is enable me to quickly tell from a results report or an AGM statement what the state of play is. I can tell in just a few seconds whether to carry on looking at the company or forget it immediately. Once you have installed this you will wonder how you ever did without it.

How does it work?

I use a neat tool which is available for use at ADVFN. The tool can be set up by clicking on "News" in the top menu bar. Then somewhere below you should see 'highlight phrases'.

You can add any number of words or phrases and those will be highlighted in any text you want to read. You can also put the words in any colour you want.

It will quite simply pick out the negatives and positives.

Here's what I do – and what you should do as well:

- Put 'challenging' into the first box, in **red.**
- Then 'difficult' into the second box in **red.**

Continue inputting all the words and phrases in the following table:

Colour	Word/phrase
red	challenging, difficult, down by, unpredictable, lower, poor, difficult trading, tough, below expectations
yellow	in line with expectations
green	exceeding expectations, positive, favourable, profit up, excellent
blue	debt, banking facilities, bank covenants

Finally, click OK, to store all the phrases.

Now look at the last company report of all the companies you hold in your portfolio and you will see those phrases highlighted in the different colours. (What I mean by this is, click on the latest news stories on the company in which you're interested till you get to the last report.)

Now it's really quite simple:

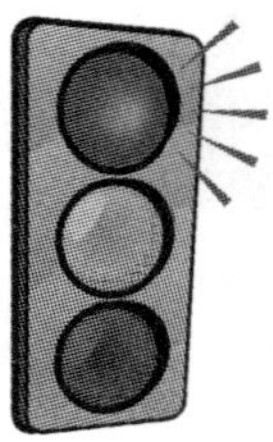

Any company report that you see with lots of **red** is a probable sell or, at least, not a buy

Any with **yellow** a hold

Any with lots of **green** are potential buys

The more greens the more positive, the more reds the more negative.

Now you may scoff at what might seem an over simplistic idea. And, of course, my system is only the basis to start some more in-depth research.

But I don't think you can beat it for a quick judgement!

I'm not saying for a minute that you should buy every company which has loads of greens or sell every one that's red, but it should give you an instant 'flavour' of the report. As you get used to the system, you could add your own words or phrases.

What about the blue highlighted words?

Well, that's all to do with working out whether the company's got too much debt or could even go bust. More on that shortly.

Watch out for "challenging"

You may notice the first word that gets highlighted in red is "challenging".

It's the one word companies like to use when there's trouble. I guess it doesn't sound too bad but it's amazing how they all use it to really say:

> *Well, er, we're in the...you know what!*

> Too many 'challengings' means one thing: the company is probably in some kind of trouble!

So after discarding any shares with too many red negative words, the next thing is to weed out some more. This is because I subject each share to a quick but stern filtering process.

Generally, I will discard and not proceed further with any share that:

1. Is AIM listed (but not always)
2. Is losing money
3. Has a big spread (more than 5%)
4. Has a small market size (a market cap of under £30m)

This weeds out the high risk stocks. There's nothing wrong *per se* in having the odd high risk stock for small stakes once you're experienced, but if you're new-ish it's best to stay safe.

When I say no AIM, there are some okay AIM stocks, but because I trade mainly in ISAs (and AIM stocks aren't allowed in ISAs), I don't go for them unless I think they are very special. And then they'll probably end up in my pension fund.

3. Dividend check

Next thing is to check dividend payouts.

- **Rising dividends** put a big tick in my book. I check these under the 'Financials' button.
- If I see a **falling, or cut dividend,** I would probably end my research there – it's not a good sign.

A company that always increases its dividend year after year is a very good sign!

4. Chart check

Next is a look at the chart for the last year – that's at the bottom of the Quote page on ADVFN.

Is the line higher once it reaches the right-hand side, or lower than when it started? The former is a good sign as the share is in an uptrend. If it's lower, I'd have to look into it further but it puts it in dodgier territory.

I'd also take a look at the three year chart too. I'll come back to charts a bit later, but for now I want to see a share in a good-looking up trend.

5. Company background check

The next step is to find out what the company does and look back through the history of the last couple of year's news stories.

I like to see rising profits and turnover, and a gradually improving share price. I look to see when it reports next. Is it next week or in three months? If it's next week, could there be a nasty shock on the way or will those already in the stock be ready to take profits?

Any big share movements reported? Any institutional buys? I check all this out. ADVFN makes it rather easy as you can click on all the news stories going back over a long time.

What I'm doing is trying to build a picture of the company concerned, and this is what you should be doing. Keep clicking, keep reading.

Just because you see one thing you like about a company, don't just buy it on an impulse.

> Don't ignore things you don't like the look of because you suddenly fancy buying it anyway. Stay cool and objective.

6. Directors' dealings

Many investors believe it's worth keeping an eye on directors' buying and selling shares in their own companies.

The reason is: if a director is buying a lot of shares, it's assumed he or she has some confidence in the future of the company – and that no one should know a company better than its directors.

Conversely, if a director is dumping shares, perhaps the confidence is simply not there and one has to be careful.

Generally, directors are allowed to buy and sell shares in their own companies, but they are not allowed to trade in shares of their company in the six weeks preceding a results announcement (this is known as the *closed period*). So you will often find directors buying or selling shares on the day of results or one or two days afterwards.

Many investors believe that by following buys or sales by directors they can make money. That is by buying into companies when directors are buying, and selling (or shorting) when directors are selling.

Interpreting directors' dealings

Of course just because a director buys, does not necessarily mean the shares are going to rise. You have to examine the buys and sells in tandem with doing proper research into the companies. Following directors' dealings slavishly in my opinion may not lead you to stock market millions!

Why do directors buy their shares?

Sometimes they buy because they think their company is doing well. Sometimes it's simply to give a vote of confidence and encourage investors to back the company. And often it's simply because they think they will make a lot of money and they have to do something with their money.

Why do they sell?

It could be because they feel the company's future for the moment is not all that bright. But it could simply be because they need the money to pay school fees or buy a house.

> Following directors' dealings slavishly in my opinion may not lead you to stock market millions!

The problem is, directors are usually rather enthusiastic about their companies and so might buy even if the shares are overvalued. Sometimes directors buy to try and prop up the price of their company if the share price has been falling.

For example, the infamous Robert Maxwell was busy buying shares in his own company, even though he must have known the company was in deep trouble.

Directors know that by buying their shares there will be an announcement and that could cause investors to buy in.

> The key, I believe, to working out whether a director buy or sell is worth following or not, is the *amount* of shares bought or sold.

If they are buying a huge amount then I am more interested. Or if they are buying a lot of shares in relation to their current holding. It is always worth looking at how many shares they already hold to put their buy or sell into context.

For example, if a CEO of a company sells one million shares, does that mean it is time to follow suit?

Not necessarily, if, say, the director still owns fifteen million shares. He might just have needed the money to buy a better house! But if he'd sold half his stake, I might get a bit worried.

It's the same with buys. Always check the amount of shares a director is buying and selling against the amounts he or she holds. The bigger the proportion of shares bought compared to the amount owned is what you should look at carefully.

It can sometimes be a good sign if a director buys, say, £20,000 worth of shares if they only currently hold a small amount. Not all directors are wealthy, and £20,000 might be quite a big investment for a director of a smaller company.

Here's an example of when simply following a director's buy would have caused you to lose *all* your money.

Example: directors' buying Homebuy

On 16 July 2006, a director of Homebuy bought 25,000 shares in the company and another one bought 100,000 shares. That was nearly £290,000 worth between them.

Incredibly, just a few days later, on 10 August, the shares were suspended "Pending clarification of financial position". And just one month later, the company called in administrators and effectively went bust.

Shareholders never got a penny back. Those directors lost all their money. A salutary lesson in making sure you do proper research and don't just follow dealings. The company was in fact heavily in debt and the banks pulled the plug. I had seen and was encouraged by the buys, but because I had researched the company properly I did not buy because of the huge debt.

Example: directors' buying Harvey Nash

But here's a different story. On 7 June 2007, a director of recruitment group Harvey Nash bought 10,000 shares to add to his holding of 22,000. He bought at 79p. Just a couple of weeks later the shares had soared 15% to 92p. You can see here the amount bought was just under £8,000. So not a huge amount, but he was adding around a third more to his holdings.

It could be argued that it is worth monitoring director sells because it could be a sign not everything is rosy. Especially if the sale is for a large amount of money, that can be a warning sign that all is not well with a company.

Example: directors' selling; Abacus

On 7 December 2006, a director of Abacus sold 200,000 shares at 184.61p (nearly £370,000). He had held 922,000 shares so was reducing by quite a bit. A definite warning signal.

By May 2007, the company issued a profits warning and the shares sank.

Directors' selling; Abacus

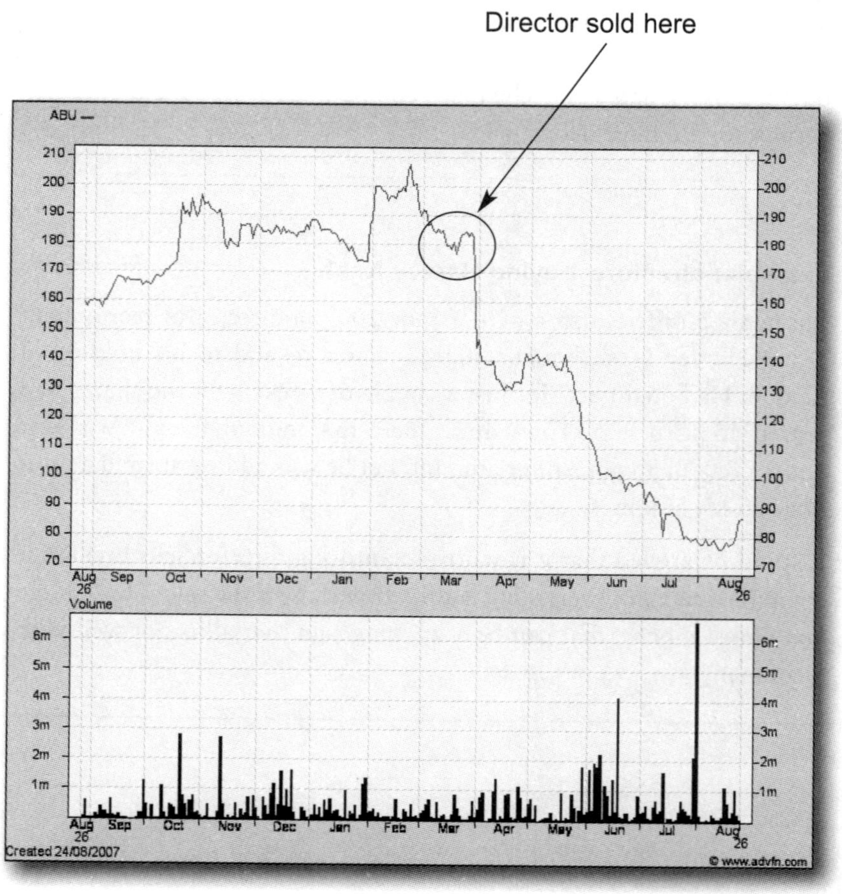

Here's a director deal that came to my attention and I did buy shares in the company on the back of it.

Example: directors' buying; Renold

A director bought a cool 1,000,000 shares in his company, Renold, at 90p (worth £900,000). It doesn't matter how rich you are – that's a pretty big deal! He made the deal in November 2006.

I bought in too, and the shares have soared since to over 130p. That buy certainly showed confidence and that was borne out with some good results in early 2007.

Summary – directors' dealings

To sum up, watching directors' dealings is something every investor should do. And sometimes seeing a deal can lead you to examine a new company that you haven't come across before.

But you should never slavishly follow a deal. There is no substitute for doing your own research into a company and just using a director's deal as good bonus information.

7. Check the company website

I always check the website of any company that I'm thinking about buying.

> If the website is crap, one has to wonder if the company is able to compete in the 21st century.

This might seem obvious but I bet most investors don't bother. A company's website can tell you an awful lot. It should also help you to confirm that you know exactly what the company does to make its money! By the time I've finished reading a site, I try to make sure I can say what the company does in a sentence.

If the website is crap, one has to wonder if the company is able to compete in the 21st century.

If the company uses the website to offer goods to the public, how good is the presentation? Would *you* consider buying goods from its website and, if not, why not? If the site doesn't tempt you to buy, it could have the same effect on others.

Look up the company concerned and its site on Google. Perhaps try putting in the company name and adding 'reviews'.

Are customers getting their goods on time or are they slagging off the company?

All bloody good research!

If the company doesn't use its website to sell, how does it treat its shareholders? Does it have a good news service and does it contain up-to-date news about the company? It ought to at least have a copy of its last financial report which you should be able to download. You should be able to send an email to the company as a shareholder.

Simple test: send an email stating you are a shareholder and you want to know the date of the next AGM.

See how long it takes them to reply, the quicker the better. If they don't reply, what does that say about how they feel about their shareholders.

The other reason for visiting the company's website is to give you extra research material. You may learn more about the company, which might entice you to buy even more shares!

8. PE ratios

> I like my PEs to be in the region 12-20.

You'll hear a lot about PE ratios and you may be surprised to learn I don't take an awful lot of notice of them. Also, I just know the moment I mention them you'll close the book and go off and do something else. Have you gone? For those of you left:

What the hell is a PE ratio and why do people go on about them?

It means price-earnings ratio and it is calculated as the share price divided by the earnings per share.

But forget about the formula, it's what it really means that's important. The PE ratio represents the number of years it will take for the earnings of the company to cover the share price.

Interpreting PE ratios

1. *Company A* has a share price of 10p, and earnings per share of 2p. The PE ratio will therefore be 5 (10/2). So, with earnings of 2p, it would take 5 years for those earnings to cumulatively match the share price.
2. *Company B* has a share price of 90p, and earnings per share of 3p. The PE ratio will therefore be 30 (90/3). It would take 30 years, with earnings of 3p to cover the share price of 90p.

One can say that the investors in company B are more optimistic than those in company A. Company B investors are willing to pay 90p for the shares and wait 30 years (on current earnings) for the share price to be covered by the cumulative earnings. If they weren't confident, the investors would sell their shares, the share price would fall, and the PE ratio would therefore also fall.

Note: above, I say that investors are willing to wait 30 years *on current earnings*. But the point is that the investors believe that the company's earnings will actually increase quickly and that they won't have to wait for so long.

By contrast, company A investors are not so confident. They're only willing to give the benefit of the doubt 5 years into the future, for earnings to cover the share price.

> In general, high growth companies (e.g. tech stocks) tend to have high PE ratios, whereas low growth companies (e.g. utility companies) have low PEs.

If a company has a high PE ratio, then the investors have bid the share price up because they are bullish on the company and expect it to perform well.

You might think, therefore, it's better to invest in a high PE company because it could do really well.

Sadly it's not that simple.

The market could be overvaluing the high PE company and it could come down to earth with a bump.

Personally, I quite like lower PEs. That's because the market isn't expecting much, so if I think the company could beat expectations, the share price could soar. I like my PEs to be in the region 12-20.

A comparative measure

The main use of PEs, though, is not as an absolute measure. If a company has a PE of say 20, it is difficult to say whether it is a buy or a sell. However, the power of PEs is when you use them to compare one company's share price with another.

For example, if company A has a share price of 400p, and company B has a share price of 14p, nothing can be said about their relative values. Is company B better value than company A? We don't know. However, if we know that company A has a PE of 12, and company B a PE of 32, we *can* say that the market values company B more highly than it does company A.

But PEs are most useful when comparing companies within the same sector, as different sectors tend to have different PEs. As I mentioned above, tech stocks tend to have high PEs while utility stocks have low PEs. Because of this, it is not very useful to compare the PEs of, say, ARM Holdings (47) with that of British Energy (3).

If a retailing company has a PE of 15, while the average PE ratio of all companies in the retail sector is 20, one could say that the company is undervalued relative to the sector. There may be a very good reason for this. But if there isn't, then the company may merit further attention as a buy.

My view

Personally, I find PEs too abstract and only give them a passing glance.

A problem with PEs is that different publications differ on the PE. So the *FT* might quote a different one from ADVFN. This is because some use historical earnings, some use forward earnings...blah, blah. Quite honestly, the whole thing washes over me, which doesn't seem to matter as I still make money whatever!

Picking undervalued shares – my secret!

All the best things in life are simple, and I think the system I use to pick out undervalued shares is simplicity itself. The idea behind it is to find cheap companies that might eventually bid for.

Here's what I do.

I am a billionaire

I use this system after researching any company that looks of interest. I pretend that I am a multi-billionaire investor and could buy any company or as many companies as I want to. But of course I want to buy them on the cheap. I want to buy companies that are making profits, but if I pay cash for the companies I know these profits would probably grow. Over a few years I'd get back what I paid for the company and start to make a lot of money on top.

The idea behind my system is: if I decide it's worth splashing out a small part of my billions to buy the company, then I've decided the company is cheap. And if that's the case, I should buy the shares because, if I'm right, sooner or later someone will buy the company or the share price will go up anyway.

So, how can I work out whether to splash out a small part of my billions on snapping up a company?

The first thing to look at is the profit the company makes; and the second is the market capitalisation. In my billionaire role, my rule of thumb for how much the company might cost me to buy is the market capitalisation. So if a company's market cap is £50 million, that's how much the market currently thinks the company is worth.

ADVFN provides the market cap and the profit on its 'Quote' page on the same line, so they are easy to find.

Screenshot from ADVFN Quotes page

Fenner(FENR) — Click for Financial

Name	Symbol	Market	Type	ISIN	Description
Fenner	LSE:FENR	London Stock Exchange	Equity	GB0003345054	ORD 25P

Sector	Turnover (m)	Profit (m)	EPS - Basic	PE ratio	Mkt Cap (m)	NMS
INDUSTRIAL MACHINERY	379.0	29.3	13.0	17.827	367.2	10000

As a billionaire, I don't really care about complicated financial ratios and all that twaddle. What I want to know is: how much do you want for your company and what are the profits?

Putting it simply: if a company is making profits of £10 million and its market cap is £100 million, that would interest me.

But if a company makes a £10 million profit and is capitalised at £200 million, then I'm not so interested – even if it has some kind of stupendous product that is about to dramatically raise profits. I don't want to spend £200 million to get profits of £10 million whatever the prospects.

So my rule of thumb is a max of around 15 times market cap to profits.

OK, you're scratching your head now –what's he on about?

Let's go back to the company making £10 million. The most I want to see the market cap at is around £150 million. That's 15 times. Any more than that and it starts to look expensive – so why would I buy the shares?

Summary – selecting shares

This is a good point to summarise what will make me put a share on a shortlist:

1. That there is still growth to come
2. It has a full listing
3. Dividends, profits and turnover are rising
4. There are tons of positives
5. There are no question marks
6. It is liquid
7. I understand what the company does
8. It is under 15x profits to market cap
9. It looks cheap
10. It is in a good market
11. Demand for its products is likely to grow
12. The chart looks positive and is in an upward trend
13. Debt is under three times full year profits

Once all my boxes are ticked the share goes in my shortlist and then it's down to timing, and we'll come onto that shortly.

You may have noticed the last line there about debt – I will explain this in full shortly.

As you can see, it takes quite a bit to get a share onto the shortlist. And quite right too!

I think at this point it's time to look at some examples of shares I bought and why. And maybe a good time for you to have a break.

Reading the book in bed?

Have a sleep and come back tomorrow. Or, if there is someone there with you, jump to WAGS and SHAGS! (See page 123.)

Q. WHY COULDN'T THE DAYTRADERS AGREE WHERE THEY SHOULD MEET TO GET TOGETHER?

A. THEY ALL WANTED TO KEEP THEIR OPTIONS OPEN UNTIL THE LAST MINUTE.

WAGS & SHAGS

WAGS[2] – why they can make you money

If you're a woman reading this and think the above headline may be a bit sexist, in my defence most share buyers are men. Around 95%. So there. Anyway this is just for you, watch for SHAGS (coming up).

So, you men should think about consulting your wives before you buy anything in the retail sector.

Again, I know I will annoy some of you girls, but WAGS are good at shopping and they know what's in or out. Don't start telling me this is rubbish. It is a fact. Ladies are good at shopping and blokes hate it and that's it.

> So ask the WAGS: which shops are in and which shops are out?

For example, the lovely Mrs Naked Trader pointed out to me years ago how well Ted Baker was doing and I ended up buying shares on the basis of that.

And when she came home with an M&S shopping bag for the first time, I realized it was probably time for a Marks and Sparks recovery. And indeed that proved the case.

Some time ago she and her friends went off Ted Baker. I sold the shares. About three months later the shares started to decline quite badly!

So ask the WAGS: which shops are in and which shops are out? Watch and see which bags appear in their hands most often.

For example, as I write in the latter half of 2007, here is the latest WAGS Report:

[2] WAGS – Wives and Girlfriends of Sharebuyers.

Shops	Status
Laura Ashley, Mothercare, Waitrose	In
Marks and Spencer, French Connection, Debenhams, Sainsbury's	On probation
Ted Baker (temporarily), Next, Monsoon, Jacques Vert, Tesco, House of Fraser	Out
Signet	You are joking
Woolworths	Divorce papers

The moment you see a retailer appear on your list of possible shares to buy, check what your WAG has to say.

Now, if you're a lady reading this book and you're thinking about buying a tech share then you need to check out your...

SHAGS[3] (You get one if you're lucky)

Now, you ladies reading this who are share traders could equally look at the kind of gadgets your husbands and boyfriends are into, as they will give you a clue as to what sort of tech shares are in or out.

For example, would your man have been seen dead with an Amstrad emailer? Of course not! So you wouldn't have been buying Amstrad shares when they were on the market (sorry Sir Alan).

Questions to ask:

- What is your bloke and his mates buying?
- Who makes what they are buying and the chips that go in them?

I'm hopeless at new gadgets, and not that interested either, so I have to ask my friends. A while back I looked around and saw the kind of gadgets my male friends where into. I discovered that tech companies CSR and Wolfson made the bits and bobs that help the gadgets to work. I invested, and made a lot of money from both companies.

Right now, I'm watching carefully to see if any blokes I know are going to start buying the new iLiads (www.iliadreader.co.uk) – giving the ability to read newspapers, mags and books on a hand-held gadget. If they do, I'll be buying shares in them and the chips inside them.

A word of warning about SHAGS though. Do your own research into what tech gear they're buying, but don't follow what they buy in the share market. Sadly, SHAGS themselves tend to buy the wrong kind of tech share! Watch out!

[3] Share traders' Husbands and Gigolos

Top Ten Songs for WAGS (Wives And
Girlfriends of Sharebuyers)
1. D I V O R C E
2. Alone Again, Naturally
3. He Works Hard For The Money
4. Ain't Nothing Going On But The Rent
5. What's Another Year (for someone who's
lost everything that they own)
6. We Don't Need This Pressure On Us
7. Blue Monday
8. Just Another Manic Monday (wish it was
Sunday)
9. No More Tears (enough is enough)
1Ø. Give It Up

Charts And How I Use Them

I discussed charts quite a bit in the first edition of this book.

My views – a couple of years on – are that I still strongly believe charts *are* very important to look at because they tell you a lot of important info about the history of a share price; where it's been, what it's been doing, which TV shows it likes, and who it's been knocking around with.

But I also believe it's simply crazy to buy and sell shares on the basis of looking at a chart and nothing else at all.

There *are* some people who do this. They call themselves "chartists" and I reckon most of them can hardly afford to get their round in. This isn't going to make me popular with chartists, but who cares if I'm not popular with everyone. Evict me and see if I'm bovvered.

Chartists say things like:

> "The MACD divergence touched off by the Fibonacci Bollinger band at 202.4 shows an increasing likelihood of a golden cross over the 40 day moving average on the triangle double bottom formation..."

Which really is probably a load of cobblers. (Well it is as I made it up obviously.)

I gave a talk one day and the guy on before me, who was talking about charts, moaned like hell to me that he was having a rough time on the markets, saying he was fed up with being a chartist. He mentioned none of this in his speech.

You'll often see bulletin board punters talking chart theory because they think it makes them look good. Bit odd considering no one knows who they really are, but people are funny aren't they?

Market commentators and tipsters tend to split into two camps:

1. *Chartists* (also known as technical analysts): they reckon they don't have to know anything about the company behind the share price; they don't care what the company does, what sector it's in, whether it makes profits or not, or when the next dividend is due.
2. *Fundamentalists*: they feel you should be looking at the accounts, profits, etc.

What am I – a chartist or a fundamentalist?

Well mind your own business because I'm not telling. Oh all right, seeing as you did buy the book.

Neither!

I want to look at the whole story of a share, so I look at all aspects: fundamentals, charts, the whole caboodle.

But as you've already noticed (I hope!), I like charts for breakouts and for setting targets and stops.

Jargon

You will very quickly come across charting jargon when you begin visiting bulletin boards – there are a lot of amateur chartists out there. I see no need, especially for new investors, to get bogged down in all the terminology.

I think it's far too easy to get bogged down in chartism – and many investors come a cropper when they rely on it. They read a few books about charting and then feel they are invincible! **Of course what inevitably happens is the chart turns on them, and bites them on the bum.**

The Naked Trader Guide To Market Jargon

Bull Market – A random market movement causing an investor to mistake himself for a financial genius.

Market Correction – The day after you buy shares.

Stock Split – When your ex-wife and her lawyer split all your assets equally between them.

Stock Analyst – The twat who just downgraded your favourite share.

Momentum Investing – The fine art of buying high and selling low.

Value Investing – The art of buying low and selling lower.

Long-Term Investing – The short-term trade that kept going down.

Head and Shoulders Formation – That bloody dandruff is back.

Breakdown – What you'll have when you hold onto one loser too many.

Profits – What you used to make before you started share trading.

Moving Averages – You'll be moved all right, as they keep going down.

How charts are used

A chart shows what's happened to a share price in the past. And in doing that, it reveals what's very important: the prices at which investors are likely to buy and sell at in the future.

Charts are useful for shares that are trading in a tight range. For example, a share price might move back and forth in the range 200-220p over a few months. And you could try to play that trend: buy at 200p and sell at 220p.

Resistance And Support

As well as breakouts, you need to know about resistance and support.

And to illustrate this, I can't find a better chart than this one, which also incorporates what we have already been talking about (breakouts).

And that chart is…BSkyB.

British Sky Broadcasting

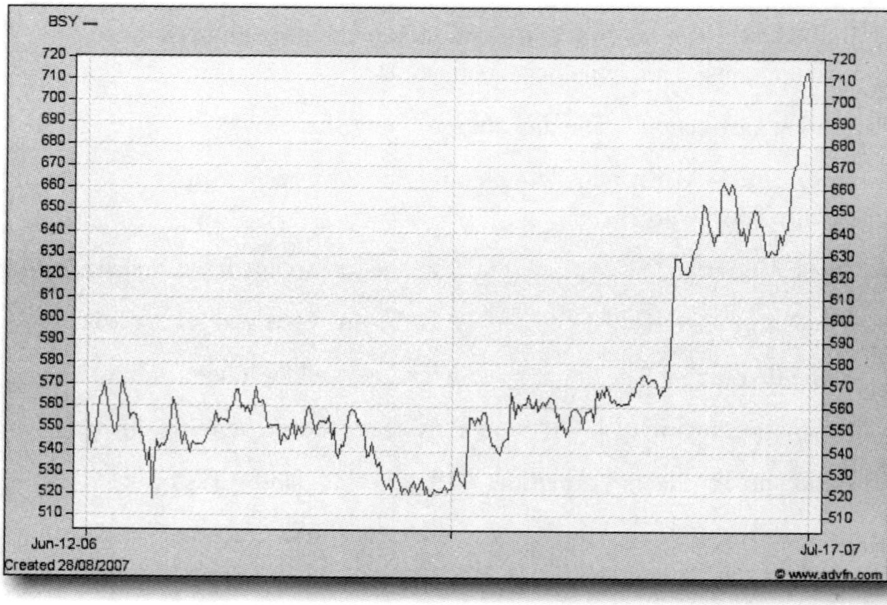

You can see that for nearly a year the shares traded in a range.

- *Support* is jargon for the place where a share doesn't tend to go below.
- *Resistance* is where the shares can't rise above. (Resistance is futile – that was for *Star Trek* fans.)

So, support for BSkyB for a year was at around 520 – you can see the shares kept falling to that level then bouncing off. While resistance was 570, when the shares reached there they could not go above.

Hey that was easy. Fancy yourself as a chartist now? Easy money, huh?

And now I want you to tell me when the breakout happened...

Yeah you got it!

BSkyB would have appeared on ADVFN's Premium Toplist breakouts at the start of May when the shares decisively broke through the resistance at 570 and so became an obvious buy. They went all the way to 650, where you can see there was some futile resistance (me Borg) before they broke up again.

Chart patterns

So now you have hopefully learned about support, resistance and breakouts. What about chart *patterns*. I'm not really so keen on these but let's have a quick look at them. The most famous chart pattern (let's call it Sir Chart Pattern) is called *head and shoulders*.

Head and shoulders

It is known as a head and shoulders pattern (and we're not talking dandruff control shampoo here) because that is kind of what it looks like: a head and shoulders! It's formed because the share hit a new high then fell off, tried to get back up again but couldn't and tried again. It really shows the share has run out of momentum for the time being and it might be time to take profits. So if you're ever going to consider looking at chart patterns, this is the one!

Head and shoulders

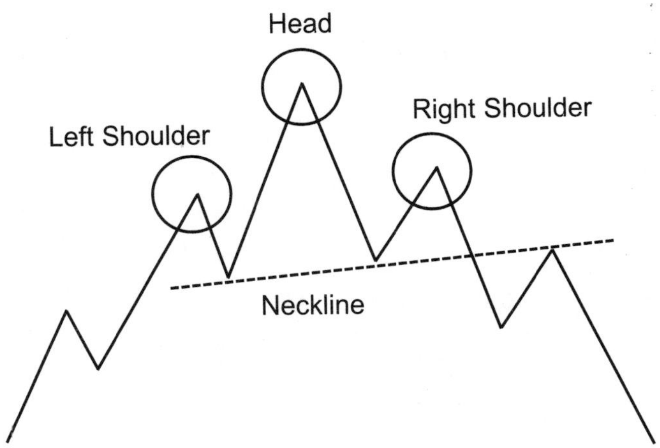

Double top

Another popular pattern where a share is expected to move lower is called a *double top* – as you can see it, well looks like two tops!

Double top

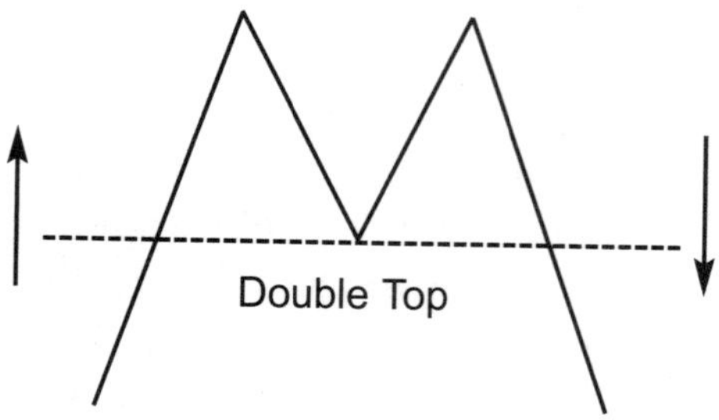

Once the share has tried twice to break up though a certain point it gets tired, needs a rest and a cup of tea and therefore goes down. So chartists argue (and boy do they argue!) it should be sold once the second peak is reached…and so forming the double top.

Double bottom

And now the naughtiest sounding pattern – the *double bottom* (ooh er missus!)

Double bottom

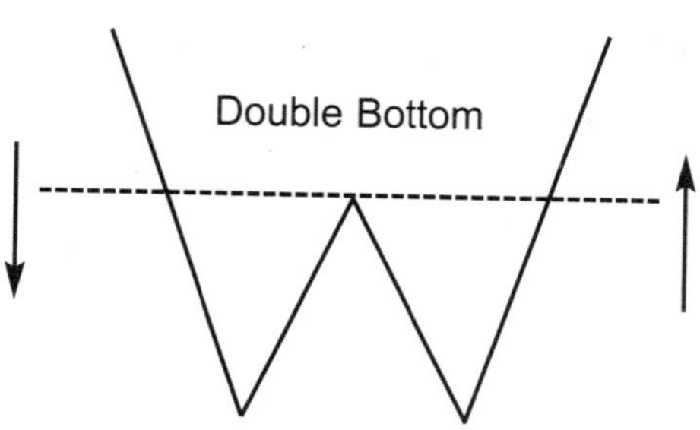

This is where the stock is expected to go *up*!

It has gone down to the same price twice and bounced off that price. That, say chartists, is a bullish signal and the share should now rise a lot as it has found support.

Oh, talking of tea, another chart pattern supposedly bullish is the "cup and handle" – i.e. the chart looks like, you guessed it…a cup and handle!

The share's gone up a lot, gradually fallen away, risen back up to form the cup shape, goes down a bit (to form the handle) and then is expected to rise sharply…

Round bottom

Then we have the err...(cough) round bottom. Lots of people like round bottoms (so I'm told). This is when a share falls away slowly, then bottoms out slowly before gently rising to form, err, the bottom.

Round bottom

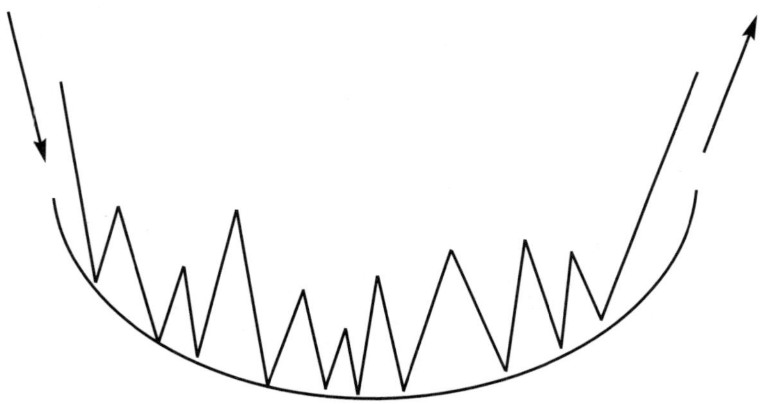

This is a bullish chart and the share should rise.

Triple top

And there's also the triple top. This is not good news. A share hits the sameish price three times. After it has hit the price for the third time it is expected to drop away sharply…

Whether you believe in all this is up to you. The chart patterns sometimes work sometimes don't, but they are worth a thought or two.

I would look on all these as things to think about before you buy or sell; as an extra rather than using them solely. Sorry, chartists!

Further reading

An excellent guide for beginners, and to help you get more advanced is *The Investor's Guide to Charting (2nd edition)* by Alistair Blair. This covers charting in depth, and if the subject interests you, the book covers most angles. And bottoms too. (Go to my website www.nakedtrader.co.uk and click 'books' to order.)

Buybacks, AGMs and Perks

Share buybacks

Sometimes you'll see a company announce that it is going to buy back some of its shares. Companies can seek authorisation from its shareholders to do this. Generally, companies seek to buy back their shares because they feel the market is undervaluing their shares and the price is too low. By starting a buyback programme, the value of the shares are usually underpinned by the buybacks and the shares might gradually see a rise in value.

But I'm not a great fan of buybacks. If the market is undervaluing the company then there is probably a good reason. So don't rely on buybacks to improve the value of the share you are holding by that much.

I would even consider selling the shares concerned, because buybacks, in my experience, don't tend to lead to fireworks for the share price.

I'm not a great fan of buybacks.

However, for those wanting a steady income from a steady share, I suppose a buyback programme would give you confidence that the share will have some support.

Shareholders' meetings/AGMs/presentations

If you're a shareholder of any company you're entitled to go to the Annual General Meeting (AGM). These are usually pretty dull affairs, but if you've got a long-term holding in the company it may be worth considering.

Sometimes companies even invite shareholders to the company premises to have a look. These are called "investor/analyst open days". If you've got the time and energy, why not have a look and visit the company?

I've visited a couple and enjoyed the visits.

Another way of finding out more about the company directly is by going to presentations.

One good website to look at is www.proactiveinvestors.co.uk. What they do is get 2-3 company bosses together on one evening to tell you why their shares are worth buying. You also get the chance to put questions directly to the bosses of the companies involved.

I've been to one or two of these presentations and thought it was well worth the time and effort it took to go along. The website tells you which companies are presenting, so I usually research them before I go. It's quite fascinating to meet the people behind a company and it can be very useful. These presentations are free and you get wine and canapés thrown in too!

Share perks

You'll often see articles in newspapers and magazines written by lazy hacks regarding share perks. When I say 'lazy', this is because articles on perks are one of the easiest features for them to write – they can re-write a perks feature written previously in about ten minutes!

Perks are special privileges you can get if you own a certain number of a company's shares. For example, hotel chains might give you a 10% discount on their room rates.

Don't buy shares just because of the perks!

You should buy shares to sell them at a profit, whereas all perks do is make you hang onto a share longer than you should. Also, many of these companies only offer perks to those with share certificates rather than through a nominee account.

And you will probably find you could have got similar discounts by phoning the company and asking them, shares or no shares!

So forget about perks.

Part 4
Trading Strategies

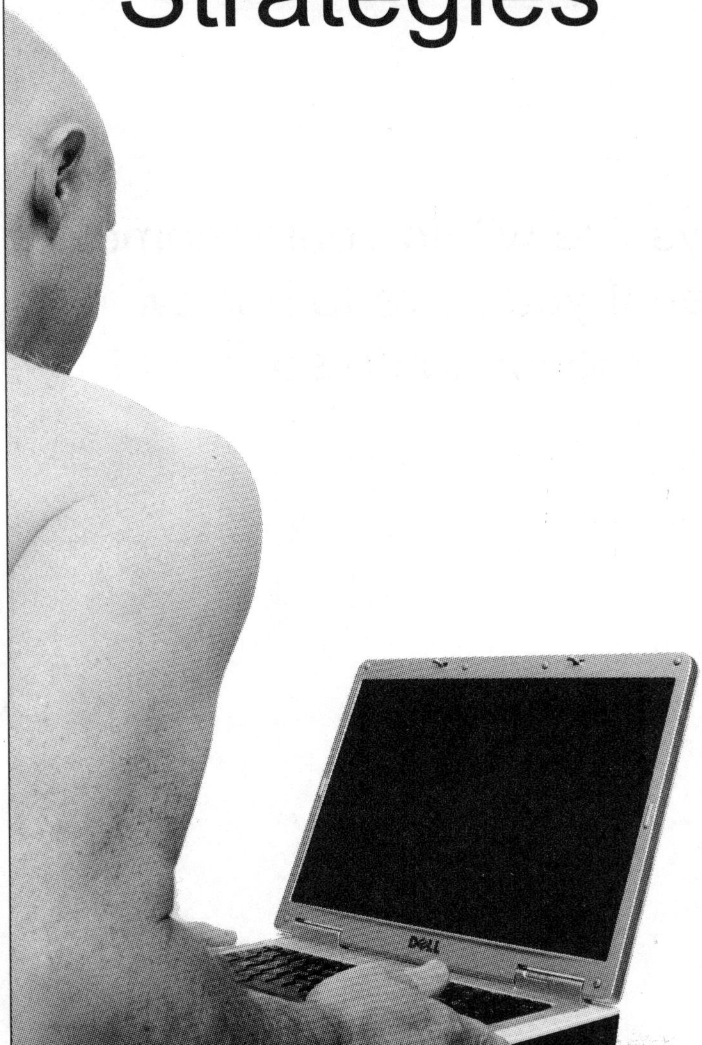

"Always live within your income, even if you have to borrow money to do so."

- *Josh Billings*

Market Timing

Timing is everything in life, and it's the same with shares.

It's pointless buying a good company if you're buying it during a general market slump, as the share will probably go down with the rest regardless of your careful research.

You have to time the best entry point you can with any share.

So I always ask myself: although maybe I found a good company that I really like the look of, is today a good day to buy or not?

Just because the company is doing well doesn't necessarily mean the share price is going to go up. You could wake up one morning and see a great statement from a company. The share price is going up and you think: with results like that this share is going to rocket!

Not necessarily.

Suddenly, just after you've bought, the price starts to head south because many investors were in this one already and have now decided to take their profits and move on, leaving you holding the baby.

So how do you get your timing right?

Patience

There is always going to be some luck involved, but the key word here is patience. If you see that great company statement, add that share to your monitor and watch it like a hawk. Take a look at the share chart over the last three years and get a feel for its movements.

Watch how it moves up and down over the days and weeks.

And pounce when you feel the time is right! Never just buy it immediately.

OK, the share might start going up and you end up missing the boat, but so what? There is always another day, another share. There is simply no substitute for experience in these matters, and as you learn to buy and sell shares you will gradually learn about timing.

> If you are very new to trading, the best advice I can give you is: if it is obvious that your timing is wrong and the share starts to move against you – just get out.

There are many things to take into consideration regarding market timing. These considerations include:

- How much buying is going on in the share?
- What is the chart telling you?
- When is the next statement due?
- What is the general state of the markets?
- Is momentum with the share or not?
- What sort of share is it and how does it normally move?

First things first: you need to *plan* your trades – to get both your entry and exit points firmly in your head.

Plan your trades

As a trader or investor you *must* try to have some kind of plan.

Too many people plunge into a share without having any idea why they bought it or how long they're going to hold it.

Make sure you plan every trade:

1. Write down every trade
2. Think carefully about why you have bought the company
3. Set a stop loss and profit target and stick to them

4. Decide on your timescale

5. Is it a short-term or a longer-term trade?

Keep a diary of all your trades and be honest. If you're losing money you can then look back and try to work out what you're doing wrong.

Not having a plan is one of many fundamental errors made by traders. Entering a trade without knowing what you want and where you are going with it, is the way to the poorhouse.

And in your plan one of the most important parts must be your timing.

Back now to timing

So what exactly are the signs I'm looking for to get in there and buy?

In no particular order I want to see:

- Positive momentum
- Good volume
- Positive chart
- It's in the run up to results
- Level 2 shows me it's a good time to buy
- General markets are rising
- It is not on the way down

Let's say I have a share I am interested in buying. I've done my research and it's just a question of when.

First, I am looking to buy when the price is *rising* on the day I am buying, not falling dramatically. I don't mean rising a lot. Just a small amount will do to show others are buying in.

Next I want to check volume by pressing the Trades button on ADVFN. Is there some reasonable buying volume coming in and has there been for one or two days? Tick!

Charts

The chart. This is where a chart becomes reasonably important. But my way of looking at it is relatively simple.

I like these charts

I am either looking for a chart that is simply gradually going higher, say a beautiful one like this:

Montanaro European Smaller Companies Trust

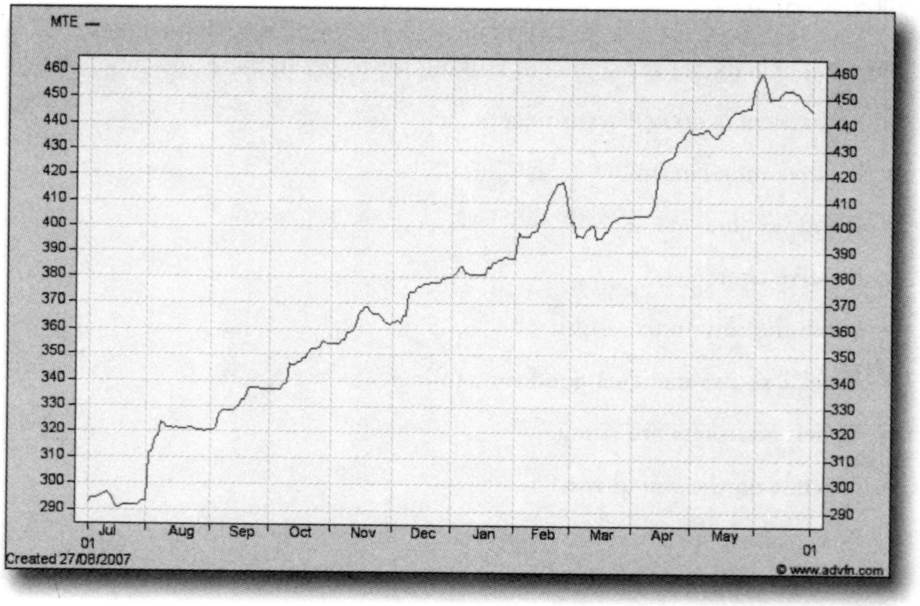

You can see this one just gradually goes up in a nice rising up trend. Lovely! Or like this:

Hunting

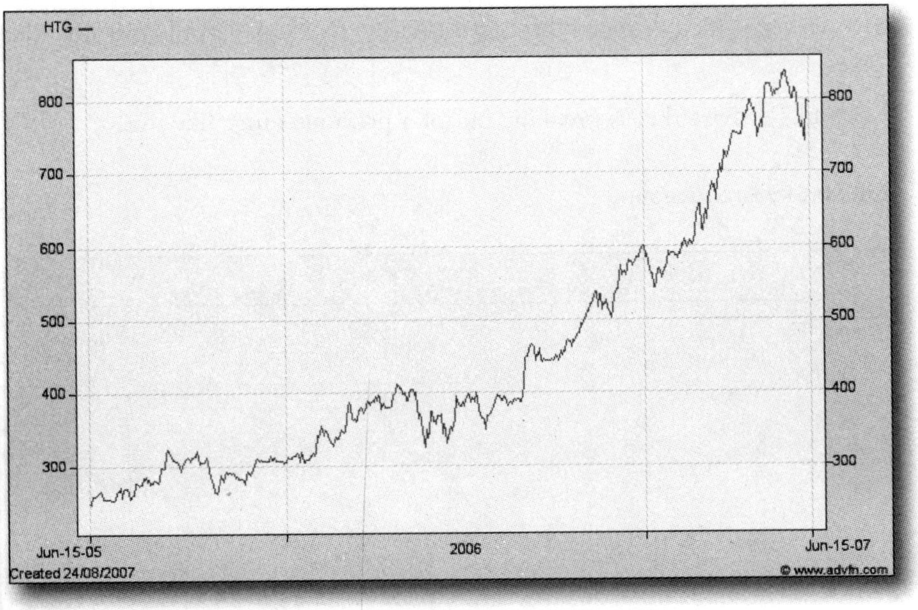

Or a share where there is plenty of buying support at a given price:

Next

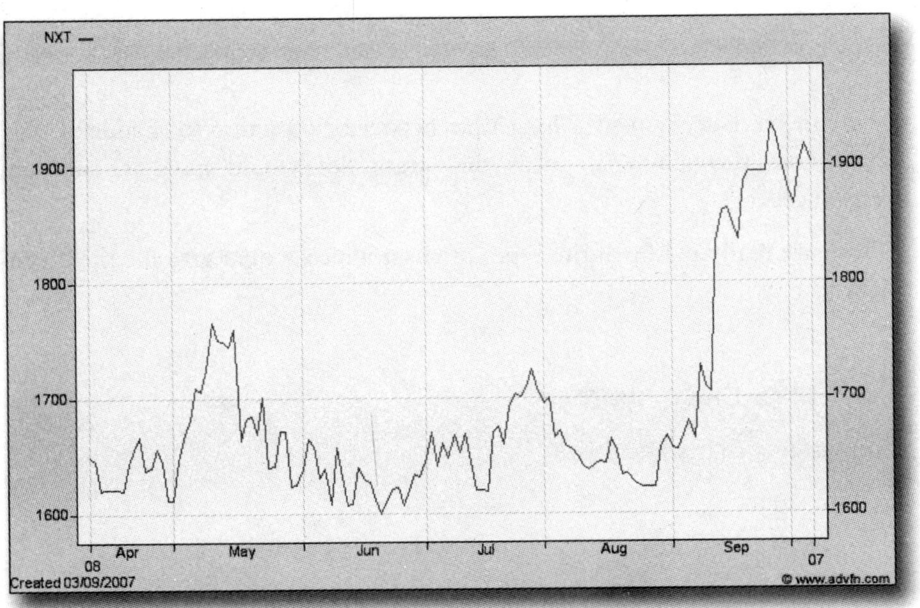

You can see here that every time the price came down to near 1600, it started to rise again. 1600 is therefore an area of support and a good place to buy. If, however, it then dropped through 1600, say to 1550, I would quickly take losses.

I also like a share that is breaking out of a previous range like this:

British Sky Broadcasting

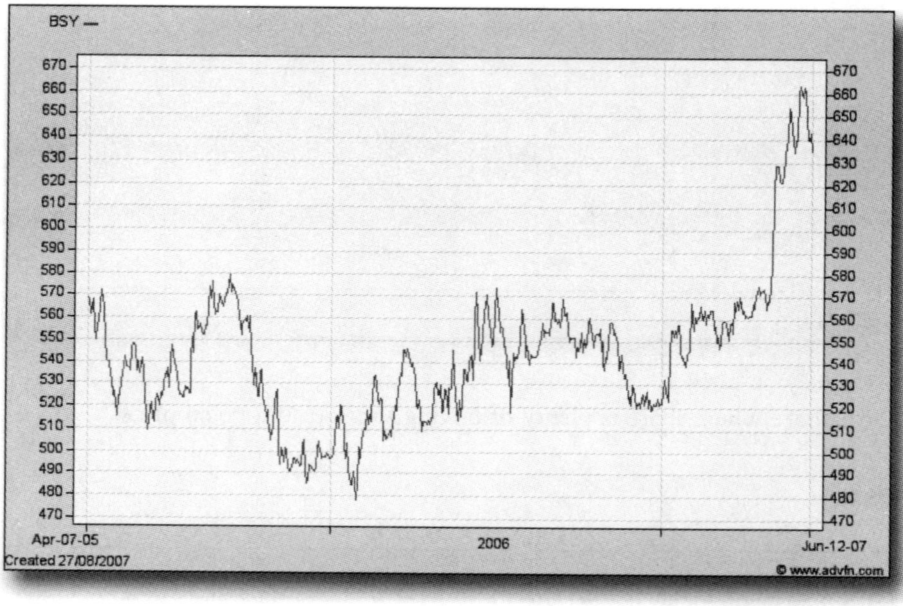

You can see BSkyB spent a long time between 500 and 570. Suddenly the share goes through 570, or as the jargon lot would have it, through *resistance.*

Those are really my favourite types of chart which would give me the green light to buy.

I don't like these charts

I do *not* like charts like this:

Paragon

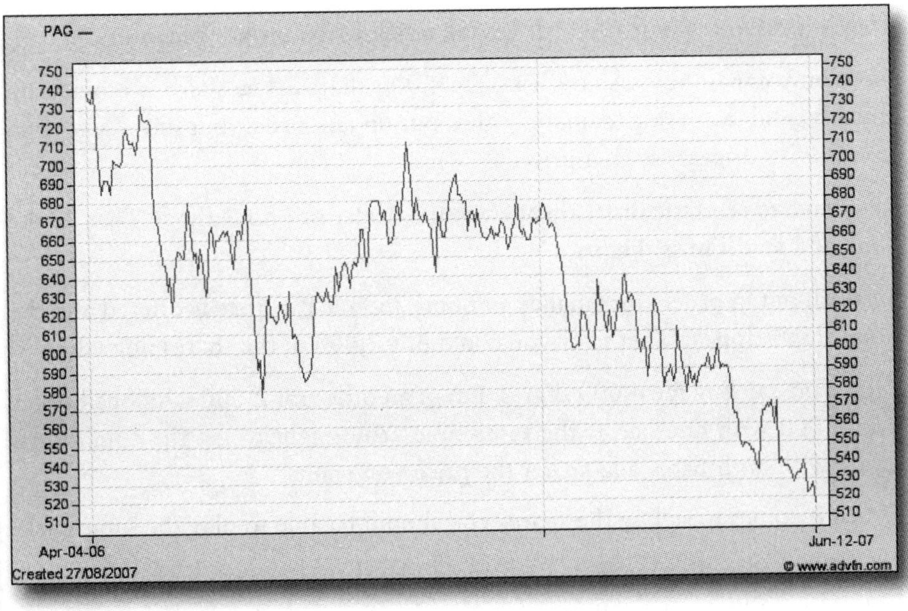

The chart shows a falling price and it's also very erratic.

Or one like this:

SMC Group

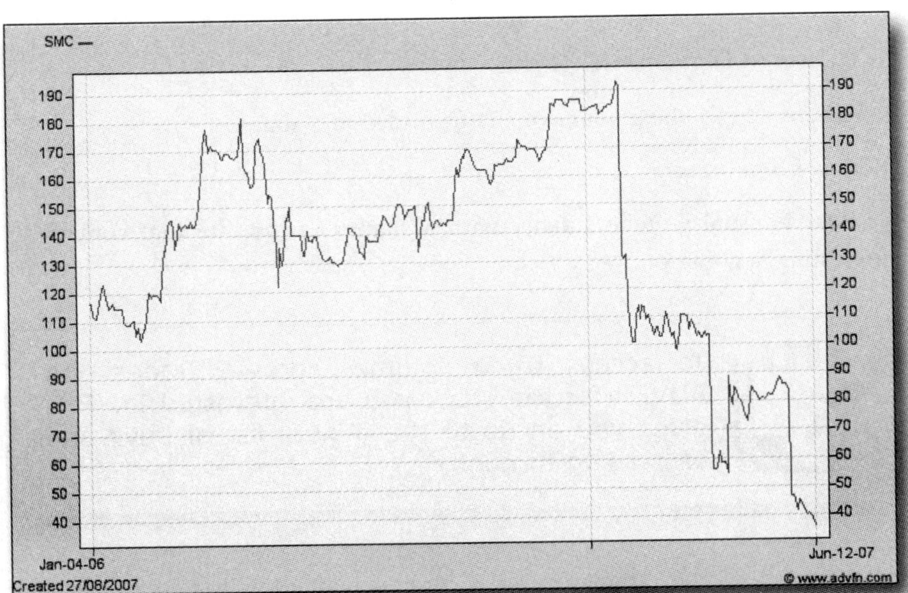

Basically, a disaster zone!

Trading tip

Here's a reason why it is worth having at least two broker accounts.

Say you want to buy a share, let's say 4,000 shares. The share is moving up quickly and is in big demand. You put in an order but no *15 second countdown* appears with a price.

You have to send the order through to the dealer or phone them. That'll take time and you'll miss the price.

Instead: put in orders for smaller amounts and see if a price is offered and the countdown appears. Let's say you could buy 2,000 of the shares immediately.

Now you *can* buy the 4,000 shares. Put in an order for 2,000 with one broker and 2,000 with another at the same time. You ought to get the countdown clock with both firms and so get the price you want.

When it comes to selling the shares you should be able to play the same trick.

I don't suppose the market makers would be that happy about it but they're not going to know it's you, so who cares?

Volumes

Trades – buys and sells

Volume is simply the amount of shares traded in a share.

Why is it important?

Because unusual volume activity with a share can indicate that something interesting is going on.

> To access trade volumes, press "Trades" on ADVFN for the stock you are interested in. This gives you an up to the minute list of buys and sells going through.

Also, you should be able to see trades coming in on your shares monitor too.

I often get emails from confused investors who follow the volume of buying and selling in particular companies. Emails like:

> *Why is the share dropping when there are so many more buys than sells?*

Apart from market maker shenanigans that I've already discussed, this is because all the buys and sells you see listed on trade analysers are only *guesses* by a computer!

So when you see trades listed under 'buys' or 'sells', that 'buy' could easily have been a 'sell'! The trouble is, market makers can delay the publication of trades that are over the normal market size of a stock. So the trade you see at 14.20, could well have been made at 10.20.

The lesson is to treat volume trade data with great caution.

ADVFN Trades page

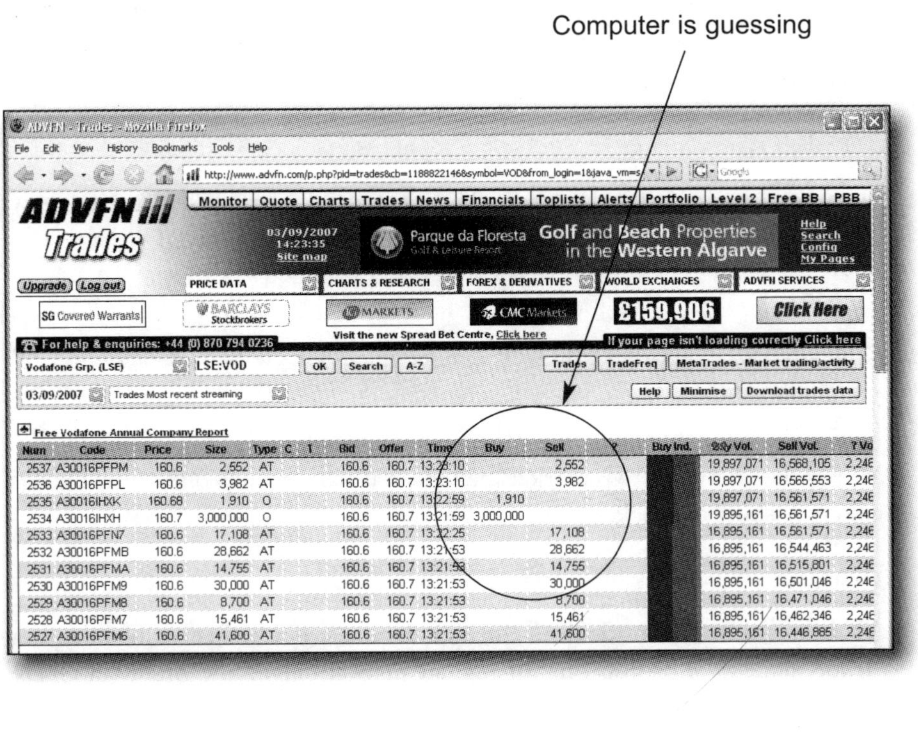

Trade codes

You'll notice that there is a letter which goes by every trade – that at least gives some sort of clue as to the sort of trade it is. Here's what the main ones mean.

T trades

This doesn't mean nice relaxed trades made over a cup of tea. 'T' by a trade, in market jargon, means 'single protected transaction'. The trade you see going through is someone who has bought or sold a lot of shares over a period of time and it all goes through as if it was one transaction.

That makes it hard to know whether the trade is a buy or a sell. But, as a general rule, if the share is rising it's probably a buy, and if falling it's probably a sell. Quite why the buyers need protection I'm not sure!

X trades

When you see 'X' by a transaction, even if it's for a big amount of shares, you can kind of ignore it. This is just a parcel of shares being swapped between two parties. One wants the shares the other doesn't. So there are no real conclusions to be drawn and the share price is rarely affected.

O trades

'O' means it's an ordinary trade. This is normally broadcast immediately, unless it is over six times NMS, in which case it can be delayed.

L trades

'L' means a late reported trade.

M trades

'M' is a deal between two market makers. It usually means one of the market makers is short of stock.

AT trades

'AT' is an automated trade dealt through the order book. Generally means it's a trade made by a professional or regular market player and often via CFDs. More likely to move the market.

PLUS Markets

Now you *might* think that you would see *all* the trades coming through, wouldn't you?

You're kidding – it's the stock market, so as usual expect the unexpected...

There is a new kid on the block as I write called PLUS Markets – this is an alternative market to the London Stock Exchange. While you might think competition is a good thing, PLUS publishes trades for shares on its website and you can't see them on ADVFN or similar sites.

So if you have bought or sold a share and wonder why you do not see your trade published on ADVFN it's because it will have gone through PLUS Markets instead.

The good news is you *can* find your trade. Go to www.plusmarketsgroup.com. Type the symbol of your share top right and you'll get the trades.

Alternatively, if you get ADVFN Level 2, PLUS Market trades are shown there live.

Of course as this book matures, the above information could change! However, as I write it looks like PLUS Markets is here to stay, but I suppose at some point perhaps a system will be devised so trades that go via PLUS will be listed together with those from the LSE.

You're kidding – it's the stock market, so as usual expect the unexpected...

OK, let's move on...

End part

So there is buying coming in, the chart looks right, there is some momentum to the share today and the price is rising on the day.

A few final checks.

When is the next statement due? If it's tomorrow I might leave it and see what results are like.

> I prefer to buy if I can around 4-6 weeks before results – this is often when shares start to motor if results are expected to be good.

I also prefer it if the general markets are rising not falling.

My next check is what sort of share is it and how does it normally move?

If it's a small company, that makes buying easier as the price doesn't move that fast. If it's a medium to large one, sometimes I have to be pretty nimble to get a good price as the buying price could move 5p or 6p just like that.

And that's where my final check – looking at Level 2 – comes in. Basically Level 2 shows me what the market makers are doing and where the support is for a share. (More on Level 2 towards the end of the book.)

Sometimes I will put in a buy order and see what price I get on the 15 second countdown. If I think I'll get a better price in a few minutes by using Level 2 I'll wait a bit.

Setting Stop Losses And Profit Targets

I didn't really go into these enough in the first book, so I am going to put that right in this one.

I'm going to start with stop losses then move on to profit targets (if that's OK with you).

Stop losses

You'll soon notice quite a lot is discussed about stop losses and their merits or otherwise.

What the hell is a stop loss?

Can you handle the truth? Can you? Sure? OK then...

Well, it's simply a point at which you agree with yourself or a broker or your cat to take a loss on a share before it goes down any more. For example:

> Dear Robbie,
>
> I agree with myself to quit this share if it goes down more than 10% because if it does it was a pile of steaming old cack which I should never have bought. And my promise to myself will ensure the cack gets sold before it does me any serious damage.
>
> Yours, Robbie

This is about preserving your capital and ensuring you don't lose more money on a share than you need to. Often shares are going down for a reason and once they start going down they can really tank.

As I said earlier in the book, one of the main reasons that people lose money in shares is their inability to sell anything at a loss. So this is where your stop loss comes in.

But at what point do you set them?

When should you be quitting a share?

Good questions. First things first. Your quitting price should not be too close to your buying price. In my view at least 10% away – this helps to ensure it's not sold too quickly because the market's gone down for a couple of days.

It also stops your broker or spread bet firm closing you out because of a sudden early morning spike down.

The place I have a good look at to decide my stop loss is the chart of the share involved.

What I'm looking for is the area where the share has some support. Then I set my stop loss a little below it. *Support* is very easy to spot usually.

Example – stop loss; Ted Baker

Here's an example – take a look at the chart for Ted Baker.

Ted Baker

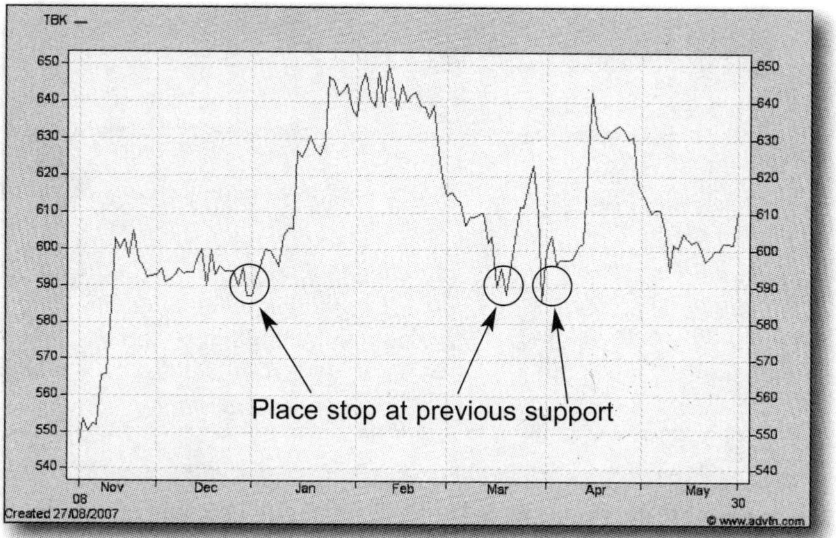

Ted is currently 610 to buy, you like it and buy at 610.

Where should the stop loss be?

You need to look at the chart. Is there a point in the past that Ted falls to then instantly goes up? On this chart it's actually obvious where the stop loss should be.

Where, Robbie? Do tell!

Well, OK, you can see every time it gets to about 585, it stops falling and buyers come in. It's done that a few times. But if it started falling below 585 that would be a danger signal.

In fact, you can see it's hovered around 585-600 quite a lot recently. It's not bovvered enough to go much below 585 though.

So stop loss?

Around 580. Gives a bit of leeway in case the shares drop below the 585 support for a short time.

You still with me or have you buggered off for a cup of tea?

Let's try another one...

Example – stop loss; DMATEK

DMATEK

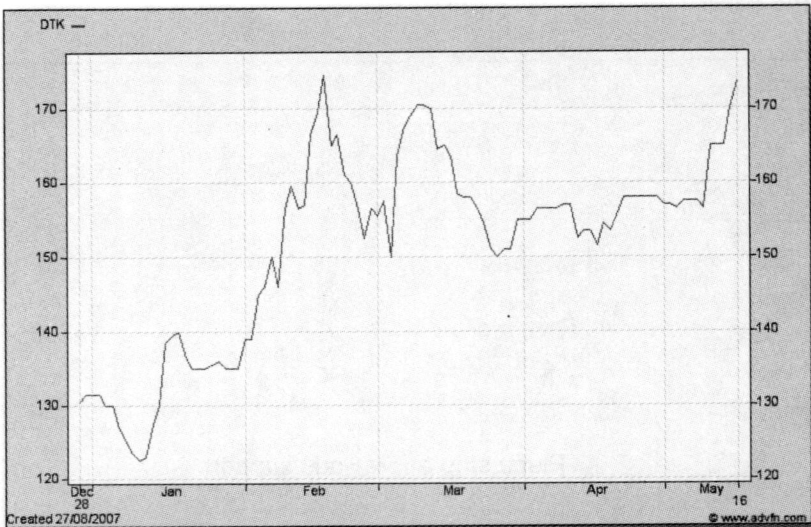

This time I want you to look at this chart and tell me where you think the stop loss should be. No peeking at what I think it should be.

Hey!

Don't look. Honestly, some people. Bet you're one of those who reads the last page of a book before starting it, eh? I've got your number, mate!

You're a buyer at 175.

You can see clearly it's been back to 150 at least three times and always bounced from there. So stop loss has to be 150, take a point or two off for a margin of error, call it about 145.

Did you get it?

What do you mean you thought 120! You're on the naughty step. Go on – and stay on for 15 minutes.

Stop losses and market makers

Something important to mention at this point:

Let's say a market maker has a huge buy order and needs some shares. All market makers are ruthless and will have a pretty good idea at where investors have set their stop losses. They will start a *tree shake* and push the share down rapidly to scare you into selling them. They will look at the share, have a guess where the stop losses are and try and take you out!

So it's always worth considering when setting a stop, that if the share moves down rapidly on no news it could be a tree shake and you may want to give your stop a little slack.

Tree shakes only last for around half a day and if your share has come down violently it will also come back quickly. You will soon get to grips with this through experience.

I have already mentioned tree shakes – beware of their effect on your stop losses.

Trailing stop losses

Some investors use what they call *trailing stop losses.* That means as the share you've bought into rises, so does your stop loss, automatically.

Some brokers are now offering to manage your trailing stop losses for you.

What does it mean?

Example: trailing stop loss

Say you bought a share at 200p, and you set a trailing stop loss of 20p. Then–

- If the share price **falls to 180p,** your holding is sold. (This is a normal stop loss). But, there's more…
- If the share **rises to 260p,** your stop loss will track it upwards, and then be set (automatically) at 240p.
- If the share then **rises to 300p,** your stop loss is re-set at 280p.

Effectively, your broker will sell if the share goes 20p lower than its recent high.

In other words, **your trailing stop takes a profit for you, taking emotion out of any decision.** I think this is a marvellous idea especially for newer investors or those who can't be at a screen all day watching prices.

You can set any trailing stop loss you like as a point difference or percentage.

> In the end it's down to experience – and trial and error. But better to set some targets than having no plan at all.

Monitoring stop losses

Fortunately most good stock brokers – and nearly all spread betting firms – accept stop loss orders. In other words, they will monitor the stop loss themselves – you don't have to worry about it.

Trailing stop losses are a bit special and are not offered by everyone. If you think they'll be important to you, it is worth checking that a broker/spread betting firm offers them before opening an account with them.

Now what about target prices?

Profit targets

I believe profit targets should be at least 20% higher than your buy price. **After all, why buy a share unless you think you can get at least 20% out of it?**

But I certainly do not automatically sell once a share gets to the target price. This is a point at which I look at the share again and decide whether it is still cheap. Is there further to go? If there is, I may well set a new target and stay with the shares or even buy more.

Because as I pointed out earlier, I am really looking for 50% plus profits – some big winners.

Example – profit target; Macro 4

So let's take a look at the chart of Macro 4.

Macro 4

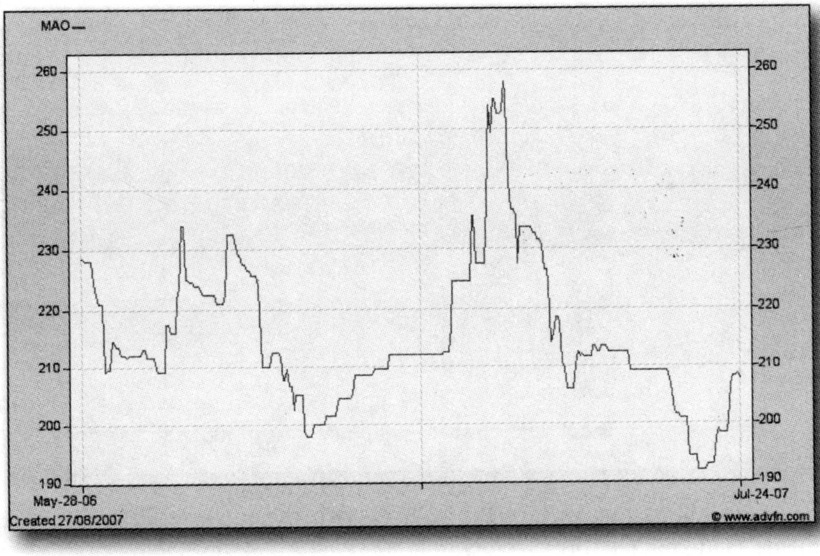

Say I was going to buy now in late July 2007, when the price is 210. I want 20% which is roughly 250. The chart shows me the share peaked at nearly 260 back in March (you can easily see the peak).

Using that chart, I would want to re-look at the share once it hit the peak again, so my target would be 255. If the share breaks up through 255 I would stay with it. If it got back to 260 and started falling away again, I would take profits.

Let's look at another example: Vega.

Example – profit target; Vega

Vega

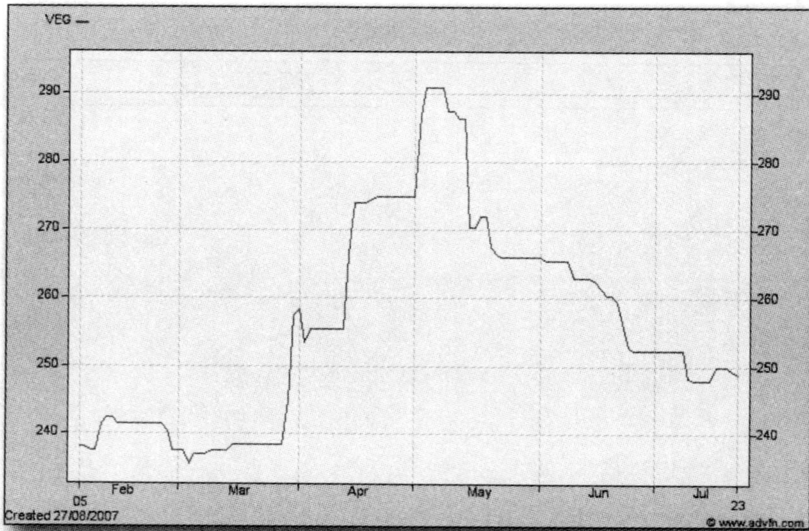

Say I decide to buy in late July 2007, with the price at 250. A 20% target leads me to 300.

However, the chart shows it last peaked at 290p. Therefore I would set my initial target at around 285 to alert me to come back and look at it again then.

If it broke through 290 I would sit with it. If it came back again after hitting 290 I would take profits.

See? It's not that difficult to use charts is it?

Summary

- Before you buy a share set yourself a stop loss and a profit target.
- And remember what I said earlier – write them down!
- If you stick to a stop loss system, your losses will generally be minimised.

You'll see if you go to my website, www.nakedtrader.co.uk, that I have a list of my current positions. Every one has a stop loss and target. You need to ensure you have done this too.

IPOs – How They Can Make You Money

This is a strategy that could have been included in the previous chapter, but it deserves a chapter to itself.

Why's that Robbie?

Cos I say so, that's why!

The real reason why, is that looking back over the last 3-4 years some of my biggest winners have come from buying into IPOs.

What the hell is an IPO anyway?

It's basic jargon for new issues coming onto the market. IPO is the abbreviation for: Initial Public Offering. Well *public* is a bit debatable, as it's not always easy to get your hands on them.

I look at all new issues coming onto the market, as I find there are gems that can prove eventual long-term winners.

New shares used to launch on the stock market all the time in the heady days of the crazy tech boom. But since 2000, the new issues market has been much quieter, although recently many resource (mining and exploration) stocks have been listed.

I look at all new issues coming onto the market, as I find there are gems that can prove eventual long-term winners. The one really good thing about *main market* new issues is they are reasonably safe investments. They are usually well priced.

At the time of writing, there are usually about 5 or 6 new issues a week and I have a quick look at them all.

However, it's the *main market* new issues I am more interested in than the AIM issues. (Although in this chapter I'll look at the AIM ones as well.)

First though: how do you keep track of what's coming onto the market and what's just been launched?

Easy peesy these days: there's a website – www.allipo.com – and the good news is, it's free.

All IPO, IPO Centre

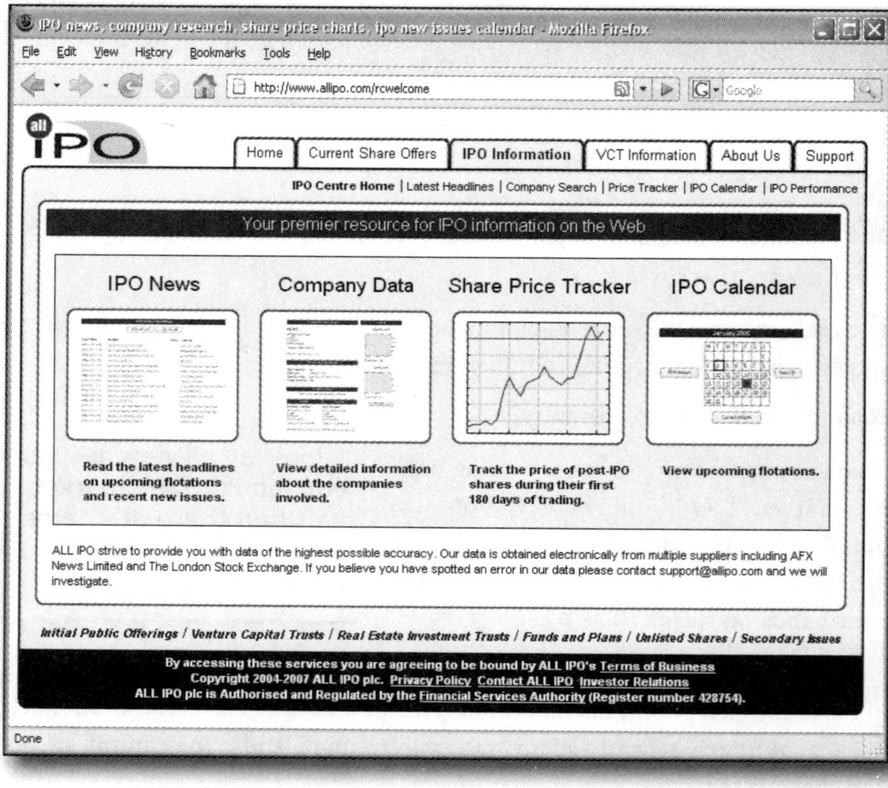

What I do is enter the main site and then click 'IPO Centre' – you can see in the screenshot there are four extremely useful choices.

The first you can see on the left, *IPO news* news about companies about to, or intending to float. I have a look at this most days to see what's on the way.

I use the Calendar page the most to check and see what new issues are coming up. Press *Calendar* and you can look back over the last few days and see what's new and what's coming onto the market each day.

You can click on each share and find out all you need to know about the company and whether it's main or AIM.

Buying into new issues

So you found a new issue and you want a piece of the action. Getting in on the first day just takes a bit of determination.

The thing is, your broker or spread firm probably won't have heard of it yet so there's no chance you'll be able to deal online.

First things first, you'll need the stock code of the company. You ought to be able to find it from around 7am on the ADVFN news service, trawl through and it ought to say:

> *Blah blah...company lists today...the code is XXX.*

If you want to buy the shares in the market you may want to buy in pretty early. So call your broker and say:

> *I want to buy this company. It's a new issue today.*

He'll faff around a bit but then he should come back and ask you how many shares you want and you should be able to deal.

If you want to trade via a spread betting firm it might be more difficult; it's a question of which firm you use. Some might give you a price and some might not be able to straightaway. Not much you can do if they won't give you a price, it's up to them really. Sometimes they've said to me they could give me a price but needed *half an hour to set it up.*

> If it starts trading on the market way higher than the issue price, you may want to consider holding off as the price could come back a bit in the days after the IPO.

Sometimes I wait and sometimes I dive in on the first day. It's a difficult call and something that takes a bit of experience and some luck too.

But the main market new issues tend to do so well that even if you buy in and it comes back a bit, it'll probably go up over time.

I don't simply buy *every* new issue – obviously not every one is going to be a winner. It's a matter of common sense. Ask yourself:

- What does it do and are its markets expanding?
- Is it the sort of company likely to be a winner?

When you click through the new issues coming up, or have been launched already, the report on All IPO will tell you whether it's an AIM or main market.

Main market new issues are in frequent, which is why they are so precious. But there is usually on average one a month. A company has to satisfy many criteria to get a main listing – the AIM market is far easier – such that it means this company is serious and wants to get somewhere. One of the many reasons I like them.

I always have a read through the statement issued. How much money are they raising and how much is the market cap going to be?

For a main issue I would generally expect the market cap to be over £200m. And I want to know the business.

The following table summarises the types of new issues I do and don't like.

New issues I like	New issues I don't like
Oil and Gas	Retailers
Oil and Gas services	A business I don't understand at all
Hedge funds	Any business where I can't see the growth
Finance	
Technology	
Renewable Energy	

Let's start with the main market IPOs and three of them that I bought in 2007.

Main market new issues

New issues I bought

Bluebay Asset Management

This has to be my favourite recent new issue. It was priced at 300p, although I didn't get any at that price. However, 330p was good enough for me. I bought loads in the market and as a spread bet too.

The shares quickly rose and I took very nice profits at 540p – nearly 210 points more than I paid for them. Bluebay looked near a dead cert:

- The company manages loads of funds
- I've observed that these kinds of companies also do OK in a market slide, as they can go short

In fact, to be perfectly honest, there wasn't a lot of research needed here – it looked to be simply a new issue with tons of upside.

Wellstream

I saw this one coming a mile off!

In fact, want me to be perfectly honest?

(No, Robbie, just fool us, we prefer it that way!)

I saw two things:

1. *Sector*: oil services
2. *Market*: main

And, well that was enough for me. Oil services new issues have made me a fortune – take a bow Sondex, Hunting and Petrofac.

These companies were in demand and right from day one I wanted some!

So, bang, at the start of the first day I was onto my brokers and spread bet firms demanding shares! I bought a huge amount – after all, history was easily on my side here.

It wasn't too long before a stream of good announcements started to come from the company as it began to win major contracts.

I bought in at about 360p. I took a huge spread bet position (£100 per point). The shares just rose and rose and climbed rapidly to over 500p, making me a quick paper profit of over £15,000.

However, I did not take profits at this level because I felt the shares had even further to go. Just as well, they went all the way to nearly 900p!

BH Macro

Another lovely hedge fund/asset manager. Guaranteed entry into the FTSE 250, where fund managers would be forced to buy. Launched at a tenner, the shares quickly put on 170p to 1170p.

This one again came to my attention via the All IPO website – all I needed to see was that it was a main listing and it was a favourable sector.

So, again, there was very little research needed to make money from this one.

New issues I avoided

I don't buy new issues just because they are going to be listed on the main market. So when a retailer came to the main market it was a different story.

Sports Direct

I didn't get this one. Why on earth would I want to buy a sports retailer? There are lots of sports retailers and it's a very competitive market.

It seemed to come to the market fully priced. I thought to myself, retailing and sports retailing especially is very competitive. Why and how would the share price rise strongly?

I just didn't have the answers to that question, so I did not get involved. Just as well. The share price slumped from opening levels over the following weeks and it became a real stinker!

AIM new issues

I do buy into the occasional AIM new issue. Generally for my pension fund as there are no tax implications, or I buy them via spread betting.

Just a reminder about the difference between the AIM and main markets first. Remember, the AIM market is cheap for companies to get onto and is lightly regulated. Therefore any old rubbish can get on. It's different with the main market, where it's expensive and only top notch companies generally apply. Also, AIM issues are generally less liquid and far more volatile.

> You have to be very careful with AIM new issues, because unlike the main ones, you can really get your fingers badly burned. So I don't often invest, but will do occasionally.

There are usually loads of AIM new issues – often 10-15 a week! So I am looking for the gold, trying to pick the wheat from the chaff. (Can't think of any other clichés right now but sure I'll find another in just a minute.)

What I tend to look for with AIM new issues is: what will catch the imagination of private investors and institutions?

The ones that tend to catch my eye are anything related to: oil, gas, energy or petrol, new technology or alternative fuel. For now. While the sector is hot! In the future I could be looking for whatever is hot then.

I have a quick look everyday to see what is being launched – **let's face it, what I'm doing is looking for the next hot wonder stock.** If you can find it, you can get very big percentage increases.

I also want it to be fairly liquid so I know I can get out of the shares if there is a problem.

Roxi Petroleum

One good example of something that matches what I'm looking for was Roxi Petroleum.

This is from the initial statement:

Roxi Petroleum – Overview

- Roxi will use IPO funds to build a portfolio of joint ventures in Kazakhstan, primarily previously discovered oil fields with both development and exploration upside.
- Company strategy is to upgrade and increase initial booked reserves through appraisal, seismic exploration, and drilling.
- Post IPO, a significant portion of the funds will be used to begin building the portfolio by acquiring 50% economic interest in two oil fields and one exploration block in the Caspian region of Kazakhstan.
- The contracted areas will total approximately 295 squared kms.
- The initial acquisitions are in different stages of development, facilitating efficient utilization of resources, personnel, and services.
- Roxi intends to add to its portfolio and acquire further fields with development potential with respected business partners in Kazakhstan.

Roxi was created to acquire controlling interests in and develop oil and gas assets in Central Asia, with a focus on Kazakhstan. The initial strategy will be to target projects which have oil discoveries and exhibit a potential for considerable development and / or exploration upside. This strategy will allow the company to rapidly add value to its projects by upgrading reserves levels and planning for the earliest possible production date.

Basically, I liked the look of the statement.

These kinds of stocks only need to have one good discovery for the shares to go crackers. On the downside, of course, they can be very risky. But for good risk-reward ratios this is the kind of AIM new issue that interests me.

I bought in at 45p and in a few weeks it was trading at over 70p.

proactiveinvestors.co.uk

Another great website which covers AIM new issues and the aftermath of their release and stories about them, especially in the resources sector, is, www.proactiveinvestors.co.uk. It's a free site and well worth a read.

This website also hosts presentations from new-ish AIM companies. You can attend, again for nothing, and meet the top bods from some of the companies. I've been to one or two of these presentations myself, they can be well worth going to – and you do get free wine and canapés!

Summary

As I said above, you have to be wary of the AIM new issues; I don't personally buy very many. But if you're careful you can make money. I would not recommend this to very new traders as you can get your fingers burned if you buy the wrong one.

TOP TEN SONGS FOR TRADERS AND INVESTORS
1. Money's Too Tight To Mention
2. Down, Down Deeper And Down (for chartists)
3. Dirty Cash I Need You Right Now
4. If I Were A Rich Man
5. The Only Way Is Up (except for the shares I own)
6. Bills, Bills, Bills (for chartists)
7. Money (that's what I want)
8. Money For Nothing
9. The Winner Takes It all
10. Breakout

Trading Tips – Times Of The Year

I tend to treat shares a bit differently at different times of the year.

Some months, the market historically tends to be strong and some months it tends to be weak. It's worth keeping an eye on history and its likely effect on stocks.

Here's a look at the different months:

February-March

These tend to be middling kind of months. After some good gains over Christmas some people take profits in February, so don't expect big advances here. I would look to have a bit of cash on the sidelines during these months.

April

Amazing how holiday times put people in a good mood. Around Easter the market does really well and it's often a good time for short-term gains. The market's stronger in April than any other month, and the probability of a positive return is a huge 78% from 1971. So it may be worth thinking about buying in mid March to catch the April lift.

May – July

I'm sure you've heard the old saying:

> *Sell in May and come back on St Ledger's Day.*

There is a bit of truth in this as May is the start of some underperformance.

May is currently challenging September to become the weakest month of the year. 2006 saw a large fall in stocks, though 2007 wasn't too bad. Still, it's time to perhaps be wary, take some profits and keep cash in hand. June is pretty much as weak as May, it's the third weakest month. And July generally isn't that better! So in summary May-July ain't great. Maybe time for a holiday!

August

From the gloom of the last few months usually comes a great August.

Of course a lot of people are away, which for a start means there is always a lot less volume. So what happens is shares can move much faster than normal on far fewer trades.

August, surprisingly, is a very good month and according to market historian David Schwartz is the third best trading month of the year. According to David:

> *Good gains can often be achieved in August. But of course with the volatility you have to get the right entry price.*

I agree with David, I often find I can make a lot of money in August.

One thing to look for is companies reporting in August. There aren't many, but if you find one that produces a strong statement, you often find the share price responds very well on smaller volumes.

Also, it is worth looking at companies reporting in early September; August is a good time to get in early in the run up to the results.

September

Yuk! September has the worst record of any month – on average it falls 1.4%. Upside is usually limited but downside can be large. If you ever want to try shorting, this is the month to do it.

October – November

Well it's not as bad as you think. A couple of famous nasty crashes have happened in October, particularly the one in 1987. Stripping out a couple of bad years, October is actually pretty good and it's often a good time to buy.

November is middling but buying the right shares in October and November can be a good move in the lead up to the Christmas buying spree...

December-January

December is one of the best months to buy shares. January too.

Why?

Because most years while it's cold outside, December and January markets are hot!

The statistics support my argument: The strongest week of the year for the market is the 51st week. And the second strongest? The 52nd week!

The probability of positive returns in December is a high 69%. The market's only had one significant fall in December since 1981.

Both mid and large cap stocks perform equally well.

Why are the markets so good?

I suspect it is down to something as simple as human psychology. We all feel good with the approach of Christmas, then there are New Year hopes and dreams. But by the end of January we tend to be left with a bit of a hangover and that's why February isn't so good.

Also, as markets often fall in October and November, investors begin to come in and buy what they perceive as bargains.

The period between Christmas and New Year often sees stocks squeezing higher on thin volumes.

While I might well be tucking into mince pies, I'm usually at my trading desk watching for opportunities to make money.

Many stocks race higher during the holidays, there is often simply no one selling and institutions are shut. This often has a good effect on stocks at the smaller end of the market.

Of course I am making it all sound too easy...it's never going to work out every year. But the use of tight stop losses should ensure if it's the year it doesn't work out, losses will be minimal.

Bad news

On the downside, one thing to watch for are companies sneaking out bad news between Christmas and New Year. It's the same as political parties hiding bad news on a big news story day.

With so many people away, the companies hope the bad news will go unnoticed. So it's worth keeping an eye on news reflecting your stocks. I get out quick if any kind of bad news at all is released at this time.

Strategies

So where do I put my money to make the most of the benign conditions?

First (and I do this most years): I buy the FTSE 100 Index in early/mid December and I sell in early January to take advantage of the fact the FTSE usually rises in this time period.

I usually just make a simple FTSE 100 spread bet long, with a stop loss in place, just in case it's the one occasional year when the festive uplift doesn't happen.

For example, in 2005, I bought the FTSE at 5495 on 15 December and sold on 12 January at 5735 for an excellent profit of 240 points. I'd placed a £10 a point stake, so that was a nice profit of £2,400.

I also like buying retail stocks short-term, only in December, as I'm not normally a great fan of retailers. These stocks often rise well before and just after Christmas, in anticipation of good consumer spending. I'm normally out by early January. Retailers usually report their Christmas figures in mid January and sometimes the reality isn't so good, or the stocks have already risen in anticipation of good figures so they begin to fall back on profit-taking.

I buy the FTSE 100 Index in early/mid December and I sell in early January to take advantage of the fact the FTSE usually rises in this time period.

I find December is also a good time to have a look at some of the smaller, tiddler stocks in the market and sometimes have a bit of a gamble.

Time For Tea And Toast

Yes, it's the tea and toast chapter. Yipeee!

It could also be entitled "Don't Panic Corporal Jones".

What do I mean by *tea and toast*? Well, I'm actually talking about periods of time when no trades are necessary. Instead of trading, just drink tea and eat toast.

You will often find that this downtime will save you a lot of money. Especially given that bread and teabags are still very cheap. If you don't like tea and toast, go out and take the dog for a walk. Or take up a new hobby.

Because sometimes markets are volatile – up 100 points one day and down 150 the next. When markets get volatile I sit back and tea-and-toast it. Or sometimes, if it gets really nasty, I hide behind the sofa. Had plenty of experience doing this during *Dr Who* (when it was really good in the 70s). Also a good place to hide if the wife's come home and I forgot to tidy up.

Every time the market has got very volatile, history has guided me that as long as I know I am holding good, strong companies they will in time bounce back.

Just remember: every time you exit or enter a trade it costs money (spread *plus* commissions *plus* stamp duty). But on the bulletin boards you can see messages like:

> *I am 100% cash now.*

So boast the writers – not mentioning it cost them a fortune to sell everything at bad prices. The next week they are suddenly:

> *90% invested again.*

Meaning they bought at bad prices too and let's not even mention the stamp duty and commissions paid.

One thing I think is worth doing when markets are going down a bit is think about exiting spread bet or CFD positions. That's because most people are in effect leveraged, which means they, say, have a £20k market exposure, but only really have £2k in the markets.

These are the kind of people that get wiped out quickly because in effect they've bought their positions by using a credit card. And the spread firm will want its money back fast.

I love buying on market dips.

If, like me, you have a decent portfolio full of good companies in, say, an ISA, you can relax more. I'm not saying be smug and not sell anything. But you can certainly keep hold of good companies for longer.

Generally speaking, it's always worth *not* being fully invested, it's worth having some cash on the sidelines. That's because then you can take advantage of a market slide by buying shares that have suddenly become bargains.

> It's usually better to be buying when everyone else is selling and selling when everyone else is buying.

And I love buying on market dips. I bought some of my favourite shares at great prices, especially during the market falls of May 2006, and February 2007.

A 'TEA AND TOAST' TRADING DAY, I SEE?
MITCH

10 Winning Strategies

This has got to be the biggest part of the book. Which is a stinker really.

Why?

Well, if you really want to know: I'm writing this chapter while holed up in a grotty hotel room near Heathrow Airport.

I gave a seminar here yesterday and I decided I was only going to get this book finished if I had a couple of days with no distractions. This is the perfect place. It's in the middle of nowhere. I can't go shopping and there is nothing to do here. So I've got to write. [Well, Robbie, we were – wildly optimistically – hoping to get this book out this century! Ed.]

Only thing is, I did have one or two gin and tonics in the bar with some of the people that came to the seminar. So I'm feeling a bit tender.

But gone are distractions such as my toddler son grabbing my mouse, heading off with it and sticking it down the loo. No *Teletubbies* playing in the background. No phone calls. No markets open. Although I do have my trusty £7.99 toaster which will provide me with hot toast while I write. Plus a Twix and a chunky KitKat.

The good news for those of you who bought my first book (too late to try and flog it now on eBay for a good price), I have in this one brought together a number of strategies you could consider using in addition to methods discussed in the original *Naked Trader*.

I realized recently that I actually have a number of differing strategies I use and I want to show you how I research shares and decide to buy them.

How have I managed to find so many good shares over the years and hang onto them?

Here are just a few of the best ones with their gains:

- Burren Energy: **+412%**
- Marchpole: **+312%**
- VP: **+318%**
- Hunting: **+403%**

The worst losers?

Nothing over 15% for a long time because of the use of stop losses.

This chapter focuses on some good winning investments I've made. I hope it will show you why I chose them and so build on what you've already learned so far.

So here for your delight and excitement (well maybe that's going too far) are the Naked Trader Top 10 strategies. These are ideas for you to have a think about. They are *headline ideas* – things I look for in companies, and over the years these strategies have made me a lot of money.

(Where the bloody hell has all the money gone though? Must be those vintage bottles of wine…! Or else that day I let the Mrs loose in Selfridges with my credit card after forgetting to change the pin number…)

Anyway, here are some strategies for you. The companies concerned will generally have to meet most of the criteria I have just outlined first of course.

Strategy 1: seek companies starting to change

Yeah, I know what you're thinking. Easier said than done, mate. Not really. It's just a question of reading through reports. I'm looking for a company that hasn't been doing that well but is suddenly changing direction or focus. You can pick up on this through a good read of some recent statements. I'm looking for companies in the doldrums that are beginning to go through a transformation. I especially like ones that state they are shutting down loss-making divisions and putting resources into profit-making areas, or indeed finding new revenue streams.

Here's an example of one:

Renold

I bought at 75p. Bought more at 90p. The price almost doubled to 140p in a few months.

Renold (2005-2007)

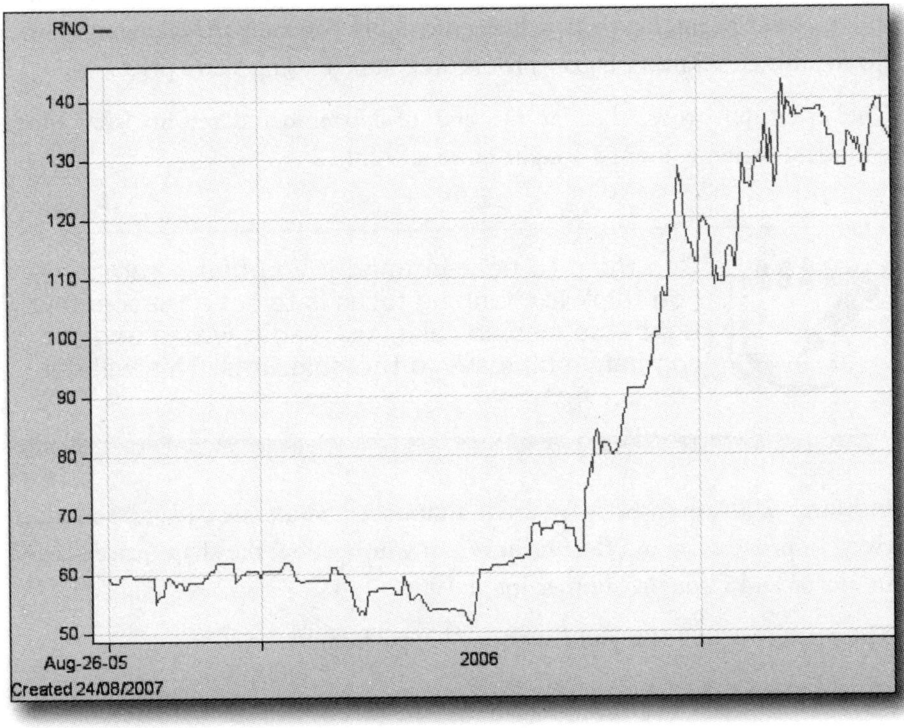

What alerted me to this one?

I just happened to notice some director buying this small company, so I decided to take a look at it and see why they were so confident.

I had a look at the last results. The company had been struggling for a while because of heavy debt. But management had just done something about that and flogged off a division to pay down debt. In the meantime, losses were turning into profit and the statement had the feel of a management that might be about to transform the company.

I particularly liked this sentence in the company results:

> "A year of progress, implementing a strategic shift to focus on the core Industrial Power Transmission business, while improving profitability and reducing the cost base."

Good. I like companies that are taking action to improve things.

Several other things to like too. The company said orders were up 16%, and the chairman was stepping down. Looks like things were improving, and management was changing.

On top of that, the financial director bought 20,000 shares along with others and this was beginning to look like a nice story – a company changing shape. To me this could mean bigger profits and an increasing share price.

The price duly rose, then at the end of November came an even more confident statement and I bought more at 90p!

One thing to bear in mind if you find a company you think is changing focus is to set a reasonably tight stop loss, in case you read it wrong and the company still stays in the doldrums. This will get you out fast.

In March 2007, even better news: it announced wholesale changes to reduce risks, improve cash and the business as a whole. Now the share price started to motor and I bought another lot at 100p.

The price rose to 140p and I was one happy bunny!

In Renold's case my stop was 70p, I would ensure no more than 8% was lost.

If you want to see the reports that got me interested, just go to the ADVFN 'Quote' page, type in "RNO", scroll down to news and go back in time till you find them. You will see what I mean.

Summary

- Look carefully at companies changing focus and/or management, or obviously putting some effort in.
- A good look through back reports will give you an idea of whether a company is in turnaround mode.
- Have a tight stop loss.

Strategy 2: find cheap shares!

How do you find cheap shares? What I'm looking for is a market cap that looks very low compared to full-year profits or likely next-full year profits.

Remember my rule of thumb: if a company has a market cap of say 100m and is making 10m profits, that looks cheap. (Trading at only ten times profits to market cap.) If it was over 15 that would start to look more expensive.

I've already talked about this when I was giving my example of whether Sir Alan Sugar might consider it cheap.

Marchpole: simply undervalued!

I bought at 60p. It rose to 189p (trebled in value).

Marchpole (2005-2007)

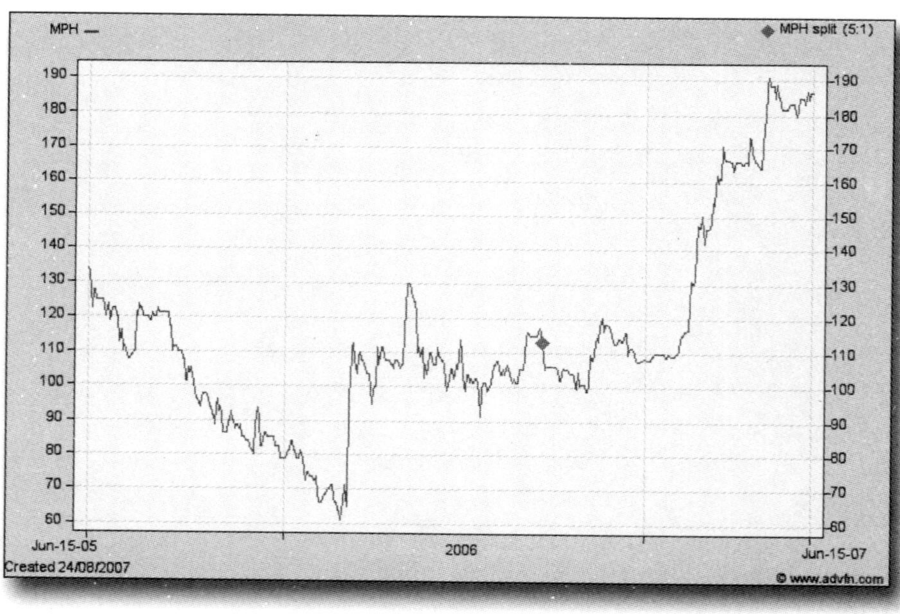

I really liked the look of this one. I especially liked one thing: the market cap was only £25m but profits were amazing – nearly £5m! That's only 5x. Statements were confident and so was the outlook.

This just looked so cheap! After some research I found it was cheap because the company hadn't had a particularly good couple of years. But it looked way oversold. You could literally buy a company that was making £5m for only £25m. The company had a good niche supplying posh clothing. Any negatives? There wasn't much, except the company had had some licensing issues which were being resolved. But not such big issues that deserved such a low rating.

> One note of caution here: if you find something that looks very cheap do make sure it's not cheap because it is doing really badly or has a lot of debt. Do thorough checks.

Summary

- Sometimes, you will through luck, find something that is just cheap.
- When you find it, buy it, unless there are some negatives around.
- Check that debt is not an issue.

Strategy 3: buy a hot sector

Sometimes you'll find one sector of the market is hot. For example, since the hot sector from around 2004 has been the small oil exploration companies.

How do you know it's a hot sector?

Well it's partly down to common sense and partly down to looking for sectors where the share prices in that sector are rising.

Oil services was a sector overlooked by many investors – oil services, that is the people who provide the equipment needed by the booming oil companies. Over the last few years, of course, oil itself has been a hot sector and I have made a lot of money buying oil exploration companies like Burren Energy and Tullow Oil.

But of course with booming oil exploration it was almost a certainty that oil services companies were going to have a great ride. In particular, I bought three oil services companies that made me a fortune between them: Sondex, Hunting and Petrofac. In fact, they still are making me money as the sector is *still* hot and could be hot for a long time to come.

Hunting was the best. My last book showed me buying Hunting at 185p. Price now...820p! I did take profits along the way but have pretty much always held some. The charts you can see here of Hunting and Petrofac say it all really.

Hunting (2005-2007)

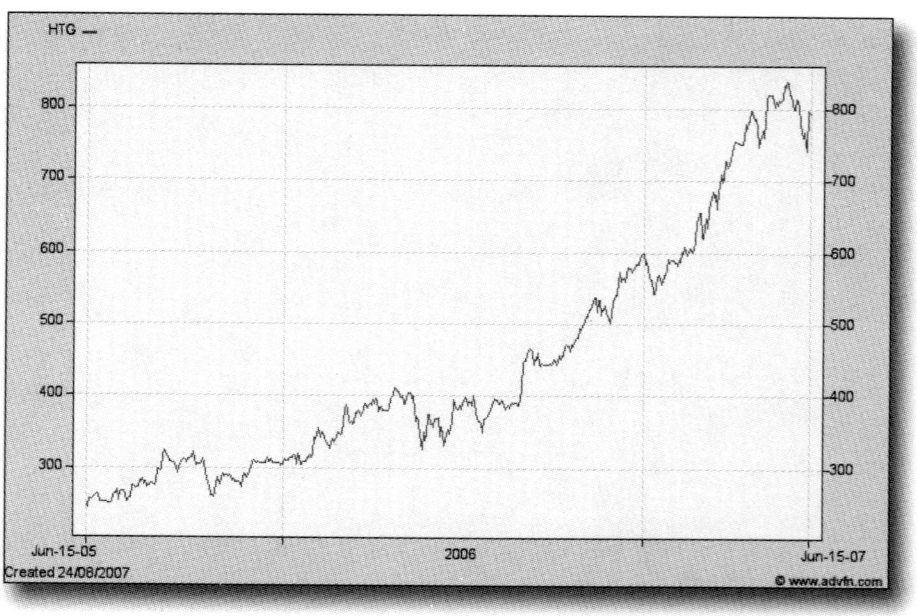

Petrofac (2005-2007)

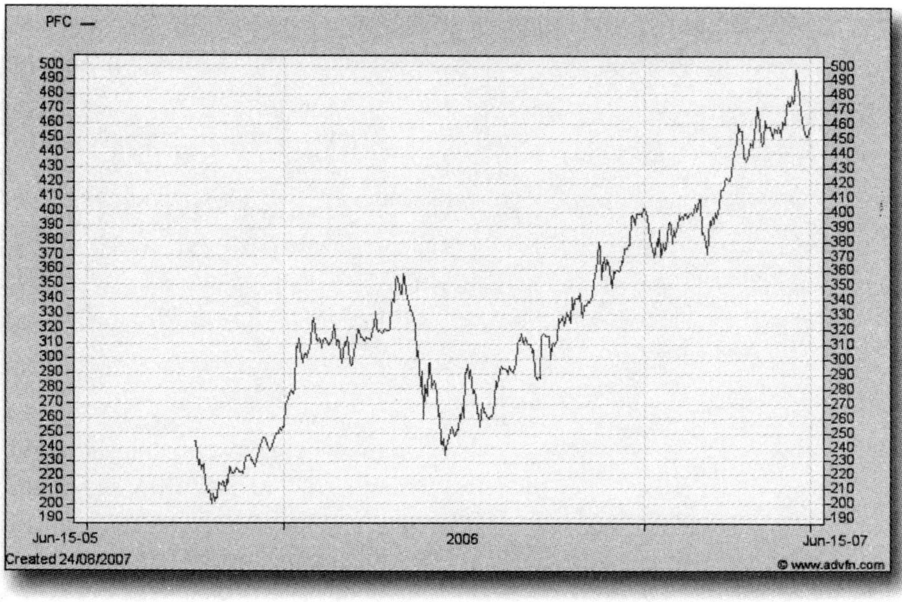

Of course a hot sector isn't going to be hot forever, but usually I try and carry on riding the waves of a hot sector for as long as I can until they start an obvious downturn.

For example, as I write, telecoms – which were until quite recently a dog sector – have begun to shine. I noticed this quite quickly and bought Carphone Warehouse as probably the best play in the sudden new hot sector.

Carphone Warehouse (2005-2007)

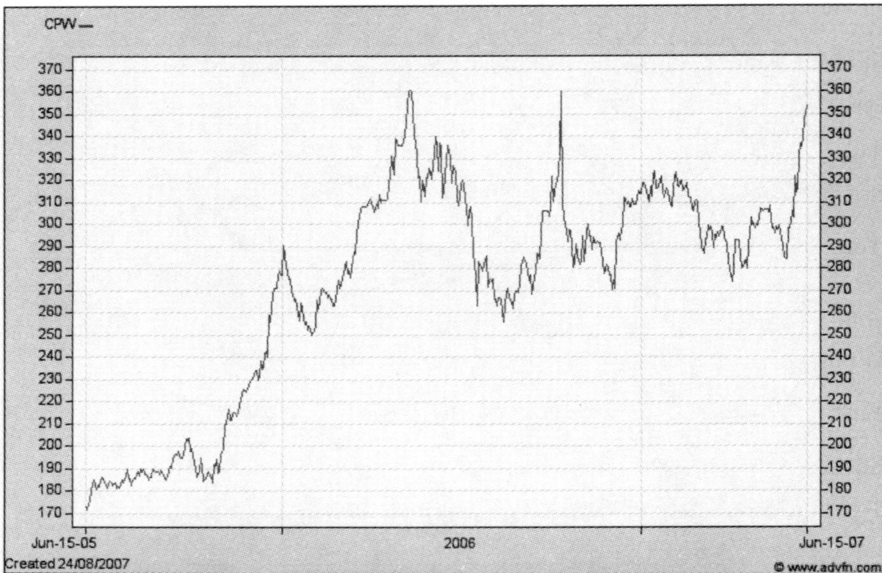

If you find a share you like, find others in the same sector. Click "Financials" on that share on ADVFN and near the top there is a clickable link "Other shares like this". Click on that to find other shares in the sector.

I don't know what the next hot sector is going to be, but I will probably find it in the course of researching shares in my usual way. When you do find it, don't be afraid to really go for it and buy well.

Summary

If you can find a hot sector, it can stay hot for quite a long time. At some point it'll lose its shine, but it's worth riding a hot sector for as long as possible.

Strategy 4: recovery plays

A recovery play strategy is all about finding a share that was once doing well, has had a terrible time but is now starting to rise again, i.e. it is recovering. (Geddit!)

The trouble here is finding the right share: one that is actually recovering and not still in the dumps and likely to get further in the dumps!

You *must* have worked out a reason *why* the company is going to/is recovering and not just jump into a share that's gone down a lot. I'm usually trying to find a company that has got something terribly wrong with it, but is putting it right and so there is plenty of potential in the share price.

But whatever you do, ensure you are not just buying a dog that may not recover.

So here are two examples: one that *could* be a recovery play as I write is Jessops, which is a chain of shops mainly flogging digital photography.

Jessops (2005-2007)

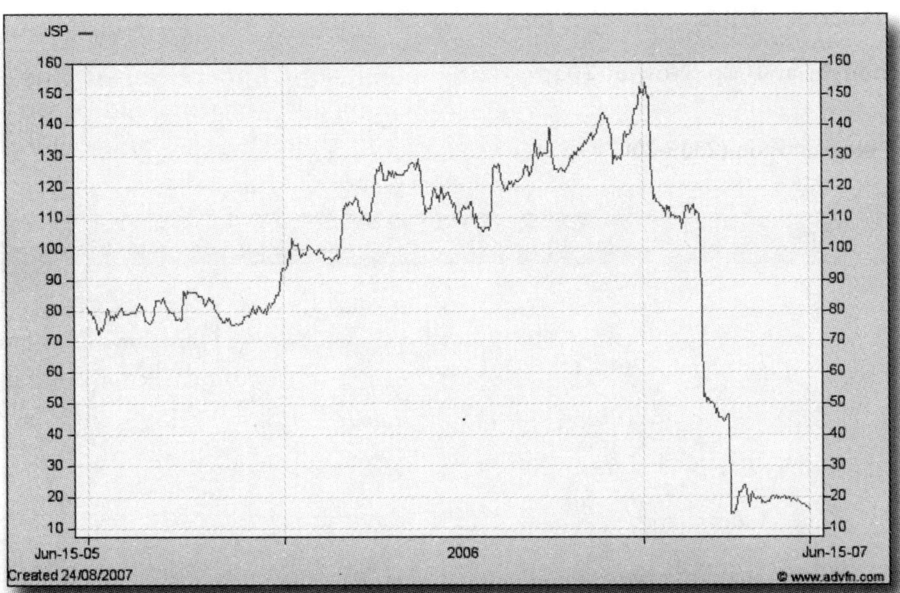

It's had a pig of a time and shares have come back all the way from 150p to 25p. But however tempting it is to consider the shares could make a comeback, I haven't bought. Because so far the company hasn't put out any kind of statement that gives me any reason that their fortunes are likely to recover.

- How will their shops fight back against the fact most people now can just print their digital photos at home?
- How can the business be turned around?
- And is there even the remotest chance it could go bust? (Well, yes possibly.)

These are the kind of questions you need to ask yourself when looking at recovery plays.

> If you find a recovery play but there is even the *slightest* chance it could go under, leave it.

Anyway, for now, Jessops is just on my watchlist.

Now a recovery play I bought and doubled my money on.

Telecom Plus

Bought at 102p. Now at 205p.

Telecom Plus (2005-2007)

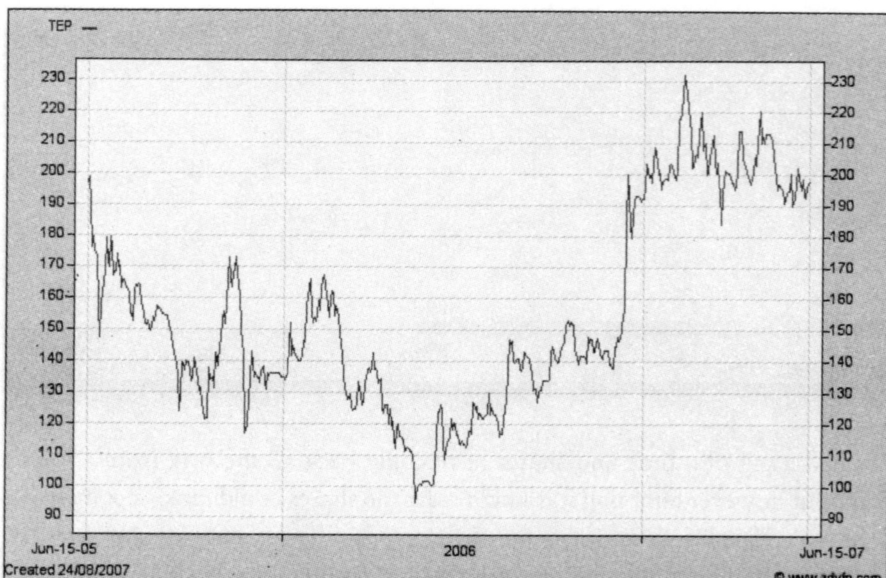

This is a company I followed for many years. I've also been an independent distributor for it for many years – but never had any special inside information. One point to make is that you'll find as you get experience you will follow a certain number of shares and get used to them and understand them well.

This company, which uses network marketing to sell low cost telecoms and energy, did very well, but then ran into trouble when the price of oil and gas soared in the markets. The company didn't expect it and suddenly, from making £10m, it started running up losses because its energy customers became very expensive. So while it was doing really well in telecoms, the energy side was draining the company of its funds – and fast!

The shares took a tumble and as the price of gas continued shooting up, the shares kept coming down. I was keeping an eye open to see what the company was going to do. At one point it looked like it could go bust.

Then there was an announcement. The company sold off its energy customers. Now, instead of buying the energy themselves, npower agreed to supply the power and give Telecom Plus a commission per customer. I immediately saw that this would transform the company and bring it back to profits. There was no way it would go bust now. **I swiftly bought shares at just over 100p minutes after the announcement.** That proved the right move as they quickly doubled!

Again, it's all about building yourself a picture of why a company is recovering. It's common sense really. If you think a company is going to recover, make sure you've worked out why rather than taking a punt. Because if it isn't the recovery story you think, it could go down further.

If you do buy in, set a tight stop loss just in case.

Summary

- Have the reasons why the share will recover clear in your head.
- Don't buy if the share price is still going down and it could go bust.
- There must be a tangible reason for recovery.

Strategy 5: play short-term trends

If you feel like you want to trade shorter-term, it's often better to specialize in a small number of FTSE 250 – or even FTSE 100 – companies. Get to learn the way they move up and down in a range and get a feel for them. This is the time you really need to look at a chart.

The main thing to remember is make sure it is a good strong company with plenty of growth potential. In other words, do proper research on it first so you are not going to be suddenly surprised by a profits warning. You want a great share that will carry on rising over time, but one that often trades in a specific trend.

Have a good look at the historical chart and see where it gets bought and sold.

A good example – and one of my favourite trading stocks over the last couple of years – has been Charter. Basically it's been in a long-term up trend. But it also goes down on profit taking so I've found plenty of chances to get in and out.

Charter (2005-2007)

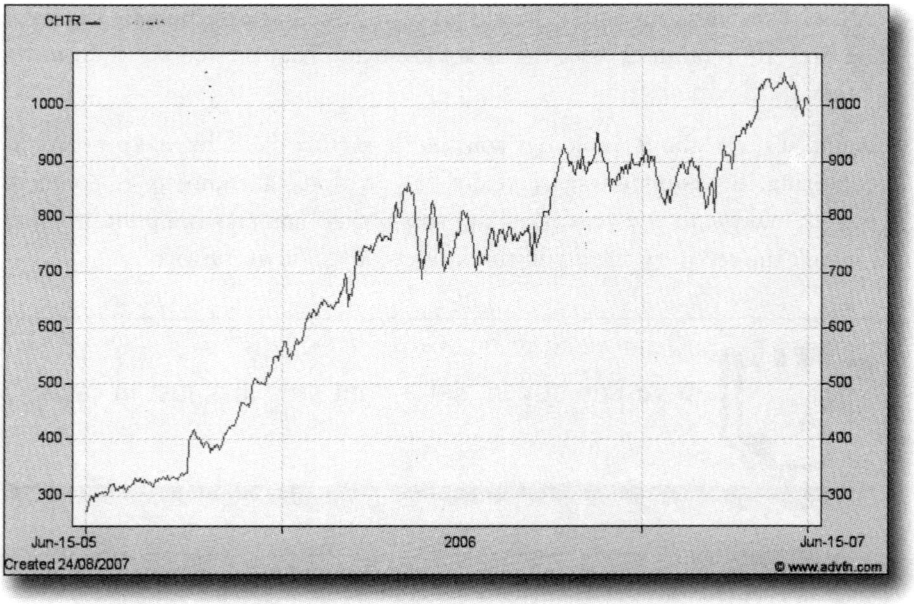

I originally bought in the early 700s, and kept those shares as a long-term hold, but I enjoyed trading them too because there were many points where the shares ran out of steam.

You can clearly see these on the chart. From Dec 2006 right through to April 2007, it ran from the low to mid 800s through to the low 900s many times and then back again. **So I bought several times in the mid 800s and sold in the early 900s to quickly bank some 10% trades.** It traded between 8ish and 9ish pounds for many months as you can see until April 07 when it surged through resistance at 930 to power up to the 1150 level. At this point I sold again and am waiting (hoping!) for it to resume a new short-term trend between 1050 and 1150.

As you can see, this took no particular chart reading skills. It was just common sense.

The beautiful thing about this kind of range-bound trading is that you can get out if the share goes below the range. In other words, when I was trading it from the 800s to 900s, if it had gone below the 800s I would have stopped trading it for a while until a new pattern had been established.

So examine a few charts – in preferably FTSE 250 stocks – and find some trading range patterns and start to play them. You are looking for a share that is oscillating between two levels for a few weeks or months. Each time you want to try to buy near the bottom of the range.

You can see from Charter there is no great skill involved at all. You are simply going between two numbers. But do get out if the range gets broken on the downside. It is of course possible to short the share too, once it hits the top of the range – in which case get out quick if the range breaks to the upside!

I mention FTSE 250 stocks because they are liquid and the spreads are normally tight, ideal for short-term trading. If you tried this with smaller stocks, the bid-offer spreads would be greater, which would reduce the profit.

> If you can only look in on stocks once or twice a day, it may be worth having a stop loss with your broker or spread betting firm say around 2% below the bottom of the range, in case something happens when you are not at your desk.

Summary

- Make sure it is a strong company, and of sufficient size.
- Confirm it is in a range then buy at or near the bottom of the range and sell near the top.
- Get out fast if a range is broken on the downside.

Strategy 6: buy boring companies!!

For goodness sake who wants to buy a boring company?! We're macho traders and what we want is excitement! Something with lots of whiz and flashing lights...

Not true in my case.

When I look at a company's website and see a load of boring looking cogs and widgets I get excited, because often it's boring companies that make superb gains over the years. I guess when I say "boring companies" I probably mean engineering companies.

Companies that make, say, conveyor belts like Fenner which has risen well over the years. Or Volex, whose stated mission on its website is:

To be the world's leading supplier of electronic optical fibre cable assemblies.

(I hope you didn't fall asleep while reading that.)

My upside on Fenner has been *huge!* I originally bought it as featured in my first book at 86p – it has hit 250p since and I have been with it most of the way. It has always matched my criteria for buying shares. Just me and the institutions in this one because of the boring nature of the business!

Fenner (2005-2007)

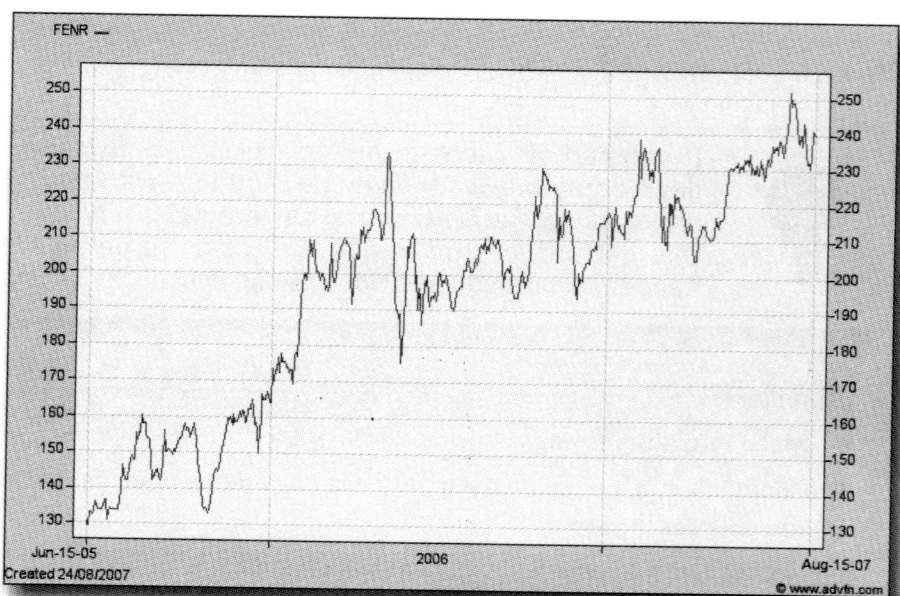

There are loads of boring looking sockets and cables on Volex's website. But that didn't stop its share price going from 50p to over 200p in two years. A nice return! I was a bit late to the party having bought around 175p. But its boring cables get me going!

Volex (2005-2007)

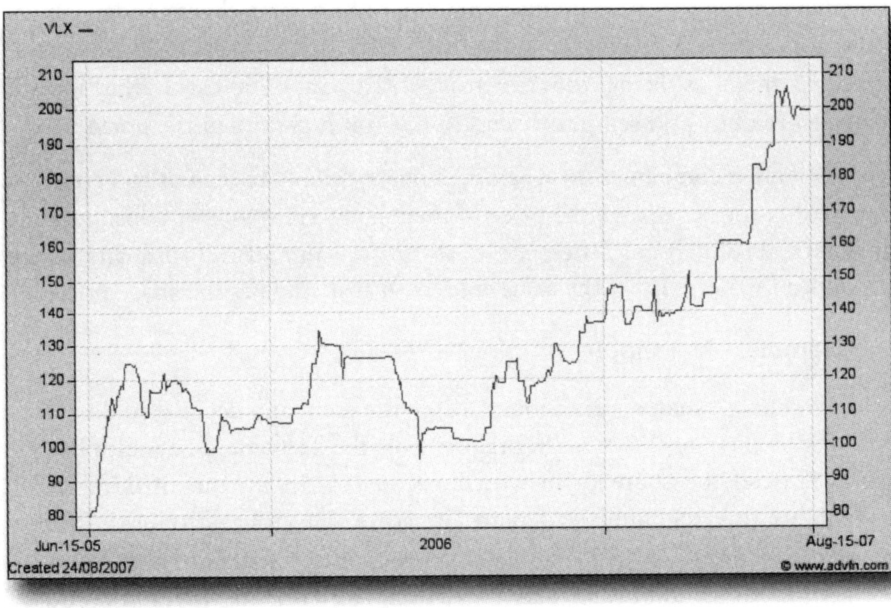

So the surprising thing is: boring products often sell really well. Just because you come across a company that has a product that starts you yawning doesn't mean you should overlook it!

It's amazing how these engineering companies can pay out in time. My timescale for boring but steadily gaining companies is about 3 years, and you'll find they can become the great bedrock of, say, a self-select ISA. They are always there, gradually increasing your wealth.

Summary

Think about having one of two boring companies in your portfolio – buy and hold them. They will keep you going during the bad times and steadily help to increase your wealth.

Strategy 7: buy shares "doing the splits"

What the hell are you talking about Burns? Buy fit shares? Nope. I'm talking about share splits, consolidations and bonus issues.

This is what it means simply.

Companies whose share prices are under 50p or over 1000p sometimes get stuck in a rut simply because investors don't like buying shares under 50p, as they come with a *penny share* tag, and with shares over 1000p investors perceive them as being too expensive. Also, in both cases, the spreads between the buy and sell prices tend to be a bit higher than the norm.

So what some companies do when their share prices are seen as too cheap or too dear is simply change the price of their share via a split or consolidation. It makes absolutely no difference at all to the value of the company or the amount in value held by the shareholders. It just changes the share price.

Example – Marchpole

Marchpole's shares were around 25p – the company decided to do a 1 for 5 share consolidation. In other words, the 25p would be multiplied by 5 – so the share price would become 125p instead of 25p. To balance this, the number of shares in issues was reduced to just a fifth of the previous number. This instantly took it out of penny share status and made it more attractively priced for private investors and institutions. And the price motored.

The effect on a Marchpole holding 10,000 shares at 25p was:

- *Before consolidation*: of 10,000 shares held at 25p; value = £2,500
- *After consolidation*: 2,000 shares held at 125p; value = £2,500

If you hold shares that are being split, your broker will just change the number of shares held in your account on the morning of the split.

How do you profit from a split?

I find the best thing is to buy the share before the split. Research has shown there is an average rise of over 3% in a share price on the day of a split and many shares outperform after a split or consolidation.

Another example is Henry Boot, a property company whose shares were trading at an expensive looking 1200p. They did a split bringing the price down to a much nicer looking 250p.

It is simply a fact that investors hate to buy at 1200p but love to buy at 250p. I guess it's all silly in a way and psychological.

Henry Boot (2005-2007)

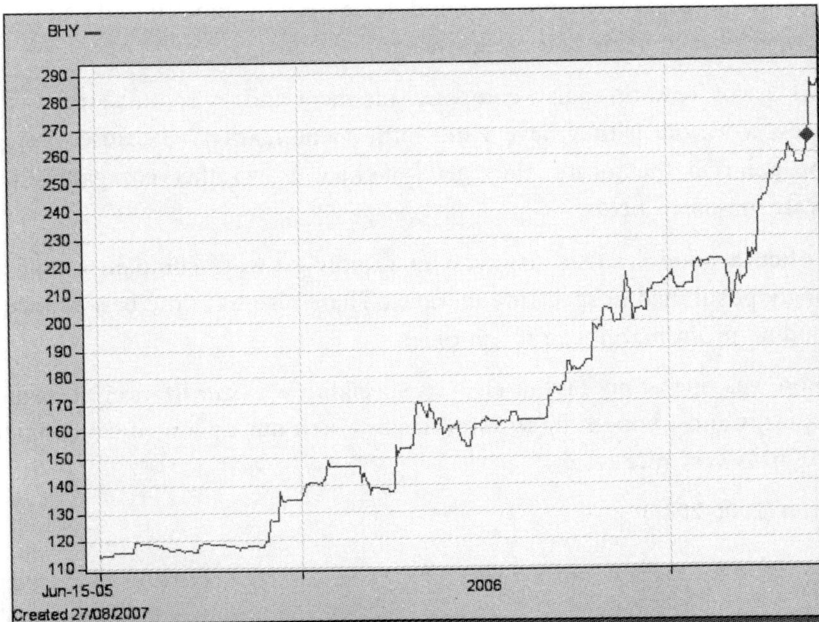

Note: after a share split or consolidation, charts of share prices will automatically adjust the old prices (to provide a continuous share price). For example, on 2 January 2007, the share price of Henry Boot was 1080, but in the chart above it is shown as 216. If this wasn't done, it would be difficult to read charts and apply any technical analysis.

Of course you should not buy a share just because it is splitting – you must still only buy after you've done the usual research and you're happy with the share anyway.

But I've bought a number of shares before their price has changed and found it's been well worthwhile.

Summary

Shares that change their price, often rise after the change and it is often worth buying in before the price changes.

Strategy 8: companies doing well in specialist markets

I like finding companies that are strongly positioned in specialised markets. There are quite a few examples around. It's especially good to find companies who specialise in areas that are growing.

So when you read through a company statement and try to understand what it does, work out if they have a nice little niche market – because often, at some point in the future, they get bought out by other companies who operate in related fields.

It's often a good strategy to invest in rapidly-growing companies that are strongly positioned in speciality markets. These also have the best chance of defending profit margins in tough times.

Isotron was one of my favourites – its speciality was sterilization of medical equipment and I bought in at 550p. It got taken out by a medical company at 900p! A very nice result.

Isotron (2005-2007)

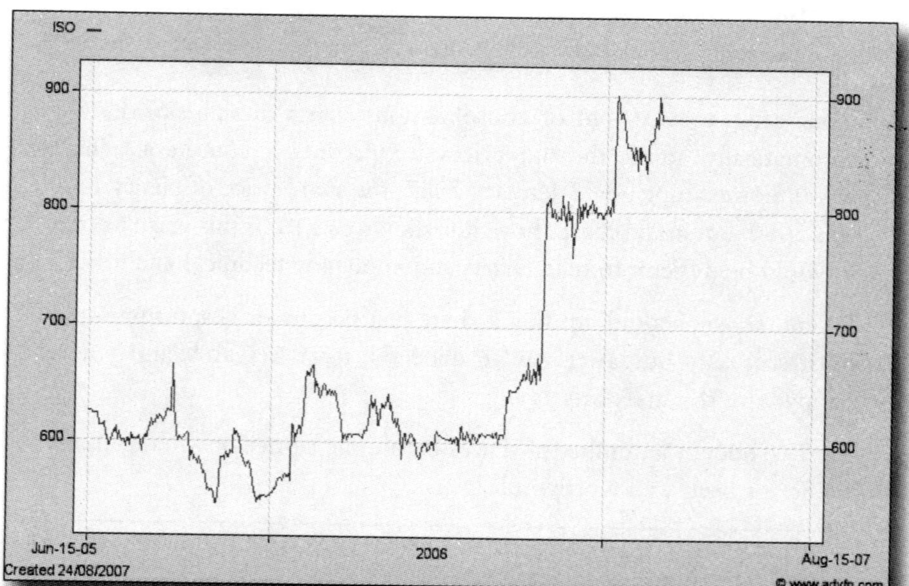

Another good example is a company I bought into a couple of times, MTL Instruments, a small company which is a major player in the development and supply of safety explosion protection devices. In an increasingly safety-conscious world, this sector is growing in importance. And its niche here should ensure a steadily growing share price with a good chance of a bid at some point.

MTL Instruments (2005-2007)

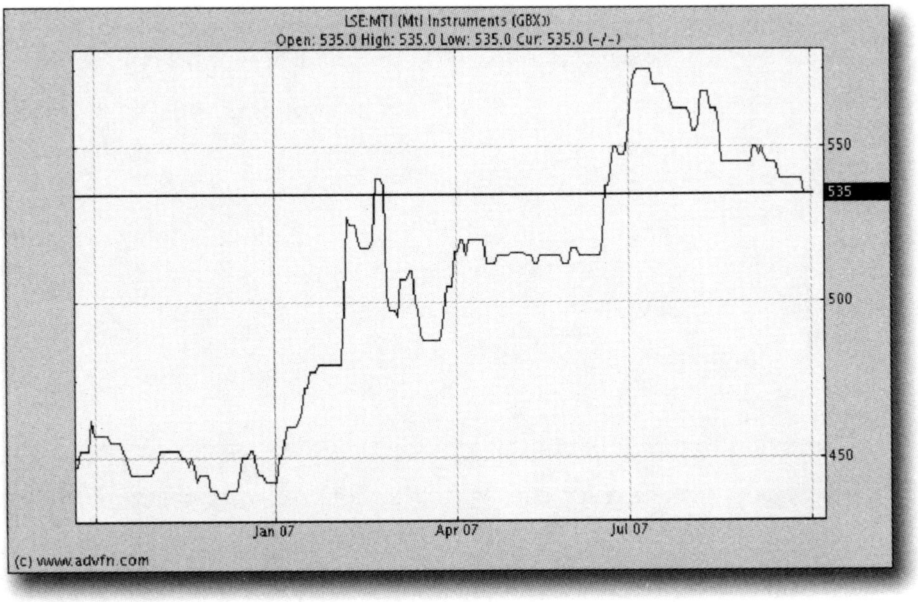

Another company I made a fair bit on is Latchways. This company specializes in safety equipment for those working outside – again, very much a speciality market but a very strong one with not much competition. I bought these around 750p – they recently hit 1200p.

Latchways (2005-2007)

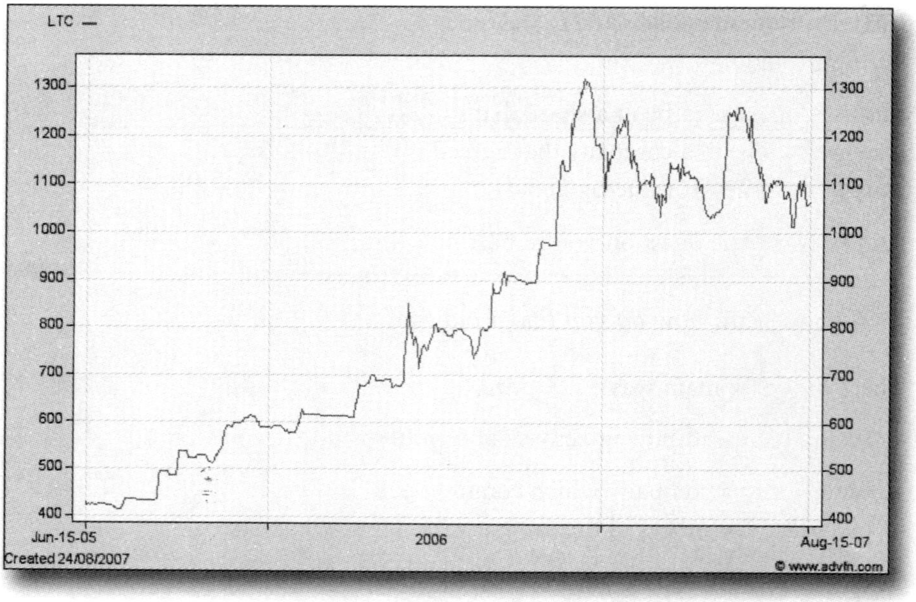

With these speciality markets I am looking for companies that are growing their turnover and profits, which should make them very attractive to other, bigger companies who might want to bid for them.

I generally expect to hold a speciality market company for some time as it can take time for its value to be perceived by the market.

One thing to beware of: there is a difference between a growing speciality market and a company that has one product that nobody wants!

Summary

- Look for growing companies in unusual or specialist markets.
- Buy and hold.

Strategy 9: finding bid targets

Let's sing the bid song:

> *There ain't nothing like a bid, nothing in the world...*
> *There ain't nothing you can name, that is anything...like a bid...*

(Err, that was supposed to be to the tune of "There ain't nothing like a dame" but never mind.)

I usually manage to be in a share that's bid for about 5-6 times a year. Why's it so good to be in a company that agreed to be taken over? Because the share usually increases in value by 20%/40%.

And I'm sure the question you're busting to ask me is:

> *OK, wiseguy, how do you find a bid target?*

There are three main ways:

1. Seeing increased buying activity in a share
2. Buying into a company which common sense tells you would make a good bid target for others in the same area
3. Quite simply, keeping your eye on bid gossip in the papers.

Let me give you three examples of shares I made very good money on in three different ways.

Domestic and General

Bought at 1090. Sold at 1402.

Domestic & General (2005-2007)

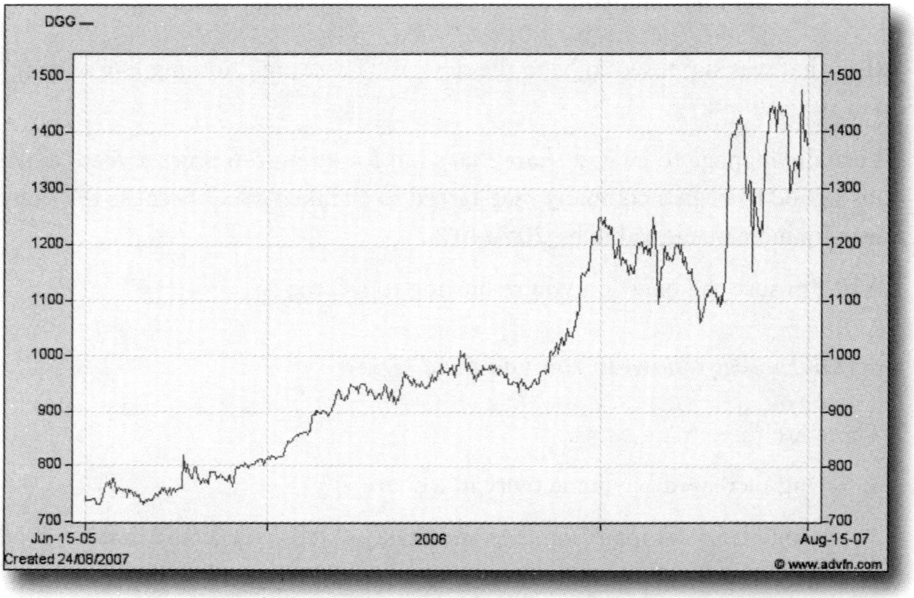

So how did I suss this one out as a possible bid target?

Well, it was simply that I thought it was the kind of company that another company might be interested in. I liked its business anyway. It is the company behind all those extended warranties. If you buy anything electrical from the major retailers, odds on D&G would be providing the warranties. And it looked a super business considering electrical items these days, like TVs, usually run for years without breaking down. D&G are the guys who come out to mend anything that goes wrong.

And the business looked cheap – worth something like £420m with profits of over £35m.

Sussing this out as a potential bid target was mainly common sense. A lot of companies could be interested in adding a warranty business to their existing operation. An electrical chain like Dixons or, as it turned out in the end, Homeserve – whose business is to go to homes and repair water-related items. A perfect fit.

Homeserve became interested in buying D&G; the share price rose sharply and I gratefully took some nice big profits.

So when you think about buying into what looks like a cheap company think about whether it could be a good fit for another company and you could well have a bid target on your hands.

Bid targets: volume

By *volume* I really mean trading activity for a share above the norm for that company. It's certainly worth scanning the ADVFN *Volume Toplists*. These lists give you access to shares trading more than their normal volume.

Although insider trading is illegal, you see time and time again lots more shares than normal in a company being traded in the run up to a bid. Because, let's be honest, those in the know gossip about it, and so the news gradually spreads.

Birse

Bought at 12.5p, sold at 16p (more than 30% profit).

Birse (2005-2007)

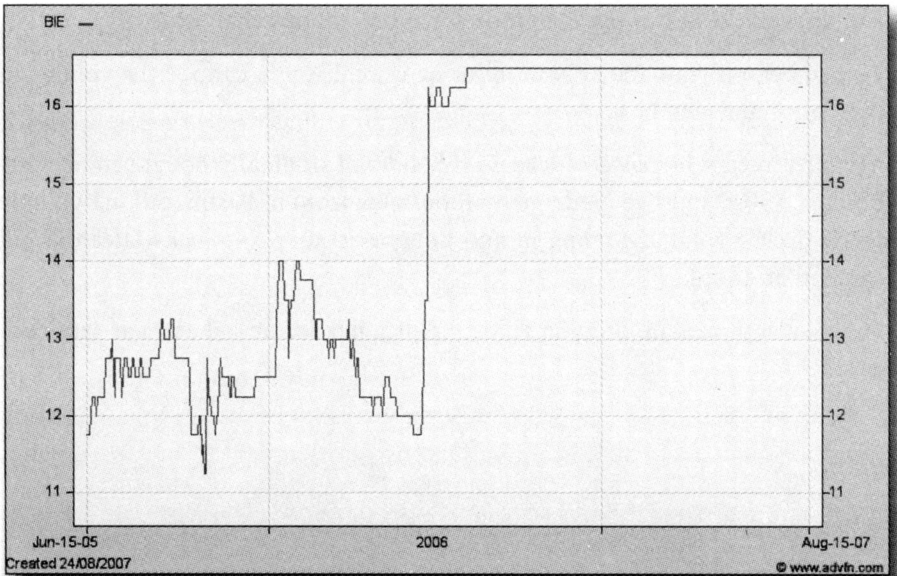

I happen to have had Birse on one of my watchlists . I'd traded it before – a small construction company that had had its fair share of problems but looked quite cheap.

One morning, I suddenly saw a 300,000 share buy appear, after many days with hardly any activity at all. Hmm, I thought, why would someone suddenly be buying nearly 40 grand of a small company like this? The next day another big trade appeared and I thought:

Hmmm, something could be brewing here...

And I simply tagged along and bought some shares. As far as I was concerned, if people out there were interested in buying loads of shares then I should probably be too.

Around 6 weeks later I was nicely rewarded, as ADVFN newswires revealed a bid for Birse at a 25% premium and the shares shot up.

This has worked for me a few times in the past and is especially good in smaller companies. If you get to know shares on your watchlist, as time goes on and you gain experience you will, like me, develop a nose for abnormal buys or trades coming in – and it's usually worth acting and fast.

Seems to me that those in the know tend to be in the know around 6 weeks before a bid is due in the smaller companies.

Of course there are also plenty of risers in the bigger companies too, in the run up to bids. Best thing is to look for more volume than normal.

Remember, on your ADVFN monitor or watchlist you can see the volume in the right-hand side box.

My most recent bid success was with Sondex. I originally bought in my first book at 130p, and I've made many thousands from it. Again, talking volume I saw decent volume coming in and bought at 309p...4 weeks later the bid came in at 460p!

So this was a mixture of good volume plus a hot sector (oil and gas services).

ADVFN watchlist

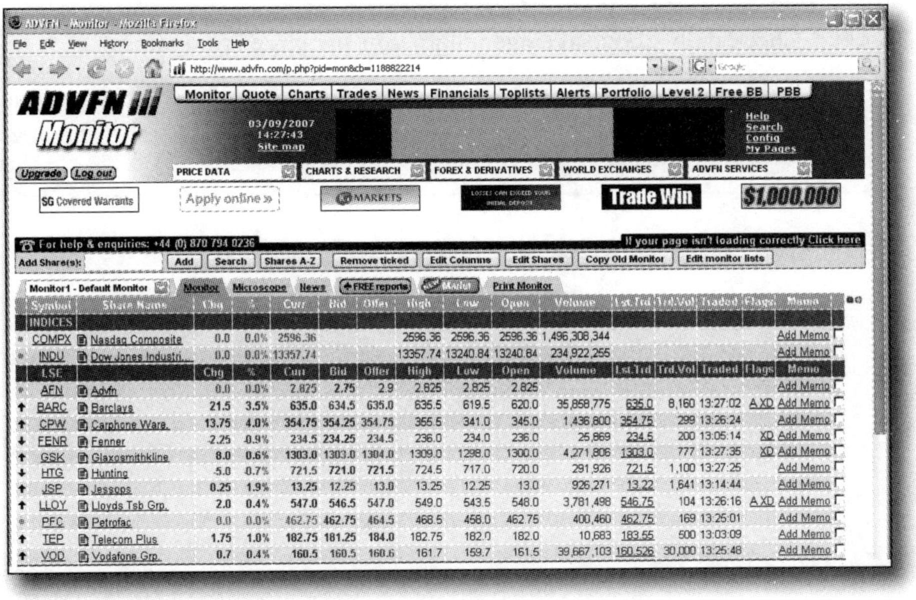

Bid targets – keeping an ear to the ground

Catching a bid is often a case of picking up news and gossip from the ADVFN newswires, other web sites and general bits and pieces from the newspapers.

Often, when a company is mentioned in a gossipy way in the press as a possible bid target, there is still time to get on board. It's a matter of timing and a bit of guesswork.

You have to decide whether a counter bid is likely from some other party – this happens quite a lot. For example, the Boots share price was around 770 when rumours first went round about a bid. It was possible to get in then. The price rose to near a tenner and then a counter bidder came in and the price rose to 1130p.

Carpetright sat at 1000p or so while bid stories circulated for quite a while. A few months later, a private takeover was mooted and the shares rose 350p in a few minutes.

Of course it is not all plain sailing. If you come to the story late and then a bid does not materialize, the shares can come down quite a bit. If the price is already close to where a bid might come in, you may have missed the action.

Summary

- Watch for sudden buying activity in quiet shares
- Check daily above-average volumes in the larger companies
- If you think shares are cheap so might a bidder
- Keep an eye on newspaper gossip

Strategy 10: buy shares moving up to the main market from AIM

One of my favourite strategies is to look for AIM shares that have just moved onto the main market, or are about to move to the main market.

2007 saw many companies deciding to move onto the main market, which is good news for investors like me who use ISAs and can start buying into these companies. Early evidence suggests that shares move up in price once listed on main.

For example, Sinclair Pharma, Imperial Energy and First Quantum Minerals all moved from AIM to the main market and their prices rose.

A lot of it is because both ISA investors and fund managers can start to invest in shares they wouldn't have wanted to get involved with before. In 2006, only 3 made the move. 2007 sees at least ten making the leap, and this looks like gathering pace as more companies take the plunge.

Two of my favourite buys like this have been Oilexco and International Ferro Metals.

Oilexco went from 400p to near 700p in the run up and after the move to main, and IFM went from 80p to 150p. I was a little late to the IFM party but still bought at 120 and am showing an increase already of nearly 25%.

Oilexco (2006-2007)

Why is it a good move and why do the prices tend to rise?

Because for the first time big institutions can get involved (many don't buy AIM shares). Those like me who buy most of our shares in ISAs can buy for the first time too.

It also shows the company is serious about its growth prospects and wants to be a big player, which is one of the main reasons for making the leap.

Companies with a value above £150m will get a place in the FTSE Small Cap index and those above £500m or so will get in the FTSE 250 – inclusion in both indexes will see tracker funds buy in.

So whenever you see an announcement that an AIM share is planning to move to the main market, it's pretty much a buy signal. I would say probably one of the best buy signals there is!

Of course, again you need to make sure you do the normal research and not buy just anything, but if you like the company, get stuck in when you hear they are going to full from AIM.

Summary

It's a great signal when a company goes to a main listing from AIM. Very well worth noting and thinking about buying.

Other strategies

Before moving on, some other strategies and ideas in brief.

Government contracts

Buying companies which win government contracts. Always worth having one or two in a portfolio. They tend to be rather solid shares, generally stay in long-term uptrends and don't go down too much in bad times.

Examples: Mouchel Parkman, Serco.

These government contracts tend to last over a good number of years, therefore some income and profit is pretty much guaranteed.

Tech companies

I am always on the lookout for a good tech company. If you get the timing right, they can really bring in the money.

CSR and Wolfson were two tech companies I bought into at an early stage; I trebled my money, and more, in both. I ended up taking profits after they rose too much and went ex growth.

What's the next hot must-have gadget/phone/music machine and who's going to make the chips that go in them?

That's the research you need to do now, and how I found those two companies.

Oil exploration

Oil exploration companies are going to continue to be in demand for a long time to come. While they obviously have their risks I have made some good money from these. Researching them is a little harder and I find it difficult to get my head around production rates etc. But as long as they are producing oil and the oil price stays high they can be a decent earner for any portfolio.

Long-term up trends

This is a simple strategy based on charts: buying a share simply because it has a lovely long-term up trend. As long as your research shows no negatives it can be worth trying to join the party. A 7-10% trailing stop loss can pay dividends.

Small drug companies – avoid

One strategy I tend to avoid: buying into small drug companies. They tend to be rather highly rated and are generally loss-making. They are relying on one or two drugs to get approval – if this doesn't happen the share price sinks. Too high risk for me.

Part 5
More Knowledge

"The great rule is not to talk about money with people who have much more or much less than you."

- Katharine Whitehorn

SIPPs

SIPPs (self-invested personal pensions) mean you can take control of your own pension fund rather than letting the professionals look after it.

I think they're brilliant. The question is:

Should you take the plunge and run the fund yourself?

The answer is: could you do any worse than the fund managers?

I watched the pension fund I had with the company I worked for, BSkyB, go up for a few years and then sink like a stone between 1999 and 2001, at which point I'd had enough. So when I left full-time work I immediately transferred all the money from two frozen company pensions into my SIPP and began trading.

I'm glad I did as I've built it from £40k to £165k. Much of that rise was detailed in my *Sunday Times* column "DIY Pension".

So I run my own pension fund, buying and selling shares. Of course, I'm confident when it comes to dealing in shares, but other people need to think carefully about whether to run their own fund.

> One rule of thumb is: Only go for a SIPP once you have about £25k or more to put in your pension – it's not worth it otherwise, taking costs into account.

For this section, I'm going to assume you feel reasonably confident about investing. So I'm going to discuss how to set up a SIPP and what to do with the money once you get hold of it.

Setting up a SIPP

Setting up a SIPP – how can I put this? Well, it's a pain in the bum, to be frank, especially when you want to transfer in frozen or current pension schemes. It takes ages and there are lots of forms to complete. It also takes a lot of hassling. The reason is, of course, the people currently running your fund don't want you to quit and run your own. They want to continue receiving their nice fat juicy fees.

Assuming you mainly want to trade shares you need two things:

1. An execution-only **stock broker**
2. **A pension trustee**

The trustee basically looks after the money and keeps it secure for you usually – for a yearly fee of around £150-£300. You then trade the shares as normal and hopefully watch your fund rise.

It's probably best to choose the broker first – maybe the one you use for normal dealings – they should have a list of trustees they recommend and work with. Trustees are much of a muchness, so just choose the cheapest.

It's slightly easier if you want to start from scratch, without transferring in any money.

You can transfer in as much of your salary as you want, you then get 20% added, or 40% depending on your tax bracket.

> Trustees are much of a muchness, so just choose the cheapest.

If you're a 40% taxpayer and put in £10,000, the government adds another £4,000.

You just send the money to the trustee, it's put into your stock broking account and away you go. Buy and sell shares using the money as you wish – and that includes AIM shares which aren't allowed in an ISA.

Transferring frozen schemes

You can transfer in frozen schemes. You have to chase up the company the schemes are lodged with as they need to send you forms (yawn!) You fill them out and return them – the company should then release the money to your trustee.

It can take weeks and you need to keep hassling all the time. The other issue is it can be difficult to transfer in a *final salary scheme*. Some trustees won't let you do it because final salary schemes are supposed to be the bee's knees.

If you have a final salary scheme it could be argued you don't need a SIPP, because the FSSs are excellent payers. This is something you will have to look at closely. These days there are hardly any final salary schemes around, they have mostly been closed.

Anyway, all the hassle is worth it in the end. It's a great feeling to be in charge of your own destiny.

You can carry on trading your SIPP till you're 75, at which point the government reckons you'll be too ga-ga to trade any more, and you have to buy an annuity.

But from the age of 55 you can take 25% of the fund as cash. Oh, and there is a limit of £1.4 million on a fund – after that you get taxed. Thanks a lot Gordon.

SIPP charges

What usually happens: the stock broker you pick will charge you their normal dealing rate per trade. The trustee you pick will charge an annual fee – expect something around £150-£200. Don't pay much more than that.

The best thing is to go for a broker with a reasonably low execution-only rate per trade and then ask them for their list of trustees and the trustees' charges. I don't see much reason not to go for the one that charges the least!

Trading in a SIPP

Trading in a SIPP is exactly the same as trading your shares normally. You buy and sell shares as per usual – however you can't get at the money till you're 55 (if you're over 55 you can take 25%).

Once you have your SIPP what sort of shares should you deal in?

You really ought to be sensible. You probably have many years to go before you want to cash it in. Don't go crazy – buy some decent, sensible shares with good yields. You're looking for a decent lift for the fund over time. You have time, and do not have to worry so much about the ebb and flow of the market and can look longer-term.

Look for shares you'd be happy to hold for a while and follow the practices I've already outlined in this book.

Aim for growth of around 10-20% a year – the fund will soon grow nicely at this rate. Don't take too many risks as you may be relying on this money in the future.

As well as buying shares within a SIPP, you can short too. This can be done by buying covered warrants or CFDs. You'll need to research these carefully. I do think as you become more experienced it is worth looking at CFDs and covered warrants within your SIPP, with a view to a little shorting.

For example, when the market headed near a high recently I bought a few FTSE put covered warrants. This means if the market tanked short term I would make quite a lot. This would help to cover any losses in the longs.

Just recently, I have been using my SIPP to buy high risk AIM stock, which has worked quite well for me. However, it is easy for me to do this because I have built up tons of money within my ISAs which I can take at any time and I have decided to try and grow my pension money more quickly as I can afford to take the risk.

Summary Summary

- You can run your own pension fund
- You can make contributions and transfer in frozen pensions
- You need a stock broker and a pension trustee
- It can take time to transfer in funds
- Buy any shares you like, including AIM
- You can short shares using CFDs
- Be cautious with your fund – you may need the money

BROKER'S MANTRA: SOMEONE IS A CLIENT... UNTIL THEY HAVE GONE BROKE.

Bulletin Boards

It can be a lonely business buying and selling shares. But that's where the internet bulletin boards (BBs) come in. They are great fun to read and worth a look if you are researching a particular company.

The four most active and biggest bulletin boards are:

ADVFN – www.advfn.com (click 'Free BB')

Hemscott – www.hemscott.com (click 'Info Exchange')

MoneyAM – www.moneyam.com (click 'Investors' Rooms')

Interactive investor – www.iii.co.uk (click 'Community')

All BB contributors have chosen a nickname, so you have no idea who they are. If you want to contribute, you just register on the site, pick your nickname and you are away.

On ADVFN and MoneyAM, each topic is called a 'thread', and they appear in order of last updated. There are the main bulletin boards which are free, and they both have premium BBs where you pay a small amount to access them. The premium boards attract a more serious investor and tend to be much better.

BBs are like a big pub where blokes (generally) talk about shares in the same way they talk about football in the pub.

The main rule regarding the BBs is: treat them as light entertainment!

Bear in mind that many BB contributors are trying to push the share they've just bought. So treat everything you read with some scepticism. Especially comments on very small companies.

- A **bad sign** is if there are dozens of posters all enthusiastically discussing every tiny movement of a share. Even worse, if there are posters claiming it'll be a ten bagger and the like, or posters saying they've bought some and are going to buy more, etc. And worst of all is when there is loads of inside bitching and backbiting between posters!
- The **best sign** is a reasoned, quiet but informed BB. It means the share concerned is actually more likely to be a winner.

Some bulletin boards are good, some not so good, and others a complete waste of time. There is a good function on the ADVFN BB called a filter. If you find a particular poster a waste of time you can filter that poster so their posts just disappear from your screen. Handy!

My view on using them?

Well, I think the BB on the company you've just decided to buy is worth a quick look in case there is some additional info you missed. You never know.

Sometimes you might find some handy research done for you. For example, if it's a retailer some posters may have visited stores and reported back their findings. Quite often with oil stocks you can find very informed posters who know their way around oil exploration, digging for oil and the like.

Sometimes, really good BB posters will make life easy for you and will cut and paste in company statements and reports, dividend dates, etc.

However, don't take everything you read as accurate! Remember you are just using the BB to place another piece of the jigsaw.

Ramping

Rampers is a term applied to those who continually talk up a share they are holding in the hope others will buy in and so raise the price of the share in question. They then hope to quickly sell in the strength generated and make a profit.

They will say or write anything to make you buy. They will often claim to have inside information or say there's a 'bid coming' or there's an amazing 'chart breakout'. They pick on the smallest shares in the market and make clever remarks about them intended to suck you into buying.

> The lesson here: don't believe everything you read, especially if comments are made about an illiquid company with a small market cap.

There are different sorts of posters to bulletin boards:

1. The **complete idiots** who just like using naughty words or having fights with others.
2. The really **good posters** who are well-informed and come up with decent and well worked-out predictions.
3. The **wind-up merchants** who don't even trade and just like winding people up. Watch out for posters who can't post during the day. This is a big clue that they don't really trade much but want to appear authoritative.
4. The **in and out types.** They will breathlessly post their trades one minute saying what a great share it is, then ten minutes later saying they sold because it wasn't moving. Best ignored.
5. The **gurus.** Often with their own blogs; they try to set themselves up as the wise ones. They will post trades but will quietly not mention the losers. Beware.
6. **Complete fantasists.** They really think they are the bee's knees. Avoid.

Given time, you will work out which is which!

Summary

- BBs should be used mainly for entertainment purposes
- Don't get conned into buying worthless shares
- Treat everything you read as suspicious
- It is worth reading a board before you buy a share

Bulletin board shorthand

Abbrev.	Explanation
BH	better half
ATM	at the moment
BBL	be back later
BFN	bye for now
BRB	be right back
BTW	by the way
FWIW	for what it's worth
GGG	giggle
GRH	grinning, running and hiding
GSHIWMP	giggling so hard I wet my pants
HTH	hope this/that helps
IDK	I don't know
IMHO	in my honest/humble opinion
IOW	in other words
LMK	let me know
LOL	lots of laughs/laugh out loud
NP	no problems
OT	off topic
OTOH	on the other hand
PLMK	please let me know
PTM	please tell me
ROFL	rolling on the floor laughing
ROFLMHO	rolling on floor laughing my head off
SGTM	sounds good to me
TTYS	talk to you soon
TIA	thanks in advance
TIC	tongue in cheek
TTFN	tata for now
WYSIWYG	what you see is what you get
RBIEH	Robbie Burns is extremely handsome
IHD	in his dreams
;)	wink and smile
;	coy wink
:)	normal smile (number of mouths is proportional to happiness)
:(	sad face
:D	very big grin (or VBG)
>:)	evil grin
:O)	clown face
:P	poking tongue out

All the above can also be used for text messaging too!

Level 2 And DMA

When it comes to timing a trade, I always use Level 2 for a final decision. In fact, I wouldn't personally ever trade without it.

Level 2

What the hell is Level 2 and is it worth having?

Two very good questions which I will try and answer for you now.

Level 2 only used to be available to professional traders in the City, but thanks to new technologies and price cuts by the stock exchange, it's now available cheaply to anyone that wants it.

I have to say Level 2 is bloody hard to explain simply, but I'll do my best to give you some kind of insight. If you are just starting out I wouldn't worry about it just yet until you find your feet. But if you're starting out you *could* decide to take it – the reason being it will help you to understand more about how shares move and why.

You will find it an eye-opener and you will quickly understand much more about how and why shares move up and down. There's no way I could trade without it. I think even if you're very new to the markets it's worth considering finding out about Level 2.

So what is it exactly?

Without Level 2 you simply see the current best sell and buy price. But you have no idea what other bids and offers there might be in the market. Let's say you were interested in buying or selling Harvey Nash. Without Level 2 here is what you see.

Simple (Level 1) price quote for Harvey Nash

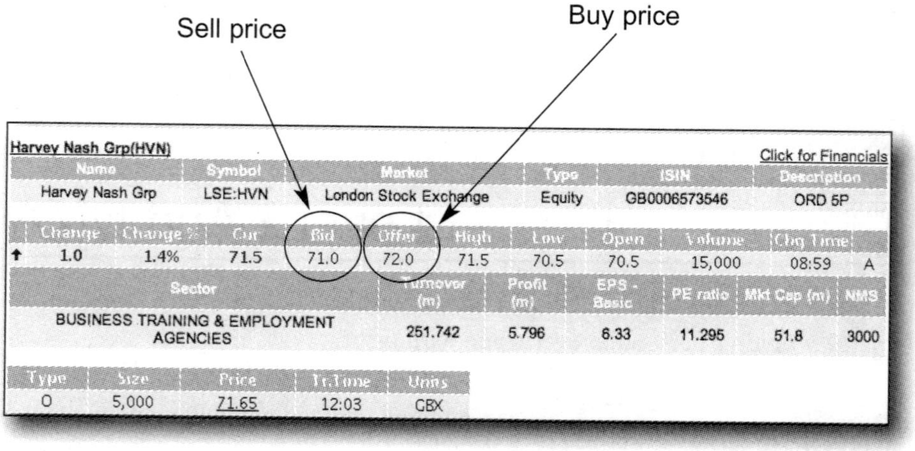

You can see the sell price of Harvey Nash is 71p and the buy price is 72p. These are the *best* prices, meaning:

- 71p is the *highest* selling price in the market
- 72p is the *lowest* buying price

This is all very well. But those aren't the only selling and buying prices in the market at that time. For example, there could be loads of traders willing to buy Harvey Nash at 84p.

Now here's a Level 2 quote for Harvey Nash. You can see it is completely different. You can now see the other orders in the market.

Level 2 price quote for Harvey Nash

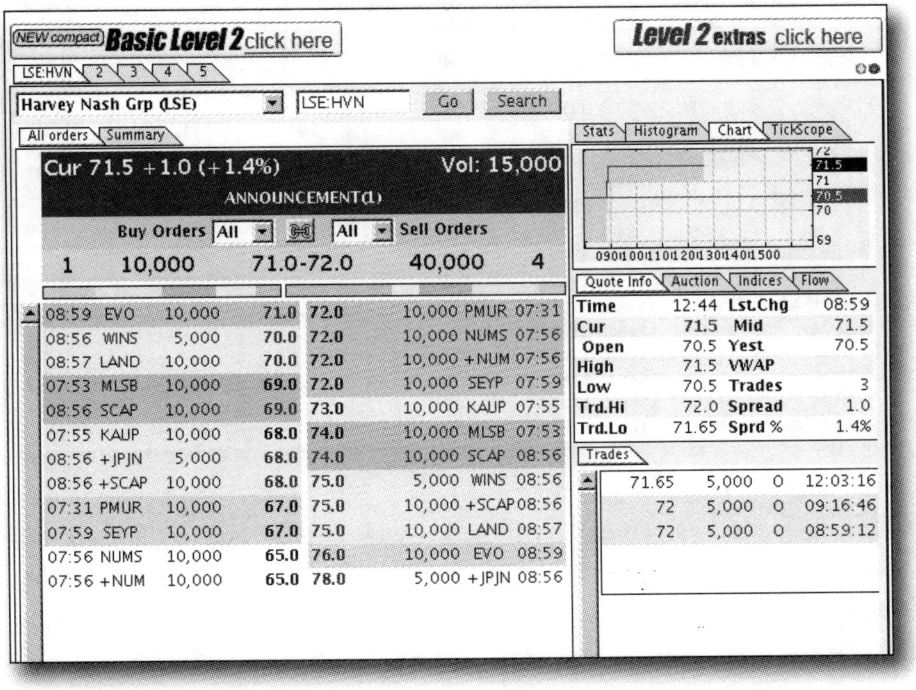

What's the use of it?

Well, you can see the orders begin to rise or fall *before* it makes a difference to the Level 1 price. And what that means is, you can get in and buy or sell *before* the crowd knows there is going to be a price change. I find I often get in ahead of a big price jump.

On this Level 2 screen you can see the market makers such as Winterfloods (WINS) and Evolution Securities (EVO) and all the others. On Level 2 you can see them start to move their prices up or down. This means you can buy or sell *before* most people know the price is about to change. Which is rather handy!

Moving onto the bigger stocks, here's a view of the Level 2 for Charter.

Level 2 price quote for Charter

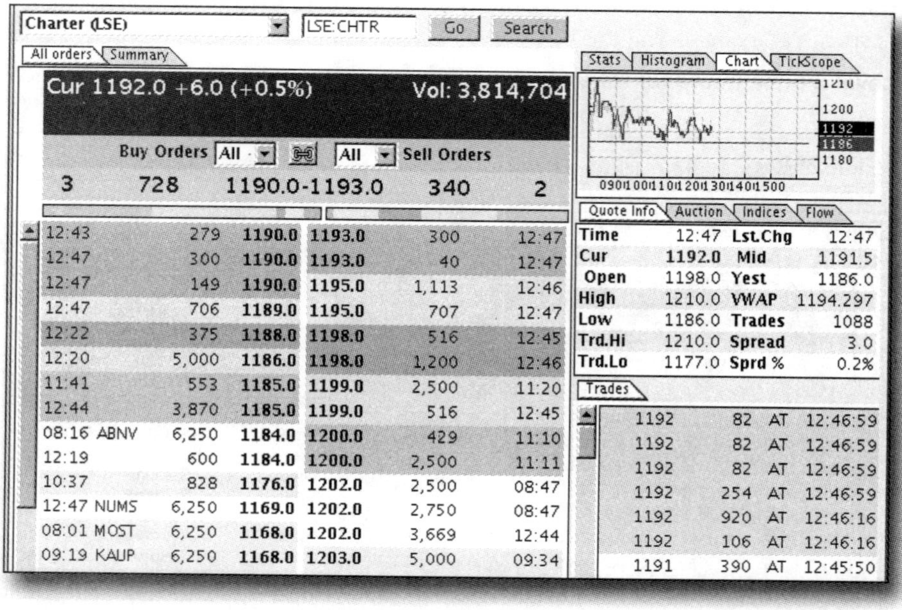

With bigger stocks you still have market makers (you can see they are still there), but there can also be all and sundry putting in buy and sell orders.

The prices and amounts of shares you can see are all real buy and sell orders. The price of the share moves when someone has bought or sold the amount you see on the screen.

What may confuse you is it says "buy orders" on the left and "sell orders" on the right. This is from the point of view of the people putting on the orders. For you, you are "buying" the right-hand side prices and "selling" the left-hand side ones. In other words, when someone puts in a "buy" order they are buying from you – who is the seller!

A quick way to remember this, you always:

- *buy* at the **higher** price, and
- *sell* at the **lower** price.

In other words, you always buy or sell at the more disadvantageous price!

You may look at this Level 2 screen and think: "Bloody hell, I'm never going to understand it."

But once you're used to it, it's much easier than you might think. What you're looking at here is not only where the market makers are, but with larger stocks you can see all the buy orders and all the sell orders. By seeing how big the buy orders and sell orders are, you can judge where support might be on a share price. And this information really is invaluable.

The other invaluable thing about it, is it teaches you how and why share prices are moving – you can see everything going on in the background that affects a price.

Level 2 will stop you from taking profits on a share too early and buying a share at the wrong time.

The best way to understand Level 2, though, is really to get it and play with it on your favourite stocks.

How do you get Level 2?

It's available (at the time of writing) at anything from free to £500p.a. If you trade an awful lot, some brokers and spread bet firms will give it to you for nothing – a rule of thumb is roughly 30 trades plus per quarter.

If you don't trade that much, it's a lot cheaper than it was, and costs keep coming down all the time. Probably in 5 or 6 years or so it'll end up being free.

I personally use the ADVFN Level 2 because I like the layout. Also, at the time of writing, it is the only Level 2 that includes all the trades made through PLUS Markets (the rival system to the LSE), so you can see all the trades.

> ADVFN is happy to offer *Naked Trader* readers a pretty big discount of about £120 on its Level 2 – email me at robbiethetrader@aol.com for details, and put 'Level 2 offer' in the subject line.

Direct Market Access (DMA)

More and more brokers and spread betting firms will allow you direct market access.

What's it all about, Alfie?

It means you (yes, *you*!) can be a market maker, and you can put your own buy and sell orders directly into the market.

Let's say a share price quote is currently 500-502 (500 to sell and 502 to buy).

Now, normally, if you wanted to buy the shares you would have to pay 502 – as that is the buying price.

But DMA allows you to input an order direct onto the order book, which means you could input an order to buy at 500.25. You would then become the best (i.e. highest) selling price, and the share would officially then be quoted as: 500.25-502. If someone then wanted to sell some shares, your price would be the best and they would sell to you at 500.25.

Brilliant for you because you are effectively buying them at the sell price.

Alternatively, if you wanted to short the shares you could put in a sell order at 501.75p and effectively sell at near the buy price.

Most direct market access is done via CFDs. All the orders, including yours, will show up on your Level 2 screen.

As I said, you can get DMA at many places now – I have used E-Trade and GNI Touch. GNI Touch has the best system and you can pretty much place your orders on any share you like.

If you're very new to trading don't worry too much about DMA just yet. But Level 2 is worth looking at.

Spread Betting

Introduction

When I say the words "spread betting" to someone, their eyes glaze over.

Much easier to say the words: "Would you like another pint and some crisps?" Then the eyes light up.

However, I'm going to explain spread betting in a very simple way here. Don't be scared of spread betting – it is easy to understand if you concentrate for a few seconds.

I'm writing more about spread betting in this book than the last one because I'm using it myself more and more – and so too are many private investors. Profits made by the spread betting firms are growing and growing, as more and more people use them. And I'm not surprised as spread betting has become an important arsenal in the tools available to private investors.

OK, here goes...

With spread betting, instead of buying or selling shares in the market, you are betting on the shares to go up or down with (what's essentially) a bookmaker. Which is why it's called spread *betting*!

So, you're having a *bet* something is going to go up or down rather than making an "investment" in a company.

But why bother with it at all – why not just buy or sell shares in a normal account? What's the big deal about having a spread betting account?

Well, there are some amazing attractions which I list overleaf.

Attractions of spread betting

Attraction #1: it's tax free

Oh yes! How about that for a knockout attraction?

Gordon Brown (or whichever dodgy geezer is in charge by the time you buy this book in the bargain bucket) cannot get his hands on any profits you make. No capital gains tax. Make as much as you like.

It's tax free because it's considered to be gambling.

Attraction #2: you can trade on credit

Quite amazing when you think about it. It's a bit like having a "spread betting credit card".

For many trades, spread betting firms give you what's called *margin*. What this means in practice is many firms will let you buy shares on tick!

There is no sign up at the spread firms like in shops in dodgy areas to the effect of: "Don't ask for credit or you'll get a punch in the mouth." Indeed, the motto is more like:

> *Please ask for credit and we will give you as much as we can.*

Why are they so keen to give us credit? Well, spread firms should make a profit out of every trade. Therefore it is in their interest for you to bet as much and as often as possible.

And boy, they give you a lot of credit. Give them £10,000 and in many cases you will be able to trade up to £100,000 of shares! In other words, you only have to put down 10% of the money to trade.

So you could buy ten grands worth of a stock for just one grand. You're thinking: "Ah, now I can see why it's getting so popular..."

Attraction #3: bet on things to go down (short)

If you think the market is going to crash or you want some insurance against it happening, you can go *short.* (More on shorting a bit later in the book.)

Attraction #4: play the indices or commodities

With spread betting you can make money on whether the FTSE goes up or down, or the DOW. Or gold. Or oil, yen, sugar, or loads of other things.

Attraction #5: spread betters get the hot girls[4]

If you spread bet you will end up with a hot girl.

And, sorry, of course if you prefer boys, spread betters get all the hot boys too.

Of course, as with anything that sounds too good to be true, there's always a downside isn't there?

So what are the downsides to spread betting then, Mr Naked?

[4] Sorry. I made up attraction five in order to show a couple of good lookers to brighten up the book and get more sales in Waterstones. It's called marketing, I'm sure you will understand and forgive me.

Downsides of spread betting

Downside #1: wider spreads

Well, it's fair enough – the spread firms aren't a charity and part of the way they make money from you is they charge you a wider spread when you open your bet and when you take a profit or loss on it. So it costs. In other words, if the spread in the share market is 500 to sell and 501 to buy, expect the spread betting prices to be 498 to sell and 503 to buy. That's why they should make a profit every time you bet!

Downside #2: longer-term trades get pricey

The longer you keep open a spread bet, the more it costs you. Every three months or so you have to close your bet and re-open it, which means you pay the spread again. And the further out you set the expiry date for your bet, the bigger the spread. More on that in a mo'.

Downside #3: losses are unlimited

If you don't set a guaranteed stop loss when opening your bet (which costs you even more on the spread) your losses aren't limited to your stake.

We'll discuss all of the above shortly. But first I want to show you how easy it is to spread bet (either shares or indices). The best way to describe spread betting is to dive right in and look at an example.

Example: long; held to bet expiry

BSkyB shares are going up and you want some of the action. The shares are currently priced at 500-501 (500 to sell 501 to buy) in the stock market.

However, your ISA is maxed out, and you only want a relatively short-term exposure (say three months), so you decide to take out a spread bet.

You phone the spread betting company (or use its web site) and find the BSkyB spread betting price is 500-505 (i.e. 500 to sell, and 505 to buy).

Now it's very simple:

- If you think the shares are going *down* (you want to short them). Then sell at 500p.
- If you think the shares are going *up* (you want to go long). Then buy at 505p.

In this case, you think BSkyB shares are going up, so you would "buy at 505".

BSkyB price	Profit (£)
480	-250
485	-200
490	-150
495	-100
500	-50
505	0
510	+50
515	+100
520	+150
525	+200
530	+250
535	+300

The next decision is how many pounds a point you want to stake. If you're very optimistic you'll bet a high amount, but if you're more cautious (and risk-averse) you'll bet a low amount. In this case, let's say you bet £10 a point.

The table shows what your profit will be, depending on the BSkyB share price at expiry of your bet.

For example, at bet expiry if the BSkyB share price is 530, you will make £250. (This is a cash profit that would be deposited in your spread betting account.) But if the BSkyB share price was 485 at bet expiry, you would lose £200.

The formula to work out your profit is simply:

```
stake amount x (final price - price bought at)
```

So, if the final price is 515, the calculation is:

```
£10 x (515 - 505) = £100 profit
```

If, instead of betting £10 per point, you had bet only £1 per point, then the profit numbers in the above table would be divided by 10. Or, if you had bet £100 per point, then the profit numbers in the above table would be multiplied by 10.

It's usually easiest just to think in terms of numbers of points made or lost. For example, if the BSkyB share price is 520 at bet expiry, then you've made 15 points (520 - 505). Then simply multiply the points you have made by your original pounds per point.

Example: short; held to bet expiry

In the previous example we looked at the case when you were *bullish* (optimistic) on BSkyB and so went long (i.e. you *bought* a spread bet). In this example, we'll look the case where you are *bearish* (pessimistic) on BSkyB and so will short it (i.e. you will *sell* a spread bet).

To quickly recap, prevailing prices are:

- The **share price quote** is: 500-501
- The **spread betting quote** is: 500-505

In the first example, you bought the spread bet at 505. This time you will sell at 500. Again, you will bet £10 per point.

The table shows what your profit will be, depending on the BSkyB share price at the expiry of your bet.

BSkyB price	Profit (£)
480	+250
485	+200
490	+150
495	+100
500	+50
505	0
510	-50
515	-100
520	-150
525	-200
530	-250
535	-300

As you can see, the profit profile of the trade is the reverse of that in the first example. If the share price falls to 490 at bet expiry, then you make a profit of £150. But if the share was at 535 at bet expiry, you would lose £300.

The general formula for calculating profits for *short* trades is:

```
stake amount x (price sold at - final price)
```

So, if the final price is 495, the calculation is:

```
£10 x (505 - 495) = £100 profit
```

As before, just think in terms of points made or lost. And then multiply that by the pounds per point to get the cash profit.

Example: long; closed before bet expiry

All spread bets have a date at which they expire. At expiry the bet is settled at the prevailing price in the underlying market. In the first example above, if the underlying market (BSkyB shares trading in the stock market) was priced at 520 at bet expiry, the spread bet is settled at 520. Expiry of a spread bet can be considered like the end of a horse race – when the result is known, and the winnings paid.

However, unlike a horse race, spread bets can be *closed out before expiry*.

Think about that for a moment – that's quite a useful facility.

Imagine placing a bet on a horse race and after two bends your horse is out in front. Wouldn't it be good if you could stop the race right there, and collect your winnings immediately. But you can't, you have to hold on to the end of the race, and possibly see your horse being overtaken by others.

But this isn't a problem with spread betting. You can, effectively, "stop the race" whenever you like. This is what is meant by closing out at expiry.

This can happen because the spread betting firms are quoting prices all the time – even after the "race has started".

Let's look at the first example again.

You bought the spread bet at 505 for £10 per point. After a few days the spread bet price is 515-520. The price has moved up and you want to close your bet immediately and bank your profit, instead of waiting to expiry of the bet.

No problem. You close your bet by making an opposite bet. In other words:

1. if you *bought* the bet originally (i.e. had a *long* position), you would close it by *selling* the bet.
2. if you *sold* the bet originally (i.e. had a *short* position), you would close it by *buying* the bet.

In this case, you are long, and so you would close the bet by selling the bet (at the same pounds per point: £10). To recap, the spread bet price is 515-520, and so the selling price is 515.

The table below summarises the prices and action taken to open and then close out a bet before expiry.

Market action	Value
original spread bet price	500-505
spread bet bought at	505
stake (pounds per point)	£10
spread bet price a few days later	515-520
spread bet sold at (effectively closing the bet)	515
points made	10 (515-505)
profit	£100 (£10 x 10)

So, we can see that this facility is very powerful indeed. It allows the spread better to get out of the market before bet expiry.

You can't do that on the horses!

Expiry dates

Most expiry dates for spread bets are set at three-monthly intervals – March, June, September and December. The expiry date itself is usually the third Tuesday of the month for shares, and the third Friday for indices. However, you can set a different time if you want: daily; weekly; fortnightly; or monthly.

I (and most traders) usually go for the next quarter, unless it's close to expiry in which case I'd go for the quarter after. The further away the expiry date, the bigger the spread. Unless you're a skilled day trader, I'd avoid the daily expiry, often called *rolling expiry*.

For example, say it's 5 January, you would probably want to go for the March expiry – always best, I think, to give the bet a couple of months to play itself out.

But one other thing to note: although you have chosen an expiry date you can *extend* that date if you want to. That's called...

Rolling over

Normally, your spread bet will expire within 3 months, when you will *have* to take your profit or loss – not a bad discipline. But you *can* keep a trade open by what's called a *rollover*.

A rollover means you close out the current trade, and open a new position in a spread bet with a further out expiry date. Effectively, you roll over the position. You take your profit or loss and a whole new trade is set up. Unfortunately, you have to pay for this via a new spread, but most firms will give you a decent discount on that.

> Some people argue that you should just let all bets expire on their expiry date, clear your slate and start again. Some merit to that I think.

Phew – that was a lot to get through. Still with me? Look if you're not don't worry, put your feet up and read it again. It will sink in I promise. Took me a while to get my head round it too.

Dangers of over exposure

When you're spread betting, you get exposure to shares without putting up all the money you'd have to if betting on a normal share account. That's good and bad news.

For example, I could buy £10 a point of BSkyB giving me, in effect, exposure to £5,000 of shares without having to put up the five grand. Most spread firms will allow you to trade that with only 10% upfront – so you'd only need to have £500 in your account.

> This is where you have to be careful and make sure you are not playing with money you can't afford to lose.

What happens if the shares sink 200 points and you suddenly owe £2,000?

Can you afford to pay?

And what happens if you open a lot of trades and they all go wrong, leaving you with a whopping great bill?

Always check your spread account. Think about a few worst case scenarios and check carefully that you are not overdoing it, buying or shorting shares on tick. You must work out what your exposure is and whether you can afford that exposure.

Here is my handy cut-out and keep guide to spread bet exposure. Make sure you don't put on a bigger bet than you thought.

Easy Naked Trader Cut Out And Keep Guide[5]

Spread betting: Check Your Exposure

Spread bet size	Equivalent size in share market
£5 per point	500 shares
£10 per point	1,000 shares
£20 per point	2,000 shares
£50 per point	5,000 shares
Your exposure: £10 per point. Share price	
500p, exposure	£5,000 (10 X 500)
£10 per point share price 1000p	£10,000
£20 per point share price 100p	£2,000

This is where you have to be careful and make sure you are not playing with money you can't afford to lose.

[5] WARNING: Please note if you cut this out of the book it might reduce its resale value by around a fiver if you want to sell it on eBay.

Opening an account

There used to be only two companies that took spread bets – IG Index and City Index – but now there are many spread bet companies with various offerings.

Many traders have two or three accounts and use different firms depending on a particular trade. Some firms specialize in tiny bets, others have minimum stakes. Some have smaller spreads than others.

> Beware of firms that offer very small spreads. Remember, they have to make a profit somewhere. You may find (and there are instances of this I know of) trouble 'closing out' a trade. The spread may mysteriously move against you when you try and take your profit or loss.

Most spread bet companies want you to win. That's because every time you put on a trade they should make money. They should simply put on whatever trade you make themselves in the market and they pocket the extra spread charged.

A winning client is more likely to carry on spread betting, and so make them a profit, whereas a client is more likely to call it a day after racking up losses.

But some companies take what can be described as an adversarial stance against you. You put on trades and they don't take out a similar trade in the market to ride the trade with you and just make money on the extra spread. In effect, they want you to lose! They want your trade to go wrong and so they cash in. In particular, they will do this against clients who mainly lose. If you're a winner, of course they will trade with you!

It's up to you to pick one or two firms – get to know them and see if you like the way you get treated. If you don't like them, there will always be plenty of others!

One way of choosing could be to scan through the bulletin boards and read about the experiences of others.

(I try to do deals with them for readers of my web site and get free bets, etc. So do check my web site in case there are any decent deals to be had.)

Credit accounts

Generally, most financial spread betting is done using credit accounts. When you open your account you can set your credit limit. As spread betting is tightly regulated, the spread firm will want to see that you have ready assets to sell should it have to ask you for money. So, if you want a credit limit of £5,000 you will have to show you have three times that in ready funds; cash, shares you own, premium bonds, and savings accounts can all be taken into account. Once a year they will usually ask you again for proof of funds. It's not that they don't trust you, but they are forced to do it by the regulators.

Net or phone?

Whether you use the net or phone is up to you.

The web sites of spread bet firms are now very sophisticated and you can pretty much call up any share you want on a site and be given the current quote.

Most firms only quote the top 400 or so companies directly on the net. For smaller companies you have to phone for a quote. Generally, the spread firms will allow you to deal in any company as long as their market cap is above £50 million.

However, the odd one or two (e.g. Manspreads) specialize in allowing you to bet on pretty much anything. (I have a deal running with them – contact me for details.)

Don't expect to be able to take out big positions on the very small companies, firms are only likely to let you have a stake at the normal market size.

When you are on a particular firm's web site, remember you have to decide when you want your bet to end. So if it is the end of June, you will probably be given three choices: daily rolling, September or December.

As I said before, it is best to give your bet 2-3 months. If you are in any doubt whatsoever, phone the spread firm, especially if you want to close the bet out.

Spreads and costs

There is no point in moaning about being charged extra spread whenever you do a deal with a spread betting firm. Remember, you do not have to pay commission when spread betting, *and* you don't pay the dreaded stamp duty *and* you don't have to pay capital gains tax on any winnings.

How do the costs compare between normal trading and spread trading?

It's quite hard to work that one out. Different spread firms charge different spreads at different times. It also depends on how you like to trade.

Let's take the BSkyB example again, and work out a rough cost comparison between normal share dealing and spread trading.

In this example we will say the shares were 500-501 in the stock market and 500-505 in the spread market when the shares were bought.

Then we'll say the shares go up to 549-550 in the normal market and 548-553 in the spread market.

Normal share trade

- Buy 1,000 shares at 501p. Value = £5,010
- Buying costs: broker commission = £12.50; stamp duty = £25.05
- Sell 1,000 shares at 549p. Value = £5,490
- Selling costs: broker commission = £12.50
- Gross profit = £480. Costs = £50.05
- Net profit = £429.95

Spread trade

- Buy £10 a point at 505p. Sell at 548p. No costs.
- Profit = £430

The comparison trades are summarised in the table below.

	Shares	Spread bet
position opened	buy 1,000 shares at 501	buy at 505 for £10 per point
broker commission	£12.50	£0
stamp duty	£25.05	£0
position closed	sell 1,000 shares at 549	sell at 548 for £10 per point
broker commission	£12.50	£0
trade profit calculation	1,000 x (549 - 501) = £480	(548 - 505) x £10 = £430
Costs	£50.05	£0
net profit	**£429.95**	**£430**

So, not much in it there – and I reckon generally there is no difference.

It is probably cheaper to use spread betting if you are a larger trader and you easily make more than £9,200 profit a year (CGT allowance for 2007/2008). Say you'd already used up your capital gains tax allowance: Top-rate taxpayers would have to pay 40% tax on that profit of £480, or a massive £192! In this case, it would be much better to spread bet than buy in the normal market.

I could come up with loads of different examples and each one would throw up a different cost comparison.

For example, Vodafone – the most actively traded share on the market – would probably be cheaper to spread bet as the spread will be very tight. But a company with a 3-4% spread might be better off being traded elsewhere.

> The rule of thumb is: the tighter the spread given by the spread firm, the more cost-effective it is.

Also remember, if you are rolling over effectively you are increasing your cost again.

Stop losses

One of the greatest benefits of spread betting is you, can set a stop loss.

This means discipline is imposed on you, and your trade will be closed out at your stated stop loss. It is much more difficult in the share market.

But there are a few points you should understand.

Let's say you've bought a BSkyB spread bet at 505p. You decide your stop loss should be about 50 points, so you set a stop at 455p. If the share goes below that, you'd rather take the loss now than rack up any more.

There are *two* different types of stop loss:

1. *Ordinary stop loss*
   The spread firm will try to get you out at the stop price, but if the share is moving fast you may end up being closed out at say, 445p rather than 455p.

2. *Guaranteed stop loss*
   A guaranteed stop loss means what it says – you will be closed out at 455p. But a guaranteed stop loss will cost you a bit of extra spread, so your 505p buying price may be adjusted to something like 507p, costing you the equivalent of £20 on your £10 per point buy.

> I would say it's generally worth paying the extra spread and getting the guarantee, at least in your first year or so.

Take this example.

You've bought BSkyB at 505p but a week later the company issues an early morning statement. The market doesn't like it and the shares open at 355p.

Under an ordinary stop loss you will be closed out at 355p – a full 100 points lower than your stop loss. That would cost you £1,000 more (at £10 per point) than if you'd used the guaranteed stop loss of 455p. Because the firm guaranteed you 455p, that's the price you'd get even though the shares opened at 355p.

> Don't forget: when you close out a trade, you must also cancel the stop loss.

While I do think it may be worth having guaranteed stops, I don't generally use them myself.

Here's another view on guaranteed stop losses from one of my readers who is a profitable trader using spread bets:

> I think of the charge for the guaranteed stop losses as an insurance premium, debited via the greater quoted spread. It's an insurance policy with an agreed excess. You have to consider whether routinely paying the premium *and* occasionally falling foul of the excess whenever the stop loss is triggered – either by the real dive which you wanted protection against, or by the all-too-frequent momentary spikes in share price movement – is justifiable in relation to your own circumstances.

> It probably makes sense, especially in somebody's first year, and particularly where s/he is unable to constantly monitor the market. But the user needs to be aware that it is an expensive form of protection – thanks mainly to those unexpected and unwanted excess charges which kick in unnecessarily whenever a transient spike occurs or is engineered. They kick in far more often than the real situation of a share price collapse. What's more, the spread bet companies know that when the annoyed punter has been kicked out of a bet by one of these many false alarms, s/he will quite likely reopen the bet – paying the added spread again each time.

One word of warning on stop losses – set them at a decent point away from your trade. That's because, during the first few minutes of trading, spreads can be stupidly wide and you could get caught and stopped out on one rogue early trade. I've had horror stories from several readers of getting stopped out early in the morning by some rogue trade. And if your spread firm is especially nasty they might even close you out on purpose!

You must handle and control your stop losses in the best way you can and learn by experience. It could well be that the best plan is to use guaranteed stop losses on all your trades. At least then you know, and can control, your maximum possible loss.

One word of warning on stop losses – set them at a decent point away from your trade.

Margin calls

This is a call you don't want to get! I'm glad to say I haven't had one since 1999!

A margin call means one or more of your positions are losing heavily and the spread firm wants to see the colour of your money. Don't worry, they are very discreet, so if you don't want your missus to know you've been losing she won't find out. They will normally ask you for the money needed to cover some of the losses you are racking up. The best solution is to use a debit card and hand the money over right away.

Is it a wake-up call?

If you get a margin call you may also want to consider whether it is a wake-up call. Have your positions got away from you and should you close out, take the loss and go flat for a few days? Are you definitely playing with money you can afford to lose?

Be honest with yourself. Don't pretend the losses aren't too bad and you're 'gonna get them back'.

> When you get the margin call, give yourself that wake-up call!

If you owe a spread firm money it is backed by the law so therefore they can send the boys round. So cough up!

Secrets of the spread betting winners

This is taken from my first book but I thought it was worth repeating for those that missed it.

At a dinner recently, I met a top market maker from a spread betting company. Luckily he was on the pissed side so I thought I'd ask him while he was in that state what makes a spread betting winner...and loser!

I asked:

> *So what are the trading patterns of the people who win...and what about the people that lose?*

His answer was rather revealing. He said:

> *The people that win don't trade as much as the people that lose!*

I've already talked about over-trading earlier in the book, but this seems to be the key to not losing your shirt.

The next secret he let me into was:

> *Winners are often those who ask for spreads on firms I've never heard of, rather than the FTSE 100 companies.*

Hmm. Interesting! Looks like those who've done their research on some of the smaller companies end up in the money.

And another secret:

> *Winners often go flat.*

He doesn't mean winners go on a diet, he means they simply close down all their trades, take profits and losses and simply have a few days without a trade on their account at all.

> *It seems to refresh their brains, and clear things out.*

He also explained sometimes a big winner can turn into an equally big loser:

> *I've seen winning accounts turn into losing accounts because the trader gets overconfident and starts playing with much bigger stakes.*

He revealed that those who hung onto trades for too long tended to lose out:

> *Spread betting is a short-term tool, those holding onto positions for too long often make a loss.*

So maybe that'll help you before you go plunging into too many trades. I just hope the chap I spoke to doesn't come after me for a fee for using his quotes in the book.

Pass the wine, there's a good chap!

Spread betting strategies

My main uses of spread betting are (in no particular order):

- Shorting FTSE 100 and FTSE 250 companies in a bear market
- Buying companies when I'm out of cash in my ISA
- Buying or selling the FTSE 100 Index at certain times
- Buying AIM stock to avoid capital gains tax

I treat most trades as short-term (anything between a week and three months).

> The major lesson I've learned with spread betting is: keep an open mind and change strategies as the market changes.

Just to make you aware of how volatile spread betting can be, a contact at a spread betting firm told me this story:

> A client opened an account and put £9k in. He turned it into £220k within a week. Sounds good. But two days later, he owed £1.5k!

So beware!

Playing the indices via spread betting

One of the advantages of spread betting is it does give you the chance to bet on the indices – although this is not something I do a lot of.

To spread bet the indices is similar to buying or selling a normal share. You're just betting on a number (in this case the index value) going up and down.

So, if the FTSE is, say, 6500, you can take out a quarterly or daily spread bet. You can buy at the offered price or sell at it. You can bet on it to go up or down. Or you can bet on the dow, Nikkei or any other index.

As I've already said, I don't buy or sell the indexes much, as to me it's just gambling. One use I do have for it is to have a short on the FTSE if the market has had a very good run and looks toppy.

For example, as I write I have a £10 FTSE short. That means if the market tanks I make some money out of it. It's kind of an insurance policy. And sometimes I buy the FTSE just before Christmas as it tends to gain then.

> If you're new to the game I would leave indices alone till you are more experienced.

Naked Trader's ten golden rules for spread betting

1. Use it for short-term trading only.
2. Beware of trading volatile indices.
3. Don't open too many positions.
4. Keep stakes to a level you can afford.
5. Be strict with your stop losses.
6. Make sure you know what you're doing!
7. Remember to trade the opposite way when closing.
8. A margin call could be a 'wake-up call'.
9. Consider a guaranteed stop loss on every trade.
10. Don't tell the wife how much you're losing.

Directory

It's worth a look around the various spread betting firms' web sites. Many of them give you an area where you can practise trading.

And why not open up more than one account?

Here's a list of web sites:

- Cantor Index – www.cantorindex.co.uk
- Capital Spreads – www.capitalspreads.com
- City Index – www.cityindex.co.uk
- CMC Markets – www.cmcmarkets.co.uk
- Finspreads – www.finspreads.com
- IG Index – www.igindex.co.uk
- Spreadex – www.spreadex.com
- TradIndex – www.tradindex.com

Recommended reading

If my explanations have given you a headache and you still can't get your head around spread betting try the beginner's book:

The Beginner's Guide to Financial Spread Betting by Michelle Baltazar.

And for the more advanced: *The Financial Spread Betting Handbook* by Malcolm Pryor.

(Available from the bookshop on my website: www.nakedtrader.co.uk.)

Shorting – making money when shares fall

One of the major uses of spread betting is shorting, where you are doing the opposite of buying a share. You make money if the stock goes *down.*

I would urge new investors to tread carefully before getting into shorting, but it's something that must be considered because it means you can make money during a period when the market is going down. And while I do urge caution, it is something you should learn about quite quickly.

There are various ways of shorting: CFDs, covered warrants and spread betting. But the easiest method is to spread bet. That would certainly be the method I would use first.

I usually have at least two short positions open.

I usually have at least two short positions open.

Markets often turn down for quite a while and shorting could be the only way to make money. I tend to only take out short positions in quite large companies. The reason is mainly the spread. The spread firms usually quote much bigger spreads in smaller companies, and for shorting purposes I find the spread is simply too much.

Obviously, the best years to have taken out short positions were in 2000 and 2001 because the market was tumbling and tech shares were being hammered. During those years I held more shorts than longs (buys) because it made sense. I believe at some point in the future I will do the same again.

But I do generally look on shorting as a short-term activity - anything from two weeks to six months.

Hedging

Many investors use shorting as what's called a *hedge*. No, that's not something that separates you from the nosy neighbours, it's a way of protecting a long position.

For example, you may hold 5,000 shares in a company, but are worried for a short-term period (perhaps the company is about to announce results). You could sell the shares, and buy them back after the cloud has passed, but that could be very expensive (what with broker's commission and stamp duty). An alternative is to hold the shares, but take out a down spread bet in the company to an equivalent value of your holding. If bad things do happen, and the share price falls, the amount you lose on your share holding will be approximately offset by the gains in your spread bet trade.

Finding shorts

So how do you find shares that are going to go down and make you money?

Well, strangely enough, you have to do the exact opposite of finding buys. You need to look for shares that are overvalued, on a downtrend, or if the market is in a downturn, a share that should sink with it.

I am personally not much cop at trading indices, but I can see the point of holding a FTSE short if you're generally holding loads of share buys. Because if something happens, like a terrorist event, and the FTSE 100 goes into freefall and your shares with it, at least you'll make some money. However, I would advise you to hold off from shorting indices until you are confident in your trading.

Here are the kinds of things I look for in shares I'd like to be short of:

- **Profit warning**

  These tend to come in threes. If a share issues a profit warning there could be worse to come. This could be a good time to short. For example, Courts began issuing profit warnings long before they went bust – you could have shorted and made a killing.

- **General downtrend**

  A share that just keeps going down, maybe breaking through 52-week lows. It often means there is something amiss.

- **High PE**

  If a company has a very high PE or it's making, say, £5 million but has a market cap of £280 million, it may be all the promise shown by the company is already in the price and it could fall heavily on any negative news.

- **Watch for 'challenging'!**

  Check the latest reports on the share you're interested in shorting. If you see the words 'challenging', 'difficulties' or 'problems', then it could be worth a go!

- **Broken down through support**

  Remember earlier in the book I talked about support levels for shares? You don't remember? You skipped that bit? Bad reader! Go back and read it again. If a share has been coming back to a price a number of times and then falls through it, a lot of people sell up pushing the price down even more, so it could be time to short. You can find shares going down through support by going to ADVFN's premium *Breakout lists* but selecting breakout *down*s instead of *ups*. You should then get a nice list of shares that are breaking down and could be worth considering as a short.

- **Big debt**

  Check the net debt of the company – if it sits at much more than six times pre-tax profit, that could be a big burden – for more on this see the beginning of Part 6.

My ideal short

The share is:

1. Breaking down through support
2. In a sector that is not in favour
3. Has issued a not so positive statement recently
4. Is unlikely to be a bid target in the short-term.

A BEAR MARKET IS A 6 TO 18 MONTH PERIOD WHEN THE KIDS GET NO POCKET MONEY, THE WIFE GETS NO SHOPPING AND THE HUSBAND GETS NO SEX.

Short example: Paragon

One example of a short I made some good money on is Paragon.

Paragon

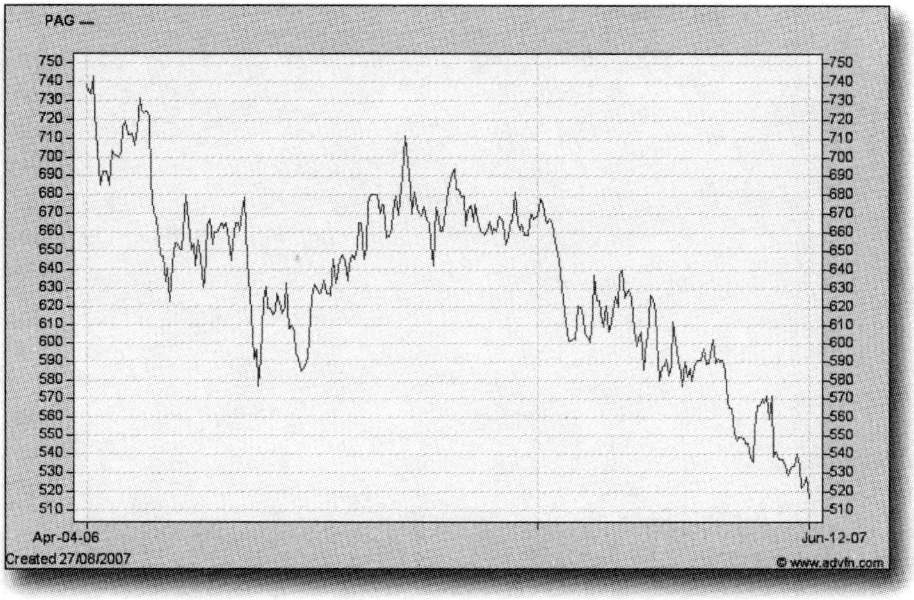

You can see it kept coming down to about 580 a huge number of times and found support there. But then it broke down through the support, so I shorted at 570p – and it kept on falling. It was in an out of favour sector (consumer finance) and it appeared a logical short.

As I write it has hit 450 and I am over £2,000 in profit.

Short example: Renishaw

Another short I went into was Renishaw.

Renishaw

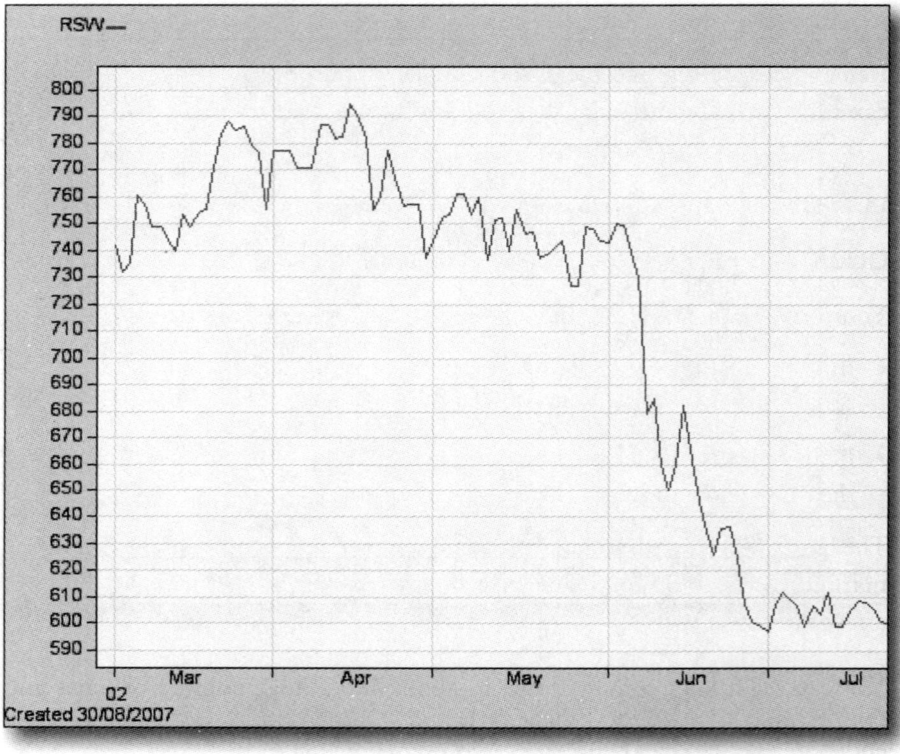

You can see a number of times that it had support at just under 750, but looked an excellent short when it broke down through that. Also it broke down yet again at 650p. On top of that, plenty of red words appeared on my traffic lights system so it seemed a very good short.

Some short DON'TS

- Don't go against the trend and short a share because it's already gone up a lot. It could go up a hell of a lot more!
- Don't short a share because some big market guru has. He's probably already in at a better price…and he might be wrong!
- Don't short shares in a strong, generally rising market. Even if you're right, and it's a bad share, it could still go up with the market.

- Don't hold on to shorts for too long – consider them as much shorter term trades than normal. If you see them starting to rise after you have obtained a good profit, it might be time to take your profits.
- If you're a bloke over 40: just don't wear short shorts in public. Someone had to tell you.

Remember: indices like the FTSE and Dow can move very fast – be very careful when shorting them that you don't get blown away by a big move.

What are the signs that the markets are going to go down?

You probably hear all the time about bull and bear markets:

- **Bull markets** are basically when shares go up most days, but with the odd sudden correction when shares fall for a short period (say a month).
- **Bear markets** are when shares are generally going down most days with the odd sudden upward thrust.

The good news is that bull markets last an awful lot longer than bear markets. Bulls go on for years and years, whereas bear ones usually only last a few years.

For example, a long bull run ended in mid 2000, and we then had a bear market for 2 years through to 2003. Many people thought the bull run had ended in May 2006, when share prices were savaged for a while, but it proved only a correction. There was another small correction in February 2007.

> The thing to remember is: don't believe anything you read in the papers or hear on TV from commentators. Just because they wear a natty suit (£129.99 M&S) doesn't mean they know what they're talking about.

They'll use loads of jargon to make themselves sound good but they have no more idea than you or me really.

So just because a commentator says the markets are about to crash doesn't mean he's right. The same is true if he says there is much further to go. Same goes for bulletin board gurus.

There is no point trying to forecast the markets. Best to trade the markets as they happen and don't expect to be able to sell your shares at the top and buy at the bottom – this is not something anyone can do.

Do you know what the biggest clues are that a bear market might be about to get underway?

> The good news is bull markets last an awful lot longer than bear markets.

Here they are...

Bear market signs

- Sunday newspaper headlines say things like: "Markets soar as investors pile in". "Our experts predict the FTSE will hit all time highs".
- You take a cab and the cabbie says: "Got some shares? Mine are doing really well."
- You visit the doctor or dentist and you see on his computer screen share prices instead of medical notes.
- A friend says: "I've got this really hot share tip, this company's got this *amazing* new product, everyone'll want it and you'll be in right at the bottom!"
- The bulletin boards are full of headlines like "Fill ya boots with...XXXXXXXXXX".
- Coffee shops are jammed with people paying £3 for a coffee.
- Possible tipping point: Starbucks starts doing tastings and free coffee afternoons...

You know what I'm saying. When the world and his wife are talking shares, it's time to get out.

All the above was pretty much true in late 1999 and early 2000. So these are the signs to watch for. You may think I'm kidding about the above, but it's really close to the truth!

In pure share terms, the sign a bear market might be on the way is when the FTSE and Dow become very volatile, up 100 points one day, down 150 the next, etc. Especially if the markets are close to highs. It's just the battle between fear and greed.

If fear wins, then shares will weaken and the bear market will start. However, with the ability to short, money can be made!

Other Instruments

CFDs

CFDs are becoming increasingly popular. It is easy to see why: no stamp duty, commissions are very low and the bid-offer spread is usually very narrow.

In fact, CFDs are probably now the instrument of choice for very active, short-term traders.

> I would advise new investors to avoid CFDs to begin with, as they are too easy to trade using credit and they could lead you to overtrade.

But once you are experienced there is no reason why you should not add them to your trading arsenal.

I don't tend to use them that much for the moment, because profits are subject to capital gains tax – unlike spread betting. However, I *do* use CFDs to short shares in my self-invested pension plan (SIPP). And I have found that quite profitable.

If CFDs interest you, make sure you read up as much as you can about them and only go ahead when you're sure you know everything. Make sure you understand completely what you are doing first!

What are CFDs?

Instead of buying a share you are buying it as a contract for difference. In effect, you are buying a contract with a bookmaker or broker, rather than buying the share directly.

So, if a share is say 500 to sell and 501 to buy, you should be able to buy or sell a CFD at that price. The difference is:

- You can *sell* at 500, without having to own the share (i.e. you can short easily). So you can make money on it if it falls.
- You don't have to pay any stamp duty. But you *do* have to pay an interest charge each day instead; Expect roughly 70p a day on a £5,000 long.

> Because of the interest charge, CFDs should be treated as a shortish term tool, say one day to three months.

CFDs *are* liable to capital gains tax unlike spread betting.

My feeling is it is worth looking at CFDs *after* you have used up your £7,200 yearly (from April 2008) self-select ISA allowance. Remember though, once you have used up your capital gains tax allowance of £9,200 (tax year 2007/08) you will have to pay tax on any CFD profit above this. (Bastards!)

You will find there are two types of CFDs:

1. *Straightforward* (no difference really to shares); expect to pay about £10 a deal.
2. *Direct market access (DMA)*: expect to pay nearer £20 or a percentage.

With DMA CFDs you can put your order directly on the order book and therefore become, in effect, a market maker and try to buy at the sell price.

As this is generally a book for beginners, I'm going to leave it there. If you want to know how to place DMA orders, I can show you live at a seminar. Explaining it here is next to impossible!

I do believe CFDs are going to get more and more popular. The main thing if you open a CFD account is to take it slowly. Start with one or two small trades until you are certain you know what you are doing.

Remember: CFDs are not suitable for long-term investment. If you are thinking of buying a share with a one or two year view, just buy it

I do believe CFDs are going to get more and more popular.

in the normal market as it will end up cheaper. Three months max for CFDs OK?

Covered warrants

I gave a talk at a conference a while back and on after me was a speaker dealing with covered warrants. After he'd spoken for ten minutes, my wife nudged me and whispered:

> *Look at that row over there, they're all fast asleep.*

And indeed they were. In fact, some of them were dribbling a bit. Well I guess it had been a long day.

I think it's just that covered warrants sound extremely boring, and they're also quite difficult to explain.

Which is quite handy for me as this book is for beginners and they are a complex derivative, so I'm not going to cover them here.

If you want to learn about them, go to the bookshop on my website (www.nakedtrader.co.uk) and order the book *Covered Warrants* by Andrew McHattie. He is the expert on this subject and the book will tell you everything you need to know.

Warrants *are* useful and I do use them occasionally if I need to do any shorting for my pension fund. However, for the moment…

> If you are a real beginner, I would suggest you leave covered warrants alone until you've had at least 2 years' experience of the markets.

Investment trusts

Investment trusts (ITs) are often overlooked by investors, but I've bought a few of these and made some decent profits.

Investment trusts are funds that buy shares in other companies. They can be bought just like normal shares – there's a buying and a selling price. Usually the investment trust has a theme, so it will buy shares of a particular kind and, in some cases, buy shares in other investment trusts.

For example, one investment trust I have profited from in the past is Resources Investment Trust (RIT), which buys shares in gold and mining companies. The argument being that if you buy RIT, you're getting exposure to this sector, diversified across a number of shares, and the benefits of a fund manager who knows the sector and does the legwork of research for you to select the best companies.

OK, it doesn't always work out like that, but that's the theory.

I've also done well out of the Templeton Emerging Markets Trust. That gave me exposure to emerging markets. Alternatively, if you fancy getting exposure to the Japanese market you could buy a Japanese investment trust.

One of my recent favourites has been the Montanaro IT – this one buys shares in small companies across Europe and has done very well. It would be difficult for you to buy smaller European companies; buying the Montanaro IT, they are bought for you. Easy.

There are many types of ITs specializing in smaller companies, pharmaceuticals, German markets, etc. The list is endless. ITs give you exposure to a sector you like the look of with a bit less risk than just buying one share in that sector.

Are they worth buying?

Well, why not? Personally, I don't buy that many or that often, and I treat buying them like any other share. You have to research investment trusts in a completely different way to buying a share.

Investment trusts rise and fall in line with their *net asset value* (NAV). This is a rough calculation of the value of the fund at a point in time. These get published monthly, weekly and even daily.

Certainly, having one or two ITs in a portfolio could be a solid move. But if you choose a risky one it will certainly be worth imposing a fairly tight stop loss.

Investment trust summary

- Research like normal shares
- Check the net asset value
- Find out the top holdings
- Work out how risky/volatile the trust is
- Make sure you want exposure to its particular market

Part 6
Trading in Real Life

"The best way to keep money in perspective is to have some."

- *Louis Rukeyser*

It Shouldn't Happen To A Share Trader...

But it does...

This chapter is about mistakes, cock-ups, blunders, gaffes, screw ups, clangers...you get the idea. It includes the top ten mistakes made by traders and investors, my biggest idiocies, and some horror stories from private investors.

If you've been losing money on the markets, I reckon you should find it all pretty enjoyable (or possibly painful)! But seriously, it's amazing what you can learn from making mistakes. I know I have learned a lot. And it really is true how many of us make exactly the same ones.

The secret is to learn from them.

Avoiding the stinkers (don't eat prunes)

Imagine the scene:

> It is a lovely day. The sun is shining in a blue sky. Everything is perfect. You get up, have breakfast and sit down at your computer to check your shares.
>
> First thing you see is the FTSE 100 is up, signalling what might be a good day and all your stocks are up. Blue everywhere.
>
> Except...hang on a minute...there's a news story on one of your stocks which doesn't seem to have traded so far today.
>
> Oh no! What's this? A lurching feeling in your stomach as you read:
>
> *"Shares suspended at request of company!"*

> What's going on? Well, you hope it's good news. Maybe the company's about to be taken over and the share price is going to soar.
>
> But you kind of know something bad is up. And that possibly the share you're in...could be going bust.
>
> *Eeeks*
>
> How could you have made such a terrible mistake? It's a great share, it's been going up, directors were buying, it wasn't even, really, very risky! How are you going to tell the wife or partner you lost ten grand just like that?
>
> You're stunned. Your great start to the day has suddenly gone tits up. As has maybe the share.

This is an important chapter. I am going to show you just how to avoid being caught in a share that goes bust, taking all your money with it.

The best example I can give you of a share that went bust and how you could have avoided being in it, is a company called Homebuy.

Homebuy

Lots and lots of private investors got caught out by this one and lost a lot of money.

And I nearly bought some of the damn shares myself!

But I didn't.

Why?

Don't be so bloody impatient. Let me tell the story at my own pace. And don't now skip to the end of the story for the punchline, smarty-pants. Read the whole story, it's important.

Do you want me to save you money or not? Right then...

The story starts on 13 July 2006, when a company called Homebuy announced its results.

And wow! What results! Profits up 343% to £12m! The chairman said they were making "excellent progress" – all the way through the report everything looked fantastic.

Why didn't I buy the shares after the great report?

When I read the Homebuy statement, at first glance I was very tempted to buy. The company had everything in it I like, a growing business, booming profits and turnover and an encouraging outlook.

The shares looked like they had plenty of room for growth and I thought about buying some.

But then, as usual, I used my *Traffic Lights System* to check the company's debt.

That was easy, my system picks out the word *debt* in company reports wherever they may try and hide it. And debt is usually hidden away somewhere!

And my system picked out this sentence:

> Net bank indebtedness has increased from £28m to £78m.

I immediately applied a back of the fag pack rule I have about company debt, which is:

> If net debt is much more than three times full year profit – don't buy.

Full year profit for Homebuy? £12m. Debt £78m. That's six and a half times profit. Way over my limit.

Once I established that, I had a look through the report using traffic lights again to find out what the banking facilities were (banking facilities highlighted in blue by TLS).

I was shocked. The banking facilities were just £75m.

They were already at the limit of what the banks were currently prepared to lend them!

I'll come back to this shortly.

At this point there was no way I was going to buy the shares. Although the company report was bullish in the extreme, the debt was way too high.

In the days following, the shares were tipped as a buy by many magazines, newspapers and tipsheets. And then, just a few days later, on 17 July, there was a further statement. Homebuy's chairman bought 25,000 shares at 231p, nearly £60,000 worth, and the deputy chairman bought 100,000 shares costing him a massive £231,000!

I thought I'd really got this one wrong and wished I'd bought – after all, directors buying so many shares shows what big confidence they have in their own company. And this provided the impetus for many other private investors to buy shares.

Amazingly, just a few days after these directors had bought shares, and on a lovely sunny morning, 10 August 2006, investors in Homebuy were greeted with this statement on the newswires:

> Trading in the shares of Homebuy has been suspended at the company's request pending the outcome of discussions concerning further funding arrangements for the business.

Translation into real English:

> We have to stop anyone else losing money buying our shares because we screwed up and the banks are about to pull the plug unless we can think of something fast.

That was all there was by way of news until 16 August 2006 at 4.25pm when the company released the following statement:

Homebuy statement – 16 August

The Group's customer base has grown over the last two years to c.100 thousand customers, financed by its existing banking facility of £75 million which has been fully drawn down. Discussions with the Group's bankers gave the Board confidence that additional banking facilities would be available on a timely basis to facilitate the future growth of the Group. The Board was informed by the bankers on the late afternoon of Wednesday 9 August that the Group's temporary bank lines would be capped at then current drawn levels. The Group's bankers have provided the Group with a short term overdraft facility to allow some time for negotiations with potential sources of funding to progress.

Subject to review by advisors and Board approval of the Group's business plan, the Board has held discussions with certain shareholders regarding increasing the Group's additional funding capacity by £100 million by the end of 2008. That funding is likely to comprise a mix of additional equity, junior debt and additional senior debt. From that time, the Group's funding requirement is expected to reverse as the Group's cashflow turns positive. Further, the Board currently expects to have further discussions with regard to an amortisation programme for the existing £75 million term debt with its existing bankers.

During the last few days, members of the Board have held discussions with existing shareholders and a number of alternative potential sources of funding. The Group's ability to continue to trade is dependent upon the successful outcome of these discussions and the continuing support of its bankers.

Further announcements will be made at the appropriate time.

And now for the Naked Trader plain English translation:

> We've borrowed all the money the banks said they'd lend us and the bastards won't bloody give us any more money! Can you believe it? They'll give us a few grand extra for now to see if anyone else is going to stump up any more loot. FFS, we only need another £100 million to add to the £75 million we borrowed! Another £100m and then we should start breaking even! Anyway, we talked to some of our big shareholders to see if they'd come up with the money and so far they've told us "You must be bloody joking!" Bottom line is, if no-one's going to lend us more money, we're broke. Let you know soon, right now I'm off to grab as much of the office stationery as I can before we're told to clear out.

The last announcement was made on 14 September 2006:

> **Homebuy statement – 14 September**
>
> The Board of Homebuy Group plc (the "Company") regrets to announce that the Company is filing a petition for administration of the Company and its trading subsidiaries.
>
> Further to the update on future funding arrangements made by the Company on 16 August 2006, the Board has, together with its advisers, held extensive discussions with existing shareholders and funders and also a number of alternative providers of funding. Unfortunately, none of these discussions have resulted in an acceptable proposition for the funding of the Company. Consequently, the Board has today instructed its lawyers to file petitions for the administration of the Company and its trading subsidiaries.

Naked Trader plain English translation:

> We're stuffed and so are you.

Homebuy went bust and shareholders never got anything back. They lost all their money. Judging from the bulletin boards, there were an awful lot of people who lost everything.

If they'd looked at the debt, they would never have bought.

Homebuy

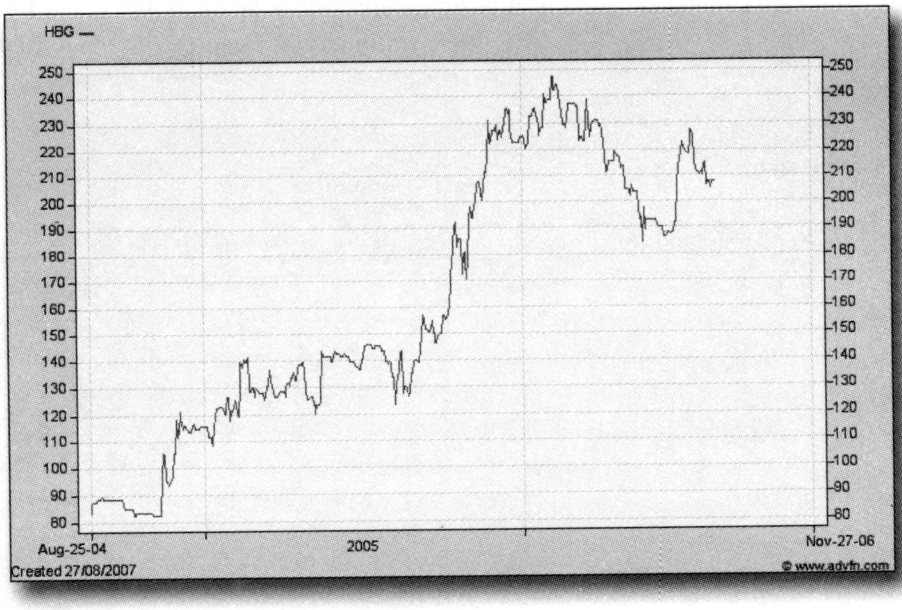

Torex Retail

This is another horror story but, again, one that could have been avoided with just a quick look at the company's debt.

I had a look at this one after a very encouraging report in August 2006. Although it reported a loss of over £3m, it said operating profits were surging and lots looked positive, and it had a "tremendous platform for growth".

But as usual it was the debt that worried me and it was this one statement that stopped me buying:

> Group net bank borrowing of £147.9 million, well within the available facilities of £160.0 million.

Eh? I read that differently. How about:

> We are only £12m away from having to borrow more money.

And, anyway, it had huge debt and was still *losing* money!

In a similar pattern to Homebuy, everything looked rosy for quite a while. Directors happily bought in and there were lots of contract wins announced. But then in early 2007, shares were suddenly suspended – borrowing was £23m higher than expected, profits were significantly below hopes.

Things got worse as the serious fraud office moved in and the company was raided.

Torex Retail

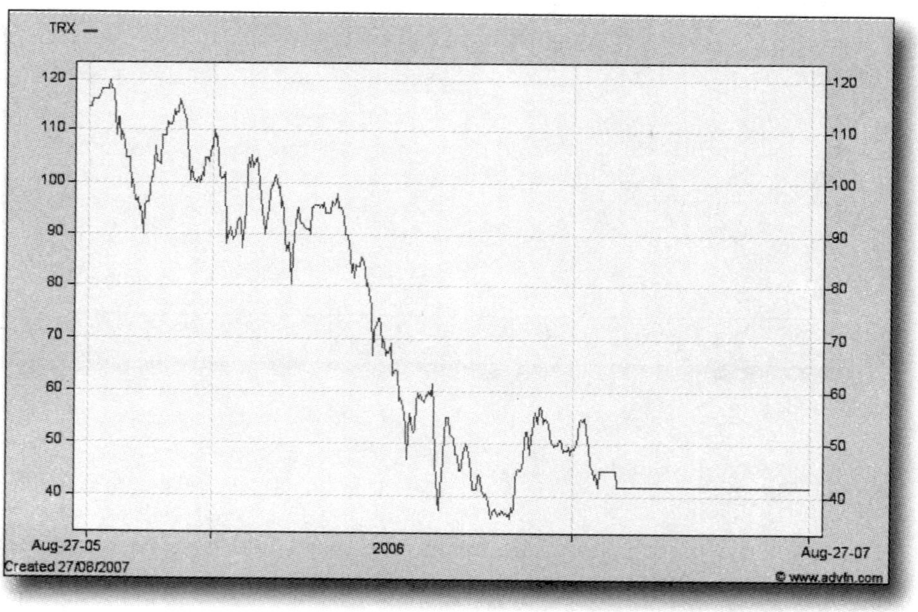

So here is the Naked Trader guide on how *not* to buy a stinker that might go bust.

Guidelines for avoiding stinkers

It's easy to say:

> *Balls to that – not many companies go bust. I'm not bothered about debt and stuff like that.*

Be bovvered! Because it really isn't much bovver and could save you a lot of money.

Here we go then, before pressing the buy button:

1. Go to the last results on ADVFN (or whichever service you use). On ADVFN, my traffic lights system should highlight the debt part of a statement in blue. It either says "debt" or sometimes it says "bank borrowings".
2. When you get down to the debt bit, write down the debt – let's say it is £100m.
3. Then find out the company's last FY pre-tax profits. Let's say it is £50m.

4. Times the FY profits by three. In this case that would be £150m.
5. If the debt figure is more than your profits times three, forget about it.

I say scoff away. When did you last see a really rich accountant?

In this example, it's OK. Debt: £100m, profits x 3: £150m. Debt is only 2x profit.

But take the Homebuy example. Profit x 3 was £36m. But debt was £78m. Way higher.

As they say in *EastEnders*:

> *Leave it!*

Accountants would probably scoff at my system and would look at PEG ratios and acid tests etc.

I say scoff away. When did you last see a really rich accountant?

Trust me, my simple system works, so there. Use it – or lose it. (Your money.)

Mistakes new investors make

No, not spelling mistakes, silly – the editor Stehpen will spot all those. I mean the cock-ups made by new investors.

If you're just about to start trading properly there are a lot of pitfalls. And nearly everyone who starts trading tends to make the same mistakes.

So you're lucky, because this chapter is all about the kinds of things you will most certainly be tempted to do. Avoid all the pitfalls that I'm going to point out and you'll be grateful to me for the rest of your life. Well, maybe a week or two anyway.

What I want to do is encourage you to invest sensibly – not exciting penny share punting.

Not investing, or even trading…just gambling

I received an email from a 19-year-old who is obviously very intelligent and could end up being a good investor. But I despair when I read paragraphs like this (I've X'd out the company names):

> I have read many contradictory info on XXX and XXX across many of the message boards you will undoubtedly be familiar with. Being 5% to 10% down on both, reading this info begins to place doubt in my mind. I do however believe these are both potential 10 bagger material. Could I have your views.?

Oh boy, I think to myself, when I take a look at the two shares he mentions to find that they are tiny, illiquid penny shares that should not be touched with a bargepole.

For heaven's sake, one of them had a spread of 13% – you lose 13% just by buying it! Both were high risk, loss-making companies that could as easily go bust as go up.

What my emailer – and so many other new investors who buy into these shares – don't realise, is they are not investing, or even trading…just gambling!

The words *ten bagger* is what really gets them going. Believe me, it is highly unlikely to happen. Trouble is it all seems so exciting to buy a share at 4p hoping it will become 40p.

True, it does happen occasionally. But for every one that makes it, ten go bust. You will simply lose money over time by buying rubbish and that's all there is to it.

And all they need is a little encouragement from penny share pushers on the bulletin boards to get them buying something they haven't researched and know nothing about in the hope of getting a big, quick return.

The other problem is, new investors, like my emailer, may have an initial bad experience. Notice he is already a bit worried that he's losing money on them and wants reassurance from me, which is not what I can give him.

> Yes, I know how exciting it is to buy those little penny shares, but I promise you it will lead to the poorhouse. So just stop it, if that's what you're doing.

Some warnings

- Be wary of **AIM shares**. Not all of them, the top 50 are OK, but be careful of the illiquid ones.

- Don't buy shares in **one product companies**; if the product stops selling, the shares will tank (as happened to Stanelco).
- Be wary of **smaller drug companies**. Their top drug may not get approved and the price could tank.
- Don't buy **shares that are falling heavily** – never try and guess when a bottom has been reached.

The thing to avoid at all costs is to buy a share just because you suddenly fancy it, without doing any research and because some bloke on a bulletin board has tipped it. You must do your own research and plan all your trades properly. Don't fall for rushes of blood to the head.

Chariot

A good example of a company that no one in their right mind should ever have bought is Chariot, which went from 220p to 5p in just two or three days and then went into administration.

Small investors all piled into Chariot because it was to do with a lottery. It sounded exciting and all that, but the risk here was obviously huge. Yet investors were egging each other on to buy the shares.

Chariot

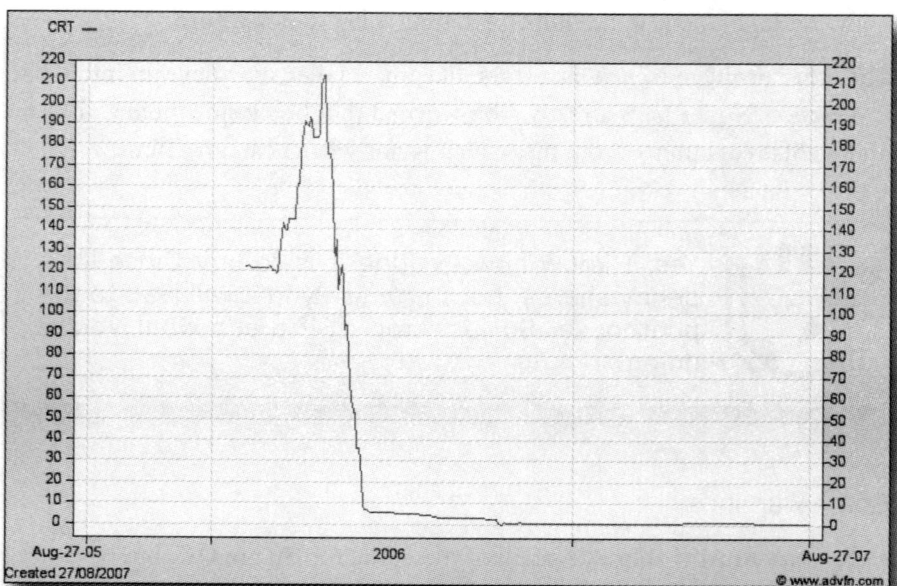

A look at the Chariot chart would show that using even a basic stop loss would have prevented most investors from losing too much. There were all the classic signs of a bad buy: one product company, wide spread, no earnings and nothing proved. You should always buy established companies that are proven profit makers.

This is a good time to point out some of the biggest mistakes made especially by new investors and why don't I make them Top Ten list...

Top ten mistakes

Here's my list of top ten mistakes made by traders.

So what did you do, Mr Naked? Just make all these up over a glass of wine? How do you really know people make these mistakes anyway?

Look, wise guy, I know, right. I know because I've met loads of people at my seminars who admit this is how they lost money. So the top ten comes from real people.

So here we go, in reverse order...

Mistake #10: buying tipped shares

When you're new to buying shares, the biggest temptation is to buy shares you have seen tipped in the papers or a magazine or a tipsheet.

Be wary!

Firstly, if the tip is a very small company the market makers will see you coming a mile off, and the shares will be marked up before the market opens. If you buy, you will probably be buying at an inflated price. Market makers could well add 5% or more to the price of the share. And once they've got you in their clutches, what's the next thing they want you to do? Panic you into selling them – and that often works.

Using these wily tactics, the market makers will have sold you shares at a high price, and then buy them back off you at a much lower one. The only person who wins...yes, you've guessed it, those dastardly market makers.

The same rule applies to any tipped share. This is where the bulletin boards come in handy. If a share is rising, check carefully it hasn't been tipped and you're not buying into a false rise.

OK, so maybe you like the sound of the tipped share, but do your own research first before buying in blindly. And if you still like it, maybe wait a week or two till the shares settle after the tip.

> Using these wily tactics, the market makers will have sold you shares at a high price, and then buy them back off you much lower.

Mistake #9: selling on ex dividend day

You must know your ex dividend dates! To warn you, ADVFN and other services have the code "XD" by the share when you get a quote. The XD date can be found on any particular share by pressing "Financials" and scrolling down.

Why do investors sell on ex date?

Because the share will have fallen from the off. Remember, shares normally drop on ex dividend date by the amount of the dividend. So a 20p dividend share will drop 20p. What often happens on ex day is you see a lot of small investors selling because they think the share they're in is going down fast!

But it's not really going down, because as the shareholder you are getting the equivalent of the drop in cash as dividend. It's amazing the number of private investors who sell because they think their share is going down for a different reason.

> So always, always check your ex dates. If a share you own is falling, it may just be because it's the ex date.

Mistake #8: ignoring profit warnings/negatives

Profit warnings

It's crazy to buy into a company that has just produced a profit warning. And it's crazy to hold onto one of your shares that has just issued one.

It's more than likely it'll issue another one, and just because its share price has gone down doesn't mean it won't be going down some more!

Why take the risk? A profit warning means the company is in some kind of trouble or having problems. Why get involved on the off chance of a quick bounceback?

I would suggest, far from being a buy, a company issuing its first profit warning is more likely a sell and could even make a good short candidate. That's because one profit warning is often followed by another and then another.

Negatives

If you see the odd negative word creeping into the company's statements, don't hang in there, get out! Get the hell out! What's the point of being in a company with negatives coming in when you could be in a company with loads of positives?

Mistake #7: overtrading/smugness

Sometimes traders have a good run and make some money.

Which is great. Except that after 3-4 winning trades they start to get a bit too smug and consider themselves masters of the universe. They feel they know everything and will never lose again.

And so, fuelled by an irresistible urge to carry on the good work they go nuts and start to trade too much. The discipline goes (after all they are always right now) and soon the wins become losses.

I guess it's the same as someone who wins a lot at the horses. He bets too much and ends up giving all the winnings back to the bookmaker.

> After 3-4 winning trades they start to get a bit too smug and consider themselves masters of the universe.

So, if you've had some nice profits, don't be tempted to change your tactics. Stick to what you were doing and use your normal stakes.

And stop being so smug!

Mistake #6: buying boys with toys/one product companies

If you're a woman reading this book, you'll know what I mean. Boys love toys! That is: gadgets, technology, *Star Trek* type wizardry, computer games, new computer software, Ipods, things that go whirr...kzzpt, blackberries, raspberries – you know what I'm talking about.

And because boys love those toys, when boys look for share, they get drawn to companies that make the toys. There is a rationale behind it in their minds. The company that makes the gadget is going to go up in value twenty times because everyone is going to buy the toy they are developing!

This was the reason why so many of this type of investor lost money in the year 2000. They'd all bought into tech companies. And look what happened! Most of them went tits up (apologies to the girls). Or, at least, they lost huge percentages of their original values.

But lessons haven't been learned and investors still buy into tech companies with one or two products that may end up being a toy that's used in every household. Unfortunately, nine times out of ten a new technology struggles, time moves on and it becomes obsolete. I'm afraid there are dozens of these types of companies – and I can promise that boys will continue to buy them in the hope of that elusive big share win.

Let me name a few of the boys' current favourite toy shares that I steer clear of.

Company	Reason for avoiding
NXT	A real darling of the tech boom – it makes flat speakers. Over the years the company continues to make losses, but the flat speaker story just runs and runs – and seems irresistible! Yet the share price goes lower and lower.
Tadpole Technology	The small punters' favourite share for as many years as I can remember. I've never understood what they do and I don't think their shareholders do either. The share price has occasional rises when it announces an exciting new development. But these never come to anything and the shares slump back. Investors just like the name I guess.
Trafficmaster	Develops telematics. ('Telematics' anyone? No idea what it is, but it sounds cool.) Beloved of tipsters and share punters for a long time. The shares go down mainly, with a bit of up, to keep the boys happy occasionally, but as for profits, they never seem to get a mention.
Stanelco	A one product company – bought at 25p by some punters and went all the way down to 0.5p! Something to do with a new kind of packaging for supermarkets. But it just didn't take off. Thousands of people bought the story while I stayed well clear.

There are plenty more. These shares are nothing more than a gamble, and a poor one at that.

> While, occasionally, a boy buying a toy share might make a bit of money catching it at the right time, generally they are the way to the poor house.

Mistake #5: catching a falling knife

Don't try to catch a falling knife – it's an old stock market cliché, but it is so true.

Don't be tempted to try and buy a share that's just plummeted. This is the stock market here, it is not like going to the sales and picking up a bargain.

I thought I was pretty smart when I first started trading and I thought trying to buy into shares that had just plunged down a lot was a great idea.

Why?

Well, it's obvious! Surely because they've suddenly dropped a lot they must be a bargain, and they're going to go up! Buying shares that have come down a lot appeals to us traders – we start to think about how much money we'll make if the shares go back to their levels of just the previous day.

I remember the first falling knife I tried to catch: a textiles company called Hartstone. This was in the days before you could get prices on the internet. I used to watch the biggest percentage fallers page on Sky Text. I saw Hartstone shares had fallen from 450p to 280p on a profit warning. And they were starting to go back up…

Easy money? You bet.

Excitedly, I bought some shares at 280p. And what a flipping genius I turned out to be. Within two weeks the shares were at 320p and I had dreams of them going back towards 450p. Needless to say, I'd done zero research. Suddenly my dreams were shattered, another profit warning was announced and the shares slumped again – to 175p. I ended up getting out at 120p and with a lesson part-learned.

Only part-learned because I still tried to catch a falling knife another three or four times after that.

It doesn't only apply to me; buying shares that are falling is irresistible. Every single day of the trading year, you can look at ADVFN's list of the top percentage fallers of the day. You will find a share that's down by 20% – and inevitably you can watch as punters pile in to catch that knife.

The best example in 2007 was Carter and Carter shares, which plunged from over a tenner to just 60p. Punters bought all the way down – don't be one of the knife fanciers.

Carter & Carter Group

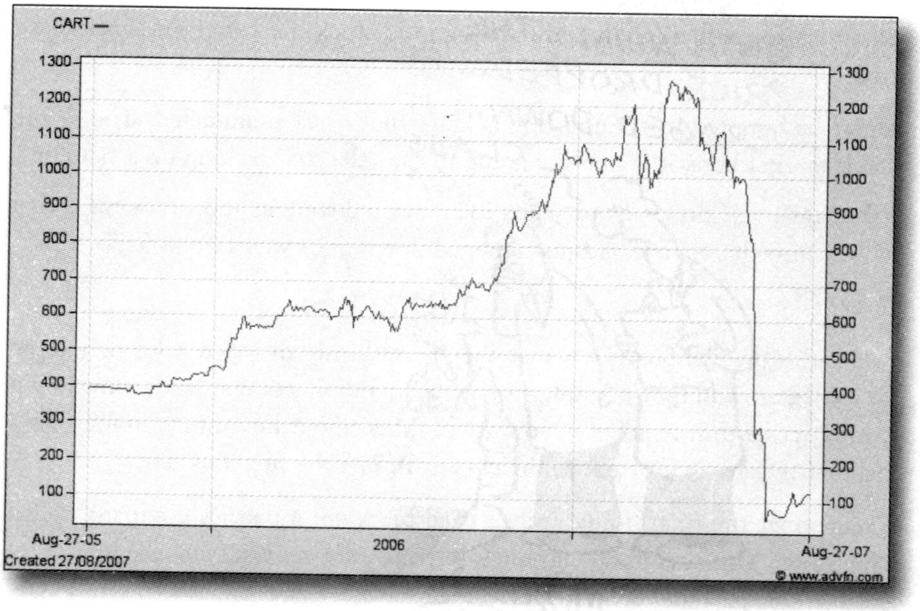

Mistake #4: tiny market caps/pennies/AIM

Don't buy shares with a market cap of less than £15 million.

It might sound tempting to buy a company with, say, a market cap of £4 million. That's because you want to delude yourself that the company could really find its feet and suddenly quadruple its market cap, and you'll be in the money.

The fact is it is highly unlikely, and it's much more likely you are buying a stinker. On top of that, they are usually very illiquid.

Some of the smallest AIM shares are the worst. They can fall very rapidly and often it can be hard to sell them if everyone else is trying to sell at the same time.

Shares valued at less than £15m also have quite wide spreads, which make them even harder to make money on.

So unless you really think you have spotted a super company at the start of its life, steer clear.

Mistake #3: averaging down

Averaging down means buying a share that you've already bought at a much higher price.

For example: you bought share X at 500p, it is now 400p and you buy the same number of X again at 400p. Your effective buying price is now 450p. This means that at any price over 450p you're making money, whereas previously your break even was 500p. Good news, no?

No. This is a terrible strategy as your share is going down for a reason and if it goes down some more you will make even bigger losses. (And you've now almost doubled up your position size so your losses are going to be twice the size they would have been originally.)

Of course what you should have done is cut your loss on share X at 440p, get the hell out and moved on. This does not mean averaging down will never work, but more likely than not it won't.

It's far better to *average up*. That is, buy more of a share you've already bought.

So take my hint: don't average down in the hope you may break even!

Mistake #2: trying to trade indices/day trading

Don't get involved with trading indices too early on in your investing life. Indices are things like the FTSE 100, the Dow, etc.

Index trading is very difficult. Indices move very fast and a winning position can turn into a big losing one in just an hour or two.

Say you decide the FTSE is going to go down or up and bet on that happening with a spread bet. The index can move fast and unless you can keep a very close eye on it, you can get in trouble. It is quite compelling. You see the FTSE 100 has fallen 70 points in the day and it's lunchtime. "Well," you muse to yourself, "it can't fall much further. It'll probably go up from here!" So you take out a daily up bet. But it goes down some more and you get closed out at a loss.

Take it from me – this type of trading is hard.

Avoid it if you are new to the markets; this also applies to betting on all indices like the Dow and the NASDAQ.

> Naked Trader says: index trading is like blind knife throwing – not for beginners.

And the biggest mistake of all is:

Mistake #1: hanging onto losers/snatching profits

I covered this a lot nearer the beginning of the book but it remains the biggest problem for newer traders. That is, hanging onto losing shares hoping they will go back up.

You have to learn to ditch the losers early. And the best way is by setting that stop loss discussed earlier. Quickly dump anything that is beginning to lose you a lot of money. If you have anything in your portfolio down by over 10% take a good look at it, and unless you really have a reason why it might come back it's usually best to bail.

Snatching at profits is the other big no-no. You need to be looking to make 20% plus on your trades even if it takes a while. If you are certain you have a good one, give it space to breathe and rise, and don't snatch at a very small profit because if you do you will never make money overall!

Don't just take a profit because a share you bought has gone up 2p.

> You'll find this *cutting losers/running winners* theme running throughout all this book. I am hammering it home to you...but it's on purpose.

It's one of the most important things to remember!!

Do I have to carry on nagging you?

And now, my big mistakes...

...and the lessons learned!

Don't imagine I always get everything right. I certainly don't! I'm not like those dodgy tipsters who claim every little thing they do is magic. But over the years I've managed to put a stop to most of my original bad habits.

Coffee Republic

My worst trade ever was in Coffee Republic. First off, I bought the shares without doing any proper research. I bought them...because there was a branch near where I lived and I liked coffee. What kind of reason was that?

I bought loads at 28p. The share price started falling from the moment I bought it. I bought some more – averaging down. Coffee's got a great mark-up I argued to myself. They'll do better. I got emotionally involved with my local branch. I started buying more coffee in the hope it might drive up the share price…

I started interfering:

Why don't you put the muffins there where people can see them

I told the manager. After all, if everyone bought a muffin with their coffee the share price would start to rise.

I bought more at 8p. Then it became a terrible spiral. I was drinking so much coffee I was having sleepless nights. The company issued one bad report after another and eventually I sold at 3p, losing £8,000.

What a relief once I sold. And sod Coffee Republic.

I go to Starbucks now.

What were the mistakes I'd made. Want the list? OK, I had:

1. Got emotionally involved
2. Hadn't set a stop loss
3. Averaged down
4. Threw good money after bad
5. gnored all the warnings

So take heed and don't do as I did.

Dialight

To show how much I'd learned from this loss, let's move forward in time to a more recent buy: a company called Dialight. This company had a product I liked the look of: LED lighting. I thought!

> *Loads of companies want to buy LED lighting, it's the future!*

I did do some research on them, but because I was tempted by the technology perhaps I ignored the fact the shares looked a bit expensive given low profits compared with market cap. But I bought them anyway. I bought at 230p. Initially things looked good and they went to 250p.

But then they started to drift back below where I'd bought them. However, I did have a stop loss this time, at 210p. Then the company issued a minor warning that things were OK, but not that great.

In my Coffee Republic days I may have held on for recovery or bought more. But now more experienced I immediately sold for a small loss at 220p.

This was the right thing to do as soon after the shares went below 200p. Hurrah! Although I had made a mistake in buying the shares, I quickly took the mistake and loss on the chin. And this is what *you* must do too...yes *you*!

Arcadia

Another slightly different mistake I made was selling a share too early prompted by fear of losing profits.

I bought Arcadia shares at 40p and felt extremely smug as they shot up to 120p:

> *Hah, doubled my money and more in just a few weeks – I'm just too bloody good:*

I thought to myself.

As I was congratulating myself, I noticed the shares went down 1p to 119p. I simply took fright for no reason other than the 1p drop and not wanting to lose the profit, sold. From that moment on the shares rose daily.

All the way to over 400p!

400p! I couldn't bring myself to buy the shares a bit higher. I watched miserably, calculating the profits I could have made.

It would have been far better to have sold half and held onto the rest. But fear got the better of me.

The lesson?

Shares don't go up in a straight line and if you have a good one which falls slightly one day, if it still looks cheap, keep holding!

Want another mistake?

('Course you do, you're lapping this up, I know. Robbie – what a plonker!)

Tanfield

I liked the look of this small company and bought in at 19p. I congratulated myself smugly a few weeks later, selling up around 35p. Nice profit.

Price now?

180p [Latest price: 195p, Ed.]. I could cry. Maybe I will…bluurrggghhhh!! I just didn't have the heart to buy back in and secretly hoped it would stop going up. A clear case of letting emotion get in the way of profit and not running the winners.

And I think this is where we will close the mistakes overview for now. Cutting down mistakes will really help you to make money. Those who want more mistakes will be delighted to know that later on in the book there are more from some traders!

Dear Naked Trader...

I get something like 100 emails a day, and I reply to them all, unless they are offensive ("You bald bastard").

As you can imagine I get many emails about the same type of topics, so I thought it would be interesting to devote a chapter to some real people experiencing real problems with the market. I don't give individual advice to people, for example I would never tell someone which share to buy or sell, but these are general issues, often misunderstandings about some aspect of the market.

Hopefully there are a few issues that you may have come across and I hope my answers will solve them for you. There may well be an issue or two you were wondering about – each letter is representative of the type of message I get about a particular topic.

System addict

Rajesh writes

> I am a great admirer of yours and your website is absolutely fantastic. (Note: This is a great way to start a letter and ensure a quick reply. If you started it: "Your book is rubbish and your site stinks you useless plonker" then it might go in pending...oh...forever!)
>
> I have found a website which uses some kind of formula to look at charts and works out when to buy and sell. Basically, it's a simple guide to buy and sell shares. If you see a green then buy, if it's red then sell. I was just wondering if you have heard of it?
>
> If you have, what do you think of the system? Is it worth investing the money in buying this?

NT replies

If only stock market investing was that easy! Don't waste time on magic formulas and systems – to my mind they are almost certainly codswallop.

You're better off doing your own research and developing your own investing style. It simply isn't as easy as red means sell and green means buy! I reckon you'll be wasting your money – use the money to invest instead!

Put everything on one share

Andrew writes

I invested all my money in one stock. I did a fair amount of research and felt I was going in with my eyes open. I bought at 16p and started reading the bulletin board on it. The bottom line is that the shares rose to 17p, a pretty good percentage of profit. Did I sell?

No, I kept reading the BB. A lack of news caused the price to fall back, so I decided to sell at 15.5p. 15.5p came along and I thought it will go up again because news is just around the corner. They kept dropping and I eventually I sold at 14p. A few days later I bought back into it at 13.5p, thinking that had bottomed out. They continued falling and I sold again at 12p. I am now into another steadier company which will, I am sure, move upwards slowly over a few months.

I'm sure you will see many mistakes with my strategy and you can't think I'm any bigger an idiot than I do myself. It does however illustrate the points you made in your book about new investors making most of their mistakes in the first year, despite all the good advice out there. I hope I am now a bit wiser than I was before.

NT replies

Well, you made a few classic mistakes – getting involved with penny shares often leads to disaster. You got too involved with the share and bought back in at the wrong time.

If you get involved with any share priced in the low pennies you are asking for trouble, and though you may have the odd winner, over time you will lose! Much better to stick with decent bigger companies. Learn to ignore shares with market caps of under £20m or shares priced under 20p.

Not much money

Dave writes

Thank you very much for undoubtedly saving me from making a total twat of myself and losing my money.

I had just set up my trading and was about to click 'deal' and start trading willy nilly all over the shop without a clue as to what I was doing, when I happened to stumble across your book on Amazon whilst doing some Christmas shopping, and starting my trading empire in my lunch break. I thought it might be prudent to read up about trading before I actually started. I am part way through reading your book now, and I must say it is both educational and highly entertaining.

I am a 23-year-old single guy and stuck in a job that I am not very good at and don't really understand, with quite a bit of debt behind me and little savings. I have about £50 a month I can afford to loose. Now, with all your worldly experience do you think trading could be the world for me or do you suspect it might be too much of a financial strain for my situation? I could really do with a little help as I am dead keen on bettering my current situation and making life a bit nicer.

NT replies

The one thing you must realise is: do not put money into the market if you cannot afford to lose it. It sounds to me as if you can't! Also, I don't think you will find that small amounts of money will get eaten up by commissions and stamp duty. My thought is to wait until you make a bit more money that you can afford to lose and perhaps when the debt is gone. Sorry if that's not what you wanted to hear but I have to say it!

Money put into the market must always be money you can afford to see the back of. I know this advice is given everywhere, but it is very important. But there is nothing stopping you from learning the ropes by paper trading. Give yourself a pretend £10k, pretend trade it and see how you get on.

Tormented by targets

John writes

I have just read your book, *The Naked Trader*. I really enjoyed reading it and thought it was full of useful information. However, one thing I am unclear about is how to work out the target price on a share and how long it will take to reach the target price.

For example, if a share is bought at 150 and you give it a target price of 220. How is the 220 figure calculated, and in what time frame is the share given to reach this target?

At the moment I have no idea how much a share is likely to rise and I am sticking with a share until it starts to fall, then I sell it if the fall is about 15%.

If I buy a share at 150 and it goes up to 220 without making any significant falls, I will stick with it until it makes a significant fall (e.g. 220 down to 200 I would sell it). With this method I feel I am hanging onto the shares too long. However, if I bought at 150 and sold at 160 I would have sold too early.

If I had a clearer idea of what I thought a share would reach I would feel a lot more confident about trading.

NT replies

Personally, I usually set bigger targets than stop losses, usually at the 20% level, however I also use the chart to set a target and try and find the next likely resistance/profit taking point, discussed elsewhere in the book. When I have a good one I do not necessarily sell.

I suggest you look at the chart of the share and set your target where buying normally tends to run out and look at it again then. Alternatively, think about trailing stops, also discussed in this book.

Dividend puzzler

Mike writes

I have been trading for a while (prior to reading your book) but now I am beginning to understand lots of things that puzzled me before.

Anyway, I am still puzzled by one question, maybe you can help?

If a share price usually goes down by the dividend amount on ex div date, what's the point in getting dividends? Surely you just get back what you lose?

NT replies

Well, only if you are a day trader...the price might go down on ex div day but of course you get the fall back in cash. And the price, if it's a good share, will carry on rising. So you get capital growth and cash payments too. My view is don't time buys or sells with dividends in mind. Just collect the dividends as they happen and they should pay off the costs of stamp duty and commission. If you're a medium-term or long-term investor you can generally ignore ex dates and enjoy the cash coming into your account. Make sure you know when the ex date is or you may sell in error on ex day because the share price will drop.

Low market sizes

Barry writes

Having read your book, I have started to invest, At the moment I am thinking of buying a share. The only problem is that the NMS is 500, which is pretty low for such a cheap share. Why would the NMS be so low? After the commission and stamp duty I am not sure that I would make a profit; what are the pitfalls of say, buying 10,000 shares when the NMS is 500?

NT replies

I can't advise you on individual shares but I can talk about NMS. When the normal market size is low – beware. It means the market makers don't hold much stock and if you buy, say, more than 4x NMS you may have trouble selling your holding if there was, for example a profits warning. It usually also means the stock is illiquid and inevitably it is probably high risk. When NMS is so low, as they say, *buyer beware.*

Trying pretend trading

Gary writes

I'm really new to trading and reading your book has really opened my eyes to who I am now and where I want to be.

I can't afford to invest now (not for at least one year), so what I'm going to do between now and until I can afford it, is to keep reading and buy and sell shares with fake money. Write down everything and see how much unreal money I can make in the next year. Start with 5 grand, see where I get.

NT replies

I think it's a great idea to paper trade for a year. Learn the ropes without any worries about losing any money. Fantastic! Remember even if you increase your 5k to 6k in a year, that's 20% – best you get is 6% in the bank.

Is a name change bad news?

Jim writes

When I first started trading, I was told that if I held shares in a company and that company changed its name I should sell the shares as quickly as possible because the share price would start to fall.

At first I thought that this idea was superstitious nonsense, but now that it has happened to me several times I believe it 100% – in fact, I now have an arrangement with my broker that if an announcement of a name change occurs without me knowing about it, he will sell the share immediately whatever the circumstances.

Is your trading influenced by any superstitions?

NT replies

I always make sure when I buy a share that I haven't just walked under a ladder. Just in case.

I asked the editor of this book, Stephen Eckett, to look at this as he is the author of *The Stock Market Almanac* and knows these kinds of things.

Here are the results of analysing company name changes over the last few years:

1. In about 50% of cases, changing the name of a company had no discernible affect on the subsequent share price performance.

2. In 35% of cases, the share price was weak, or very weak, after a name change. In some cases, the name change itself coincided with the

start of a price decline (e.g. Arcadia), or the shares were already on a long slide and the name change did nothing to stop that – possibly even accelerating the fall (e.g. The Big Food Group). Occasionally, a name change would seem to prompt a quick run up in the share price ("hurrah, with this new name everything's going to change"), offering a short-term trading opportunity, before the realisation set in ("uh-oh, no it's not").

3. In just 10% of cases did a name change coincide with a reversal in a company's fortunes, with the share price rising afterwards. Examples here are: BG Group, Kelda and Lonmin.

Different prices surprise

Edward writes

I made my first purchase of an AIM stock recently, and I'm finding that various sources display different prices for the stock. The differences aren't that great, but it makes it difficult to know what your shares are truly priced at.

For instance, HSBC: my broker gave a bid price of 407.75p, and Bloomberg and ADVFN gave a bid price of 406.75p. I then checked Yahoo! Finance, and they showed the same price as my broker, 407.75p.

Is this pricing inconsistency usual with AIM stocks? Can you offer an explanation for why this is Robbie? Should I only take notice of the price my broker is offering?

NT replies

Edward, two explanations: a) the stock could easily have moved in a second or two, or b) one of the feeds you were looking at was displaying a delayed price. Some of the websites only show 15 minute delayed prices. There should be no discrepancy in the real-time price whether AIM stock or not!

A way around NMS?

Dave writes

I was looking at a company recently and after some research I decided to buy some shares in it. The only problem is the NMS is just under half the size of the amount of shares I would like. I read about the problems of buying and selling amounts higher than the NMS. Now, this might be a completely rookie question but could I not just buy the shares in two separate transactions? It might be a bit silly but it is what will decide whether or not I buy the shares.

NT replies

Good question! Generally speaking NMS, (Normal Market Size) is there to protect the market makers in the event of shares suddenly going down and everyone wanting to sell, in which case the MM could strictly limit quotes to the NMS. But in general, you can usually deal in at least 2 x NMS and often even 5 times quite easily. I would personally feel fine buying 2 times.

You could try two separate transactions, but your broker's system may pick this up and not allow it; any further deal would have to be via a dealer rather than electronically. The other way round it is to have two broker accounts and buy NMS with each which may be the best solution.

What happens if a broker makes a mistake?

DM writes

What is the position when a broker makes a basic execution error through incompetence and you lose on the trade, or even profit? Is our relationship with our broker underpinned by contract law or some other obscure consumer related law?

I tried to find info on this subject but it's very sparse on the ground, which is strange as I'm sure that many private investors have at some time in their trading careers experienced it?

NT replies

Yes, info is scarce. I wouldn't worry too much. Clients' money by law is segregated so your cash is safe. If they make an error, which is most unusual, they are regulated by the FSA and would have to put the error right, proved as phone calls are taped. Also, the broker wants to keep your business so they are pretty good normally and there are few mistakes. So basically, don't worry too much about it!

ISA re-investing

Mikey writes

I just wanted to ask you a very quick question about self-select ISAs. If you use your full quota of £7,000 to invest in a particular share, can you, within the same ISA year, then sell that holding (for say £8,500) and re-invest it in another share?

It may seem a daft question but I wasn't sure if you could use the ISA wrapper as a trading mechanism and keep re-investing as long as you don't exceed the maximum permissable amount in any one year, or whether it had to be more for long-term holds. Thanks again.

NT replies

Yes! That is the great thing about ISAs: you can build up as much tax free money as you like. For example, in just one of my ISAs I turned £21k into £100k; now in that ISA I can trade £100k tax free. One bloke I know turned his into £1m plus! And like a normal account, when you sell something you can use the tax-free cash immediately to buy something else.

Do big sells affect price?

Louise writes

One of my AIM shares has had two 3m sells today – B trades. I assume these are broker to broker trades. Do these exchanges/sales not affect the share price? Both sales were at different prices.

Is this a positive sign? Average daily trading in the share is quite small.

Is someone gathering up in anticipation of good news or is someone offloading or balancing the books?

NT replies

With a B code they aren't sells as such; I tend to ignore these trades and they usually have little effect on the market. It's just two parties swapping shares and that's about it, (i.e. broker to broker). Someone wants them and someone else doesn't. It's the same with "X" trades.

Analyst jargon needs explaining

Graham writes

I would just like to know (it's not in your book) what precisely the jargon means that analysts use in terms of rating shares. For example, "underweight", "neutral" and "overweight".

It's obvious what buy and sell mean but other terms they use are less obvious.

NT replies

It means as a percentage of their portfolios (i.e. underweight means less than the average holding).

Brokers rarely put out pure sell notes as their punters don't like it.

Though I reckon underweight, neutral and overweight all really mean *sell*, and only buy means *buy*! Brokers rarely put out pure sell notes as their punters don't like it.

Setting stop losses

Dennis writes

I had a short trade open with a stop loss in place 5% above my entry price. There was a price spike opening today 26p above last week's closing price, which effectively hit the stop loss and closed the position. The price immediately fell back to normal levels.

I have just read the section about rogue trades in your book but I feel a bit peeved and wondered how common an event like this is. Is this sort of thing above board?

I smell a rat, or am I being too cynical? However cautious a trader you might be it, would seem there is nothing you can do about it. I mean my stop loss was not too tight, was it?

NT replies

Unfortunately, it happens a lot I believe, and why I reckon it's best to set very loose stop losses indeed with spread firms. I would have thought it's worth phoning your spread firm and arguing about them closing you out on that one, worth a try. Spread firms want to keep you as a customer so sometimes will bend over backwards to help.

I don't set stop losses on spread bets for that reason, preferring to handle the stop losses myself manually. I think 5% is probably too low, I would use nearer 10% to avoid being stopped out on spikes.

Paper trading the right way?

Phil writes

I am only 19 but I have always been interested in stocks. Just a couple of days ago I bought your book. I am wondering how little I can invest in the stock market just to test how it all works.

I am not just looking to make quick money but I want to have a good understanding of the stock market which could help me in the future.

Do you think it is worth me trying this now or is it better to wait?

NT replies

I suggest you start with just paper trading – in other words, pretend you have 10 grand and buy and sell shares and see how you get on. Some spread bet websites have areas where you can pretend trade too. Worth a look. Good luck, great age to start practising!

Is this the future?

Ivan writes

Like your website. I have been a trader for nearly 10 years with banks but mostly trading FX and futures.

Seems to me that these markets are harder for the individual to trade than stocks. Wondering if you have any thoughts on this as I am thinking of going it alone, but my experience of futures is that they usually burn people.

NT replies

Absolutely agree. I hardly ever trade futures except for a FTSE 100 upbet just before Christmas which I sell in January, usually for good profit. Trading indices is way too hard for most people, including me.

Should I spread bet first?

Vanessa writes

I am half way through your book – what a great read.

Is it better to start with regular trading and then progress to spread bets, or is it possible to go straight into spread bets as a complete wet-behind-the-ears beginner to all of this? I just assumed that it's better to go into spread bets at a much later date?

Secondly, can and do people rely on trading/spread betting as their only source of income? We have a 9-year-old business which we are very much at a crossroads with, and would like to get our fingers into a few more pies, including trading, to generate a better quality of life for us and our 19-month-old son.

NT replies

Yes, it is probably better to start off buying shares normally, before getting into spread betting. If ordinary share buying is equivalent to a Ford Mondeo, spread betting is a Ferrari!

This book should fill you in with spread betting pitfalls. Suggest you practise with tiny stakes like 1p a point!

Yes, there are some people who make a full-time living from trading. But you have to be good – I know of one, Richard, who has made a full-time living from the markets since 1987. But he is very good! Best thing with trading is to start small, learn the craft and increase stakes as you get more confident

Take aim…fire!

Reg writes

One thing I am struggling with a bit is AIM. How do you tell if a company is AIM on ADVFN? (This may seem very dim.) I have a company in my watchlist that, as far as I know is on AIM, but it is listed in the same category as the companies that you mention in your book, that I have added to my list to look at LSE. Any help on this would be much appreciated.

NT replies

Reg, click *Financials* on the share on ADVFN, adn under market segment if the first letter is "A" it's AIM! Simple as that. If it says something like AM50 it means it is in the top 50 AIM shares.

Knock on the door

Andy writes

My girlfriend has told me about how the company she works for has some big orders coming in. If I buy shares in the company is that insider trading and will I get a knock on the door?!

NT replies

There is no doubt here, Andy. Do not trade the shares or tell anyone else. It is definitely insider trading if you know price-sensitive information that has not been reported to the market. However, if the market knows about these big orders already that would be fine. The rule of thumb is: if you know something that if announced to the market would push the share price up or down, it's insider trading and illegal.

Sell on the facts?

Graham writes

Two of the shares I have an interest in reported this week. The share price of both was rising nicely in the weeks before the due date. Results were good for both, but the market reaction could not have been more different. One fell 9%, the other rose 15%. The adage buy on the rumour, sell on the fact could only be applied in one case. My question is, are there any indicators to look for that give a clue which way to go leading up to report day?

NT replies

I really wish there was a reliable indicator. The only thing is, though, if you are confident with the company and its prospects then a fall on profit-taking on results day is often followed up by rises again one or two weeks later. Usually I prefer to stay in if I still like the company and it hasn't issued a warning.

For example, I have stayed with Diploma, which dropped 40p on results day, but liked the results and remained a confident holder and did not want to sell and buy back with all the bother and commissions. But with a different stock, I sold on results day as there were some warnings!

What to do on a bid?

David writes

I bought a share and it went crazy. Turns out it was due to takeover speculation. Finding myself in a dilemma now, not knowing whether to sell or not! The shares have dropped slightly today. It looks like the speculation surrounding the takeover is unfounded, so I'm tempted to cash in as I'm 15% up in 6 weeks! Have you got any thoughts on takeover speculation?

NT replies

Always difficult. I tend to try to sell at the height of the speculation and not worry about losing a few points. For example, I sold Enterprise after some recurring bid rumours; it had gone up 100p and I figured that was a decent enough rise. Shares often fall back after the bid speculation starts to recede. Often a bid materialises some 3 months after the bid rumours surface! One course of action could be to sell half a holding so at least you banked some profits. I did this when bid rumours surfaced with Domestic and General.

The price is right

Zoe writes

Could you please explain (to a very novice trader) how share prices should be read in monetary terms?

For example, reading a list of share prices in the *FT* might look like this:

BAE: 459
Chemring: 19.03
Cobham: 211.50

How much is the share price of BAE: £4.59 or £45.90 or £459.00? I can't find a single book that explains this. Apologies if yours does and I have missed it!!

When reading share prices on ADVFN are they in ££? For example, OMH opens at 22.75. Is that £22.75 and if not why is the decimal point where it is?

NT replies

Everything is in pence. So BAE is 459p, Cobham 211.5p and OMH is 22.75p. So unless there is a pound sign by a figure it is always in pence.

I hope you enjoyed that selection of letters and you are always welcome to contact me. But do remember I can't give individual advice so there is no point writing to me to ask whether you should I sell or buy this or that share!

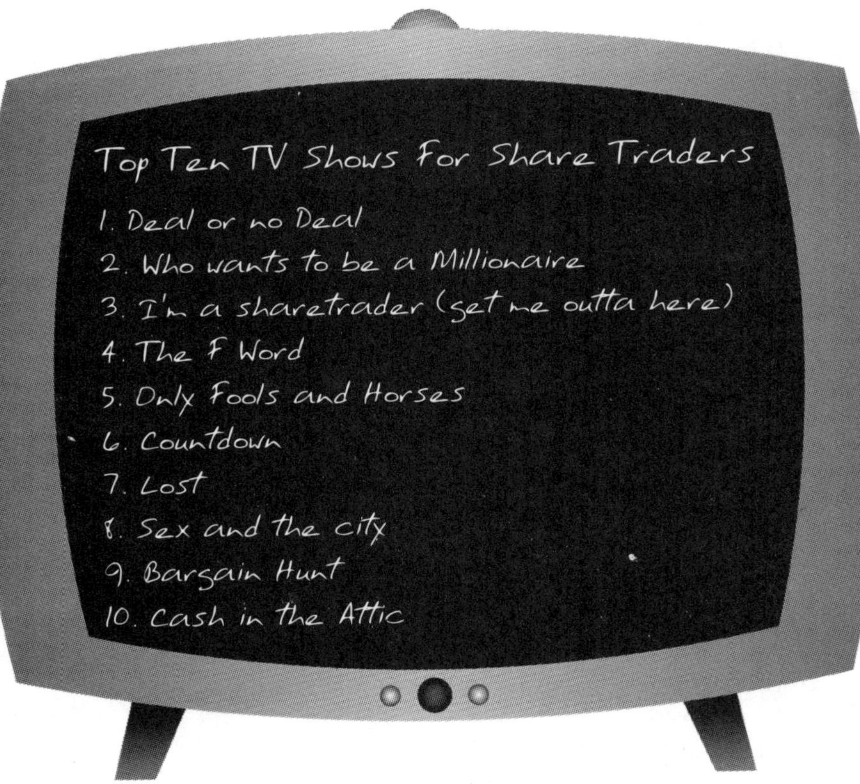

Traders' Tales

One of the most talked-about chapters of the first *Naked Trader* book was a chapter of horror stories – tales of people who had made disastrous mistakes.

I've got together a new collection for this book. But I also have some success stories to report too this time. I hope you find these tales an interesting read.

One reason for reading them is that if you've ever screwed up, and lost money, it may not have been quite so disastrous as some of these tales! Let's face it, we all love reading horror stories because we thank our lucky stars it wasn't us!

But they are also worth reading as they contain some good lessons that we all need to learn, and then remind ourselves of from time to time.

Anyway, I hope it all leads to some interesting reading!

Lost nearly everything

Peter's tale:

> In the 80s I did what you did – gave up working for wages. I went to see a friend, VP of a City bank. I insisted on seeing him in his office as a client rather than as a friend, and asked for investment advice. He said my savings were too small for them and put me in touch with a money management firm in Holland that "we use". They published a weekly letter, acted as brokers and pushed shares. I ended up suing them in Holland and Geneva (they were quite mobile) and getting judgement against them for £485k (all I had saved from my working years) and recovered...£15k in the liquidation. Lesson: who *can* you trust? Yourself. Greed is not the best counsellor.
>
> So I did start to trust myself, and made some money back investing slowly and steadily.

NT comments:

As Peter himself points out: beware of greed. But also the lesson here is to beware of share pushers; if you are going to put your money in someone else's hands, check them out very carefully, especially if they are registered abroad.

Lost the value of a house

Andrew's tale:

> In 1998, I sold a large house in Tipperary and was intending to buy another – closure three months later. It was at the time of the Ryanair float and rather than put the money on deposit, I thought I'd invest in that. A delayed flight had me receiving the money a day later than expected. That day, Powerscreen (the best run/most successful Irish company at the time) dived on bad news. Everyone said it had been way oversold. Guardian Royal had just paid 630 for 5 million shares. They hit 220. I asked around, and everyone agreed that in 6 weeks they'd be back to where they were. I put all the proceeds into it. Massive fraud discovered (CEO/CFO/CTO involved). They were sold for pennies. I lost the value of a very nice Georgian house. I now don't believe recovery stories in the middle of disaster.

NT comments:

Well, actually the lesson is not only to beware of recovery stories, the main thing here is don't put all your eggs in one basket. You bought a massive amount of shares in one company. And, of course, you also played with money you could not afford to lose. A sobering story.

Lost the lot

Paul's tale:

> I made a big loss. Hearing of my loss, a very old and rich friend (who regards £5 million on a share as a punt) said "You should listen to me. Put the money in Cortex, you'll get it all back many times over. Nomura have just put me into it". I was wary – especially since my research showed that there were serious competing technologies. Bought at 240 with the rest of my money. It de-listed. Lost the lot.

NT comments:

The lesson here is pretty obvious! Don't listen or act on tips unless you have done your own research first. Simple as that! And especially be wary of tips from friends, and people down the pub!

Believed the financial director

Rob's tale:

> I was in a little company called Gearhouse that went bust. My 5% limit rule restricted the impact on my overall portfolio, but the actual monetary loss was large for me. Although the company was in trouble, I knew people in its field who spoke well of it, and came to believe there would be a bid. I bought in for this and/or the recovery. Failed to appreciate that anyone wanting bits of the company could buy them more cheaply from the receiver, and also believed the financial director's assurances to me that the delayed annual results would be published within the statutary deadline. I realised too late that the FD could hardly have confided that the banks were about to pull the plug, and the only thing to be published would be the notice of administration. Not least, it was at a time when I could do no wrong in my trading and was taking greater and greater risks.

NT comments:

You did well to make sure you didn't hold too many. Interesting comment from you about "You could do no wrong". It's easy to feel you are king of the traders when you have a good few consecutive winners, but perhaps it made you too smug. Looks like you should simply have checked the debt levels and not relied on anyone's assurances.

Tough to outsmart the market

David's is an interesting tale. He has been investing for many years and makes money. Here are his views:

> I've been investing since I was 18 years old and I find it's very hard to outsmart the market. To do it, you have to be better than not just 50% of all investors, but probably nearer 75% of them. It's a tough, tough call.
>
> When I invest I ask myself: do I *really* know more about the share than the guy whose shares I'm just about to buy? The honest answer is

> usually "no". He's been living with his shares for a while and is getting shot of them because he doesn't think they'll go up any more...and yet here I am buying the damn things.
>
> On our side we need:
>
> *Luck*: This is much underrated. There really is such a thing as a Midas touch. Lucky people make money not because they are geniuses but because they are just...lucky. I'd rather follow a lucky investor than a smart one.
>
> *Rising Indices*: The rising tide that floats all boats, even gets the rubbish shares out of the mud. So invest when the Dow's going up (don't bother about the FTSE) and sell when it starts going down.
>
> *Graphs*: All the information there is about a share – published and unpublished, well-known or secret – is in the graph.
>
> *Stop Losses*: Keep them tight – you'll be so glad you did (well, most of the time!)

NT comments:

Interesting views! I'm not sure I agree with the luck part!

Running the gains was a knife edge

Keith's tale:

> I am not saying that it is impossible to make money in the markets, but I am saying that I think it is impossible to do this in a casual way. You have to be prepared to devote every trading hour plus almost the same in research, to be on the winning side.
>
> It depends how you look at my track record, 30% down to 7.5% down is a claw back of 22.5%. Given that the 30% was early on (the first month of trading), then it does seem to indicate that I learnt something. Still, at the end of the day a loss is a loss.
>
> What did I learn? Well, it is very boring, and very basic: cut the losses and run the gains. I found that cutting the losses was very easy, but running the gains was a knife edge.

NT comments:

Keith you are spot on: cutting the losses is so important. Interesting to note you found running gains difficult. I find that the easy part!

Lessons over 40 years

This tale is from a trader (Jerry) with years of experience – and he makes some excellent points:

> My advice, after 40 years of getting it both wrong and right is:
>
> 1. Have a bias towards risk but avoid lack of stock liquidity and its risks. Also avoid buying stocks whose sector (over the last 2 to 3 months) is trending down.
>
> 2. Shares go up and down, so don't chase an entry at too high a price. Possible ways to achieve this are to spot a good share and add it to your watchlist and then watch it, don't buy it first; try to buy when the sector and the share are rising but are not more than 4% above the previous top (probably the last month's trend top), this means you may set a limit buy for a while.
>
> 3. Manage your risk controls according to recent tops and bottoms and not according to the random price that you happen to have paid for it. Don't sell because you are afraid of the future, but do set fresh monthly stop losses.
>
> 4. Work out what sort of investor you are and stick to it. In other words, loss-making trades should be sold and not become "long-term investments".

Binary bets

This tale from Gordon:

> I found out about binary bets, which seemed very exciting. So I started getting into it. Now, more than half of my hard-earned money deposited (£1,100 – yes, it's money I can afford to lose, but who would want to throw half of it away in a week?) has disappeared into thin air within a week.
>
> The first 2 days, I won more than £400, which had made me overconfident and on the third day, I lost about £1,200 in one single trade (FTSE 100 hourly bet). Then I realised how dangerous it is in this trading world when we lose our common sense. I had thought I couldn't be wrong after studying only a few charts. Everything written in the books has been proved absolutely right. I'd paid a good price to learn the first lesson of the game: "Always stick to the plan and never

> get overconfident". Although I had the plan with my stop losses, I watched my bets almost sinking to the bottom before I realised it was time to get out. I lost my consciousness in the game. I need to train my mind to get over my emotion.
>
> I know I have been stupid trying those bets with little knowledge. I think I've committed every sin mentioned in your book. I guess I wouldn't learn anything until I experienced it. Now I've stopped all my betting and decided to study more about real trading and investing.

NT comments:

Thanks for the honesty Gordon. I believe binary betting is just that – betting. It's gambling not investing. Really glad to hear you are now going to study real trading and investing and not gambling. You can then start to make money!

Catching falling knives

Trader Tom's tale:

> I had become infallible in picking surefire winners (my capital had grown by 10 times in 6 months). But then the wins stopped. However, I could not accept that such superb judgement from such an intelligent guy with such an outstanding track record had stopped working. I took very large losses trying to catch falling knives all the way down; although I did not see it as that at the time, believing it to be a short-term correction meaning bounces should be bought. All the way down, brokers continued to produce buy recommendation after buy recommendation on stocks that were actually in terminal decline. Their forecasts of EPS gradually declined quarter by quarter, but still remained unrealistically high as later became apparent. Their forecasts helped convince me and others that the fall was just a blip. The further prices went down, the more blindingly obvious it was that the Great Recovery could only be days away! I saw what I wanted to see, and made excuses for what I did not want to believe.
>
> At least I did eventually get out with several times what I had started with – not wiped out like many others, especially those who had over-committed on margin.

NT comments:

Well, as I said before, be careful about broker recommendations. And as you say, you saw what you wanted to see not what was actually happening.

Surprised by the volatility of indices

Ben's tale:

> I lost about £700 on the DAX during very volatile trading. I went into it with the best of intentions but I was unprepared for the reality of spread betting. Trading the indices was far more difficult than I ever realised. At times I was probably gambling not trading/investing as I first intended. I was unprepared for the volatility of the indices and found that I lacked the skill to set stop losses at the right level. I set them too cautiously and was stopped out too quickly as a general rule. If I'd stayed in the market I would have been ahead, but I was again unprepared for the difficulty of watching losses accumulate. In short, while I am constantly tempted, I'm going to steer clear of trading the indices.

NT comments:

A very common tale from those who try and play the indices, and I must repeat it is *very* difficult and it is very easy to lose money. The majority of index players lose.

A little knowledge...

Eric's tale:

> My biggest trading nightmare involved 'a little knowledge being a dangerous thing', on the part of my elderly mother. She inherited 500 shares in BT in the mid 90s from her deceased brother. Shortly afterwards, I helped her to sell 200 of the shares to trade in her old banger for a new car. At the time she was in her 70s and had no experience whatsoever in share dealing. BT were riding high at this time and the share price was over £13. While I was on vacation in the autumn of 1999, she read in the newspaper that BT were overbought and that the share price would fall dramatically.
>
> She had done very well with the shares, which had doubled in value while she was holding them, so she decided to cash in the rest while the price was high. Using the contract docket from her previous sale (which I had handled for her with my broker) she rang the broker, quoted her account number and sold the balance of her shares. Unfortunately, instead of the 200 shares she actually held, she

> mistakenly sold 2,000 shares. To compound the problem, the shares continued to rise over the next few days and she received a request to send in her share certificate for the 2,000 sold shares. On my return from abroad, she rang me in a panic to ask me if I could get her out of the mess.
>
> To cut a long story short, the price had risen by 60p by the time I could buy the 1,800 'unowned' shares back resulting in a loss of £1,080 plus stamp duty (which is 1% in Ireland) and commissions amounting together to a further £600. I didn't have the heart to tell my mother that her error had been so costly so I took the hit myself, which was a very large one for me at that time. My mother is a sprightly 83-year-old now but thankfully she doesn't own any more shares.

NT comments:

This is a mistake that can easily be made – the moral is always double and triple check the amount of shares you are selling or buying and get the right amount! If you make a mistake it is *your* fault and not the broker's.

Finding a niche and sticking with it

Here's an interesting tale from Susan. I actually met her when she visited the café I used to own. She had just started trading and has come an awfully long way since then. So her tale is worth reading:

> The advertisement might have read: seasoned buy and hold investor seeks short-term trading strategy. Why was I looking for a short-term trading strategy? Because a change in financial circumstances meant that I needed to put money in the bank faster than I thought would be possible using the tried and tested buy and hold strategy. Simply, the cat couldn't wait three years to be fed and neither could I.
>
> Books, conferences, seminars – I did it all. I learnt everything from the stupidly complex to the absurdly simple. But surely, I told myself, it's best to learn from those already making money from trading. So using ideas from three 10-year plus traders on The Naked Trader thread on ADVFN, I gradually started to find my trading feet.
>
> In short, I find shares broadly going up without wild intraday swings. I buy and hold for as long as they continue up (months, weeks, days, hours or minutes). I sell any share the moment (non-negotiable and I *mean* non-negotiable) that it goes down, and buy back – hopefully

> lower – when price starts to goes up again but higher if necessary – pride has no place here. Repeat as necessary. The longest I've held a share is 5 months, the shortest is 8 minutes…or was it 10?!
>
> It's not perfect. I don't always maximise available profits, and it's time consuming, but I bank regular profits, keep losses small, feed the cat twice a day and my stockbroker and the Chancellor love me to bits. Everyone's happy!
>
> I really try to ignore the doomsters, soothsayers and sell-everything merchants because they don't own my shares and because, quite frankly, they are quite often wrong in their timing. I pay only passing attention to indices because they can go down while my shares can – and frequently do – go up. Oh, and I generally don't short in an up-market; I just don't see the point.
>
> I started with a good sized pot, have a cheap broker and tuned up the sense of humour to deal with – how shall I put it – my less successful moments. I use Level 2, live price alerts and, most important of all, I have an unshakeable belief that I can keep the cat in premium cat food forever.
>
> The first year was learning curve time, but I still banked 17%. Perhaps that advertisement should now read: top fund manager seeks big salary (and bonus, don't forget the bonus). But I'm really having far too much fun to give it a second thought and besides, the cat likes having me around!

NT comments:

It is great to see success stories and Susan's ideas have worked for her. She found her niche and is sticking to it and she shows it can be done!

A scam warning

Mike's tale:

> I bought shares in a company called Gold Mines Of Sardinia at 23p per share. They did not do much and eventually the name was changed to Chaco Resources. They have been in my portfolio doing nothing. Price gone down to 7p.
>
> About a month ago, I received a call from a gentleman who said his company represented a client wishing to take over Chaco Resources

> they had obtained 49% of shares and required the further 2%. Would I be interested in selling mine? He said they wanted to offset tax and would pay me £34,000 for my shares. This seemed too good to be true but I went along with it. He emailed me a form to sign to sell the shares and swear me to secrecy. I had difficulty emailing the form back, so I posted it to the Wall St. address. I then received regular calls from the same gentleman informing me of the ongoing events. He told me because of a share split, I now held 6,000 shares and they would pay me £96,000.
>
> Finally, he rang and said everything was in place but a bond had to be put up of which his client would pay 96% and I was to send £2,900 as my payment into the bond. My bank account details were also required to pay me my final cheque. In between, I had received my letter back from U.S.A. saying not known at this address and can make no contact via the website. So in the end I told him that I was not prepared to risk my capital and put the phone down.

NT comments:

A pretty typical scam and you did well not to go through with it. This tale is a good warning to others not to get taken in by such scams. As I keep saying: if it is too good to be true, it is!

One mistake after another

Jimbo's tale:

> I decided to actively trade 70k. I decided I needed some help and thought trading 10-15k mechanically – via one of the systems I'd been getting bombarded with – would be a good idea.
>
> Researched (or so I thought) mechanical, software-driven products and plumped for a chart-based system which appeared to show an 18% per month gain over the last 4 years.
>
> However, I wasn't completely naïve. I was sceptical and so got a lot of information on whether the trades shown were accountable and how many people were using the system. Knowing what I know now from trading, I believe the trades were cherry picked. In the last two months, only one in ten of the picked stocks have performed that well, with the rest being hampered by the fact that 90% of the tips are recovery plays on AIM, with 5% to 15% spread losses on day one.

I stopped automatically buying what was recommended, and checked out the balance sheets of every pick. And now, I've stopped using the product actively.

Enter PartyGaming. I saw the bounce in the chart. I understand internet poker and was certain the law in the States was about to be repealed. No lilly-livered diversification for me: 20k straight in at the top of the bounce. That bounce obviously had the proposed change in the law priced in; when it was understood that what was proposed was licensing in an environment, potentially prejudicial to offshore firms, it tanked.

I averaged down and am currently down 25%.

Even after reading your book and intellectually understanding that I should sell and put the cash back into LSE main board shares which I research properly, I'm emotionally attached to PRTY. As I write I'm optimistically following every quarter point rise on the portfolio tool on ADVFN. Down 5k on the 20k invested.

I also dumped an extra 3.5k into a bulletin board tipped AIM oil stock. I was hit by the 10% bid-offer spread, and then it ticked down again to the level I now know it will stay at for at least the next 3 months until drilling and steam injection reports come in. See: I do do research – just that it's after I've bought! Down 1k now, but still reading the BBs and keeping the faith.

Had some more fun trying to catch the YELL falling knife on an oversell bounce – just about got out even, down £50. Made a £50 or so on IEC in the same fashion, but have learnt now that you have to see the turn and rise with the L2 figures looking good to have only an even chance of it rising short term.

Decided to diversify in the gaming sector to LNG. Down 1k out of 10k as I raced to get in before the interims.

NT comments:

Well goodness me, Jimbo, you've pretty much done everything I warn against and…lost a lot of money. Your tale is pretty self-explanatory. You committed the following mistakes: bought software which promised you the earth but did not work; bought a risky share on impulse and then bought more; followed a bulletin board tip; and tried to catch a falling knife. I really, really hope you start investing properly because otherwise you are on your way to the poorhouse. Your brilliantly honest tale shows exactly how easy it is to get into trouble.

I would like to thank all the contributors to the traders' tales. Hopefully you will help others with your tales – and thanks for being honest.

Q. HOW DID ALL THE DAYTRADERS MANAGE TO FIT UNDER THE LIMBO BAR AT THEIR PARTY?

A. THEY HAD ALL GONE SHORT.

The Market Can See You Coming

If it seems too good to be true – it is

Don't know if you caught the recent Harry Enfield series? It wasn't much good, but there was one very good sketch about an antiques dealer in a rich area who bought crap and sold it at ridiculous prices to people with too much money because: "I saw you coming."

It's similar with the stock market. From the moment you start trading, expect a barrage of emails, mailshots and phone calls.

Why's that?

Because as an inexperienced trader/investor, a lot of people want to make money out of you. There are loads of scams out there in the marketplace. These catch out new and more experienced investors time and time again.

The one thing that you can be sure of in the markets is:

> *If it seems too good to be true – it is!*

I get emails all the time from people asking whether so and so system works, or whether a £3,000 seminar will help them to make millions. There are a lot of scams out there. There are: phone calls from people offering to buy your shares from you at an amazing price; People who want to charge you for tips; Bulletin board experts trying to get you to buy illiquid stock; Companies with systems claiming they will make you loads of money; And a lot more.

Every time a scam is offered to you it will always seem like a great deal. But trust me: all they want is your money.

> Do not give out your real email address when you register for anything. Set up what I call a dump mail. For example, when I sign up for anything and have to register I use the mail address "junkmaildump". It means the mailbox I mainly use doesn't get bunged up with spam.

It sounds horrible, but think of everyone out there in Sharesland as your enemy, unless over time you are convinced otherwise. The friendlier they appear, the more likely it is you will get led up the garden path.

Of course, it is very tempting to believe a system works and you just have to follow it to make money, or someone will tip you the right shares. But ignore all offers and concentrate on learning about the markets slowly and cautiously – do not get sidetracked by the easy way out.

However tempting it is, treat all tips, offers of advice, newsletters, phone calls, offers of shares, research documents, share systems and software with extreme suspicion.

Share scams come in various forms and guises. Here are some to watch for.

Scams

Phone calls

These often come from America. A plausible sounding bloke opens up with a question like: "You handle your own portfolio, how's it going?" When you mumble something like "it's going OK," he'll start his sales pitch. He has an incredible tech stock that is going to treble in a few weeks and he's offering *you* the chance to get in!

It could be one of a couple of scams.

This bloke will probably claim to be from a broker who can let you have this wonder stock cheaper than the current market price. What it means is he, or even a reputable-sounding broker, has bought a shed load of stock in a crap company and wants to offload some to you at a worse price, thereby making a guaranteed profit.

Or it could be worse; you could send your money off and never see it again!

Alternatively, the call could come from a UK company offering tips or shares at a knockdown price. Again the share is likely to be a small penny share and they are trying to make money out of you in the same way as above.

> Ignore all these and just hang up. You are unlikely to get rich quick and are more likely to become considerably poorer.

Before hanging up, ask them where they got your phone number and try and get off the list – otherwise, in my experience, you'll be inundated with phone calls.

Newspaper/magazine get rich ads

I'm sure you've seen these. They usually say something like:

> *Learn stock market secrets...*

or:

> *Make £400 a day from home...*

What happens is you get enticed to a free seminar. The guru will talk about things like spread betting and technical analysis and then spend the rest of the time trying to flog his work manuals, books, and another paid-for seminar or expensive software.

The plain fact (again) is: if it seems too good to be true, it usually is.

It is highly unlikely you'll make £400 a day. The guru will make money out of you by selling you his books, videos and courses. Again, all you have to do is ask yourself: if the guru is such a genius why doesn't he sit at home with his systems, rack up the millions and be happy?

I'm not saying all such systems and all software are no good. I just don't think these are a great way to learn how to make a good start in the stock market.

Seminars

My seminars are brilliant (of course), but watch out for the ones that demand a lot of money, £3,000 and the like. They usually suck you in by offering a free seminar which is where a heavy sell is used to get you to stump up for the expensive seminar, where they will reveal "the real secrets" of the market. I'm pretty dubious about these and haven't heard from anyone who has genuinely benefited or thought they were worth the money.

> There's no substitute for learning to do your own research and gradually learning the ins and outs of trading.

Scams summary

- Don't buy shares offered over the phone
- Be sceptical about 'get rich' ads
- Software may be an expensive waste of money
- Don't take the easy way – take time to learn about the markets

Tipsters – the bad

I'm afraid to say the market is littered with an assortment of what I can only describe as "dodgy geezers" wanting to take your money in return for their hot tips. Some will even offer free tips, but of course they will exploit your email address or inundate you with offers of paid-for tips.

There are loads of share tipsters around, as you will very quickly find out. They usually charge a fee for access to tips, or they come in the form of a monthly newsletter. Like entertainers, they all have some kind of shtick to pull you in. Some claim to be maverick city insiders. Others to "read the charts and the signals".

Every single tipster will quote what seems like amazing performance figures:

> *Our tips are up 40% this year!*
>
> *Amazing profit every year!*
>
> *Three penny shares that are about to rocket...!*

What they don't brag about is the ones they picked that halved in value or even went bust. So you won't see headlines like:

> *We tipped a share and – whoops – it went bust.*

There'll usually be a list of shares with percentage profits made against each one. Amazingly, you'll see hardly any losing shares. Obviously following these geniuses is a licence to print money!

Sadly, their claims are unlikely to be realistic. Some tipsters are very clever and use various manipulations of statistics to show performances that often just aren't true.

Something else you won't find in their claims: all their tips that have gone south or gone bust! You'll only see the winners highlighted and my cat could have picked some of those by sticking her paw at random on the share prices in the *FT*!

Nearly all of the dodgy tipping organisations tip very small penny shares. You won't find them tipping many bigger companies. That's because in percentage terms they only have to hit on one or two big winners (out of the dozens of companies they tip).

Here are just some of the ways they create amazing performance figures.

Tipster tricks

They often use mid prices. Never the real buy and sell prices. With the small company shares they tip, this means they are already up on the percentage game. Let's take an example. A tipster tips a share that is 9p to sell and 10p to buy. So the tipster says his tip is at 9.5p – the mid price. No one can actually buy at this price, but never mind! The tip is published in a tip sheet at the weekend. On Monday, before the market opens, the market makers have seen the tip and raise the price to 10p to sell and 11p to buy (mid price is now 10.5p). Subscribers buy in at 11p, but the tipster can now claim to have profits of an amazing 10%!! (The difference between his mid price tip at 9.5p, and the new mid price of 10.5p.)

What has actually happened is those who bought the tip are already nursing *losses* of nearly 10%. They've bought in at the real buy price of 11p, but the selling price is only 10p!

What's worse, is that the market makers know the mug punters have bought at 11p and during the next few days will drop the price, and those who bought will suffer even worse losses.

The tipster doesn't care: that now goes down as a 10% profit. On the table of winners it will show: tip 9.5p, high 10.5p, +10%!

But none of the subscribers could possibly have bought or sold at these prices.

Of course, most of the tipsters tip anything from 50 to 200 companies a year. There's no way subscribers could afford to buy that many of them.

So even when a tipster manages to tip a big winner, chances are the subscriber won't have bought it. It's Sod's Law, but they will probably buy the one that's gone bust!

None of it matters because, while people are cancelling subscriptions, there are always new mugs ready to start up subscriptions.

In particular, tipping publications love direct debit payments. That's because us Brits are so lazy we rarely cancel them, so they carry on taking money off you long after you've tired of losing money!

Tipsters – the good

OK, of course, as with everything, there *are* some good tipsters out there. There are probably five or six names that are worth paying attention to. If you can find someone tipping who trades as well, that would be an advantage. Alternatively, someone who specialises in certain shares, for example, the FTSE 350.

If you don't feel like finding your own shares, how can you find the good tipping services?

The clue is to ask around. Try the bulletin boards, put up a message: "Is so-and-sos' tipping service any good? Have you made money by following the tips?"

Bulletin board writers are notoriously difficult to please, so if you do read plaudits for a tipping service, then maybe, just maybe, it's worth a look.

If you do subscribe to a tipster service, don't just buy the tipped shares automatically. Do your own research. Look on the tips as a possible basis for further research. Monitor the service carefully and write down the real prices you could have bought or sold at and judge performance yourself.

If you subscribe to tip sheets, you must only use them to help you generate ideas.

Tips and market makers

And, whatever you do, don't buy a tip right away. **The market makers will have marked up the tips and if you buy right away the price will be far too high.** Wait for a few days for the share to settle down.

The other sort of tips you get are the free ones in investment magazines and newspapers. Again, beware of the market maker mark-up – these shares should not be bought right away. Be especially careful of buying tips in the Sunday papers, as on a quiet Monday morning these will already be higher and you will be paying too much.

In addition, remember these tips are being written by journalists. They are probably only on £25k a year. If they were any good at picking shares they'd be trading full-time themselves! They are also under pressure to regularly come up with tips and ideas, so they are not necessarily going to be much good.

Tipsters summary

- Be sceptical of the performance figures quoted
- Tips are marked up before you can buy
- Do you really need a guru?

Systems

Everywhere you look in the stock market someone somewhere will be trying to sell you a system.

These people promise you the world:

> *Spend just five minutes a day and make £2,000 a week.*
>
> *Our system picks all the trades for you.*
>
> *Trade from home and make £75,000 a week with no experience.*

But just think about it.

Don't you think if the people that came up with the systems had come up with an easy way to make millions they'd keep it to themselves and end up in Barbados sunbathing? Don't be fooled by promises of big profits for no effort. And take anything they say, like their 'record of profits', with a giant pinch of salt.

The only system is to learn about trading slowly but surely through hard work and decent research. You get nothing for nothing. Ignore the ads and bin the junk mail.

> Don't be fooled by promises of big profits for no effort.

Of course it is tempting: the system sellers are clever and they are playing on our inherent laziness (well mine anyway). It sounds lovely: a computer will do all the work for you.

To sum up the last few pages: in the end it's best to do your own research and put your own work into the market – don't let others try and do it for you.

Part 7
The End (Almost)

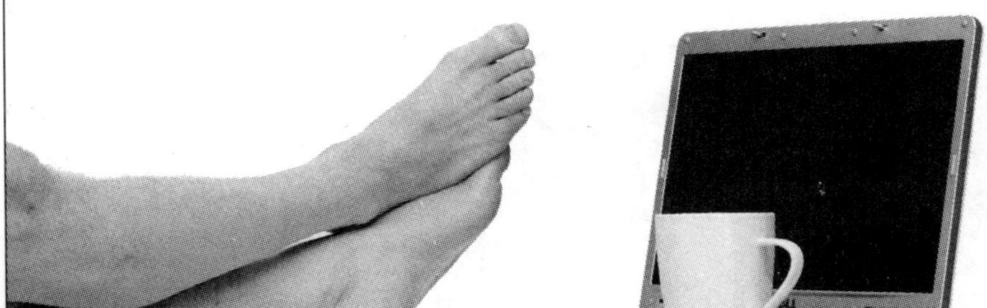

“Money won’t buy happiness but it will pay the salaries of a large research staff to study the problem.”

- Bill Vaughan

The Naked Trader Rules

I'm not really one for rules. I've always hated authority, so rules and me don't often get along. But I thought to finish up I'd set out a few of my investing rules, especially for the new investor.

You're not going to lose everything you have if you don't follow them. But after you finish reading this book and it's tossed on top of a lot of other dusty financial tomes...and you come back to it one day...these rules are a pretty good summary of what I've been banging on about.

They are in no particular order. In other words number 1 has no more importance than number 30.

Just for fun, five of them are WRONG. If you have read the book you should spot them!

The Rules

1. Only play with money you can really afford to lose. Be honest with yourself.
2. Get the whole story about a company before you buy. Learn everything about it.
3. Don't rush into anything or chase a share price. There's always another share coming along in a minute.
4. Buy penny shares – after all they can easily become ten baggers.
5. Be wary of buying into systems promising you thousands for no work. If it's too good to be true, it probably is.
6. Don't buy a share because someone on a bulletin board says it's going to double.

7. Buy tips you see in the newspapers – journalists know what they're talking about.
8. Cut your losses fast if you bought a share and it's tanking.
9. Don't take profits too quickly. If you've got a good share and it's slowly heading up, stick with it. Run your winners.
10. Don't be panicked out of a good share if it goes down for a day. The market makers may be trying to get your shares cheaply.
11. Beware of buying a share just because a director bought some. They often get it wrong. Some shares have gone bust two weeks after a director buy.
12. If you are buying more than £3,000 of a small share, check its normal market size. If that is below £1,000 of shares, you may have trouble when it comes to selling them.
13. Never catch a falling knife. That means don't buy a share because it's gone down a lot. Better to buy shares that are going up. That bargain may end up even cheaper.
14. Read! Buy investment books and then buy some more. You can never learn too much.
15. Don't buy a share after a profit warning (like London buses, they often come in threes).
16. Check the spread between the buying and selling prices. If it's more than 5%, the share could be far too risky.
17. Beware of buying before 9am – the spreads can be at their widest. Don't be suckered into buying a share at a silly price early on.
18. Don't buy and sell indices like the FTSE 100 or the Dow, especially if you are a new investor. That is just gambling.
19. Be careful of mining and oil exploration stocks. One bad report can see these shares tumble and they are impossible to value properly.
20. Don't buy companies that are making a loss. You're gambling they'll make a profit one day. It may never happen.
21. Don't buy a share because it has a perk, such as discounted hotel rooms.
22. Use all the credit/leverage you can get hold of when spread betting.

23. Use stop losses. Set them around 10% away from your buying price and don't hesitate to act on them.
24. Try to have a plan with every share. Think about what your exit price will be.
25. Shares are for buying *and* selling. Do run profits but also take them sometimes.
26. Don't get involved with things you don't understand. So don't buy CFDs or covered warrants if you don't fully understand them.
27. Beware of trading too much on margin. Think about what your losses could be and whether you can afford to cover them.
28. If you're losing heavily it may be best to cut all your positions and come back to the market another time.
29. Don't over-trade. Keep to about 8–10 open positions. Any more and you are going to have trouble keeping on top of them.
30. Beware of overconfidence. If you're on a winning run don't start increasing the size of your positions.
31. Don't only go long, do think about shorting stocks, but this is not for beginners.
32. Be careful about relying on one method of stock picking. Cover all the angles.
33. Watch for tipping points. Don't lose control of your investments and stay calm.
34. It's fun to gamble, pick a stock at random sometimes.
35. Always check your ex-dividend dates. Your share will fall on this date for the amount of the dividend, so don't panic.
36. Open more than one broking account. Then you can compare their services and systems.
37. Don't rely solely on charts, but certainly use them – along with other tools – to help your trading decisions.
38. Read the financial press – some of it is rubbish but you must keep in touch with what's going on.
39. Always "average down" and buy more shares in one you're already losing badly on as you may end up breaking even.

40. Remember the good advice of Corporal Jones in Dad's Army: "Don't panic!"

Find out which rules were wrong at the bottom of the page.[6]

Well done if you got all 5!

[6] Wrong rules: 4, 7, 22, 34, 39.

Finally...

I'm about to go, this book is nearly over (thank God, it's driven me crazy for six months). But before I do go, I thought I'd reiterate some of the main points in the book.

Simple questions to ask yourself before making a trade

Here are a few questions you should know the answers to before making a trade. If you really don't know the answer to all these questions before you trade, don't bloody well trade it, OK?

1. Why do you think the **share is going to go up**? If you can't think of a reason, why are you buying it?
2. What is your **timescale**? Are you in for a quick buck, are you looking at 2 months, 6 months or 2 years? So what sort of trade is it?
3. Why are you buying **right now**? If the share is going down, are you buying at the right time?
4. **How much money** are you going to put in and why?
5. Do you know how much you are hoping to make (**profit target**), and how much you are willing to lose (**stop loss**)?

Tipping point

Well, the tipping point is now. So you can tip me if you like for all the valuable information you've got from this book. It's worth a lot more than £12.99, so I suggest a tip of about a tenner will do. Please put your tip in an envelope and send it to me. Much appreciated. Thank you guv'nor!

A *tipping point* in gambling, investing or trading circles is the point where you "lose it". Instead of making money you have a mental crisis – you go bananas and start throwing money away and losing heavily.

What do I mean?

A tipping point is basically a small thing that tips you over from being a sensible investor or trader into a complete nutter.

It could be something simple like: you started out doing really well but one stock let you down, but you know it's a good one. So you throw more money at it. You get annoyed and take out some spread bets too. Suddenly the share lurches down more and you're losing tons of money on it. You buy more and buy some other shares on credit too – the market tumbles and suddenly you are showing huge losses. You're all excited about the share and leverage up to the max.

All of a sudden, from a reasonably good investor you've become a crazed gambler. And it's all because one stock tripped you up.

The tipping point can be anything, usually it's a small issue. Maybe you had a good run, showing a profit of say 20k in your spread betting account. A couple of bad market days later you're back down to only break even. You're determined to show a profit so take out more bets than you should, and now you're in a loss. You've tipped over.

You have to learn to stop before the tipping point catches you out.

What's the solution if you recognize a tipping point?

Cut your stakes dramatically. Or get out completely. Get rid of whatever it was that began to tip you over.

How do I recognize a tipping point?

You start to feel out of control of everything and lose control of your investments. You begin to over trade, anything to start winning again. Symptoms may even include feelings of excitement, irritation, and a bad mood only alleviated briefly by a trade.

So, one day when something tipped you, remember what you read here and do something about it before you do your brain in.

And if all the above isn't a good tip, I don't know what else is.

Final thought

A final (really final) thought.

An accountant came to one of my seminars. After I covered some basic analysis of various companies, he piped up:

> *But don't you look at acid test ratios? And what about the PEG value versus historic PE?*

And various other things. As an honest(ish) person I replied:

> *No, in fact I don't really know anything about them. But do you think all these measures are relevant?*

He then went on to describe how he analyses accounts in the minutest details and carried on for ten minutes leaving me and the audience a bit bemused because really, we didn't understand much of what he was on about. But I certainly wouldn't dismiss it as I don't mind learning something new.

And I did wonder: am I too basic? Should I be looking at a whole host of financial data? Should I try to understand everything in the accounts?

I had a chat with him in the bar. He said:

> *Actually, I think I maybe overanalyse. The fact is I can't bring myself to buy many shares because there's always one figure I don't like. In fact, I've hardly been able to trade because I get scared after all the analysis.*

He realised there and then that overdoing the analysis had actually cost him a lot of money.

So, my parting shot to you is: *don't overdo it*. You don't have to analyse everything to the *n*th degree. My simple methods outlined in this book should work. And you will, in time, work out your own parameters. Simple can be best. Ask the best chefs. And it's the same with shares.

And with that simple message I shall take my leave. Hope you enjoyed the book.

I wish you the best of luck and hope you make a fortune. Just make sure you do it over time and don't try and make your millions in a week. So long, and pick some good ones!

Make me proud of you!

And don't forget you can catch me three times a week at my website www.nakedtrader.co.uk – see you there…

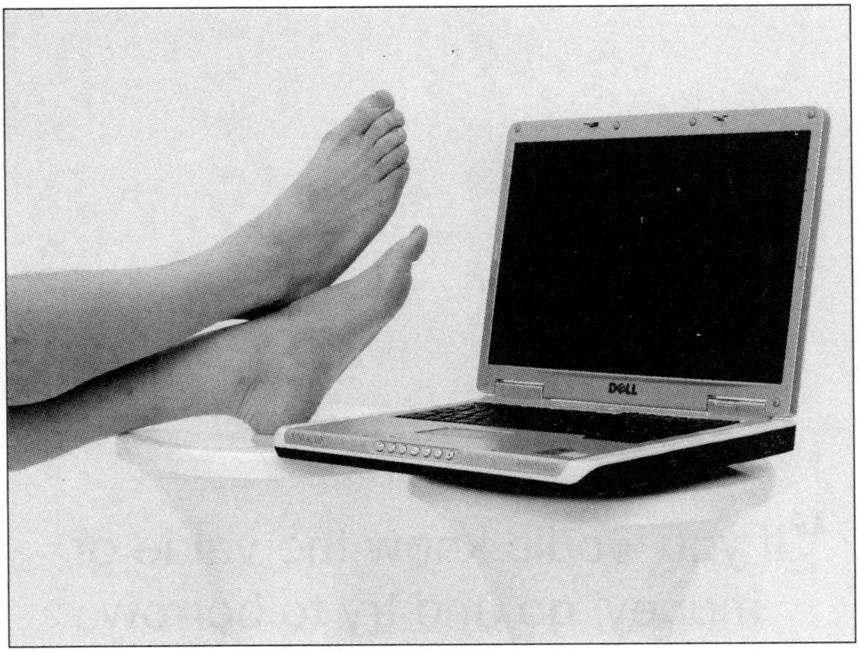

Appendices

"If you would know the value of money, go and try to borrow some."

- Benjamin Franklin

Websites worth a look

There are tons of financial websites out there, and most of them, today, are actually very good. That's partly because the useless sites that set up in the dot-com boom have disappeared. But it's also because the people that set them up enjoy finance and shares and that tends to come across.

Most good websites provide a decent amount of free information, then you pay a bit extra for premium information such as always-on access to real-time share prices. For example, once you've had some experience you may want to access Level 2 services, which will cost some money.

The sites tend to offer premium material all priced around the same level, but you may want to shop around. The best thing is to experiment. You'll probably end up using two or three sites.

For brand new starters you probably only need the free stuff to begin with. As you get more experienced, you may need to start paying for decent access to real-time information.

Indian websites

sebi.gov.in

SEBI protects the interests of investors in securities and promotes the development of the securities market through appropriate regulation.

irdaindia.org

The regulator was established by Parliament to protect the interests of the policyholders, to regulate, promote, and ensure orderly growth of the life and non-life insurance industry.

amfiindia.com

The trade association of mutual funds has useful information about funds.You can get most data pertaining to all mutual funds houses in India, like scheme corpus, fund corpus, etc at amfiindia.com

bseindia.com

Bombay Stock Exchange (BSE) website provides information on SENSEX and other indices, stock quotes, market trend and analysis, company information etc.

nseindia.com

This site is about Indian stock market. It displays latest market information regarding stocks. It contains valuable information like most active stocks, top gainers and losers, nifty stock watch,etc. It displays the required information in real time.

finmin.nic.in

This is the Ministry of Finance Government of India's official website. It contains latest notification about the Department of Economic Affairs, Department of Revenue, Disinvestment and Financial department.

rbi.org.in

To regulate the issue of Bank Notes and keeping of reserves with a view to securing monetary stability in India and generally to operate the currency and credit system of the country to its advantage.

fedai.org.in

This website belongs to the association of banks dealing in foreign exchange in India. Its frames rules governing the conduct of inter-bank foreign exchange business among banks and liaison with RBI for reforms and development of forex market.

ccilindia.com

This site belongs to Clearing Corporation of India for providing exclusive clearing and settlement for transactions in money, government securities and foreign exchange.

largedividends.com

This website gives out comparison of mutual funds in 21 classification averages. It also gives analysis of mutual funds on year-to-date return (income & capital gains distribution, etc.

personalfinance201.com

This is a website for giving personal information on budgeting, financial planning, stocks, mutual funds and other investment matters.

moneycontrol.com

It is the official site for CNBC TV18, and provides personal finance information and news on indian capital markets, stocks, shares, mutual funds, insurance, debt, loans, credit cards, etc.

crnindia.com

This is your complete online guide for stock market exploration. Get round-the-clock updates of stock market trading. Find useful stock market tips to let your investment or business set on the right track. Register with them for free to access more integrated services.

sharetipsinfo.com

Get to know the subtle aspects of share trading that makes you a decision taker. Find NSE stock tips, market tips, Indian stock market news, share tutorials, dos and don'ts of stock market investments, etc.

capitalmarket.com

Explore the Indian capital market online. Find the stock alerts, market watch, share bulletins, corporate news, sector trends, company profiles, mutual fund and insurance news, union budget news and a world of other stock market news.

stratstar.com

This website is going to guide you through stock market recommendations for trading and short-run investment on the Bombay Stock Exchange.

indiainfoline.com

This site has a colossal base of information on stock market and related areas of business. Spot the SENSEX graph and take determinative decisions as to what you should do with your equity and derivatives. Access the India Business Directory to search for city-specific business leads and opportunities.

Books

Read. Read. And read some more. I know this book is superb, but you should be reading others too.

There are many books out there and I've read a whole load of them. I've never regretted buying a single one because, generally, there's always a gem or two of decent information and points to think about.

So here are a few I very strongly recommend. They are in no particular order. They are all excellent reads for stock market beginners and old hands alike.

The Disciplined Trader by Mark Douglas

An excellent look at good trading practices, including a look at why what's in your mind can affect your trading. There are also some tips on how to become a profit-making trader.

The Stock Market Almanac by Stephen Eckett

This is a kind of financial diary published once a year stuffed full of interesting facts and stats about the market. It includes likely dates of company reports, historical trends and market anomalies. I use mine pretty much every day as it's my diary!

The Financial Spread Betting Handbook by Malcolm Pryor

Just out as I write. I'm very impressed with this one – it has all the things you need to know about spread betting and goes into much greater depth than I can in this book. A must read if you want to get into spread betting.

High Probability Trading by Marcel Link

This book tries to teach all those who want to trade the mindset of a successful trader. What you should think about before you reach for the buy button. No complex material, just good common sense.

Investor's Guide to Selecting Shares that Perform by Richard Koch

This book uncovers ten ways to beat the market, and there are some very good ideas here. A good broad discussion of methods you can use to try and outperform the indices. I learned a number of excellent tips and I agree with pretty much everything Richard says.

Come Into My Trading Room by Dr Alexander Elder

This one is the book I've read and re-read the most. Entering Dr Elder's trading room is a very interesting experience. His years of profitable trading show through the pages and many of his warnings regarding some of the pitfalls of trading are excellent. I think this one is an especially good read if you have never traded before. There is also plenty of market psychology discussed, one of my favourite topics. And talking of psychology...

Investment Madness by John R Nofsinger

Subtitled: 'How psychology affects your investing and what to do about it.' This is one of the must reads! It is highly amusing but also very sharp. You may recognize your own character traits in the book – and once you recognize them, you can learn how to stop your own character from ruining your trades. Topics include the problems of overconfidence, social aspects of investing, the 'double or nothing' mentality, seeking pride and avoiding regret.

The Investor's Guide to Charting by Alistair Blair

For those of you who decide charting is the way to work out which shares to sell and buy, this is the easiest read. Alistair explains the art of a chart and what it's all about. Find out what all the chart jargon means, like 'double tops', and whether charting is suitable for you. And what's really good is he discusses how much of chart theory and practice should be taken with a pinch of salt.

The Investor's Toolbox, 2nd edition by Peter Temple

Everything you need to know about spread betting, CFDs, covered warrants, options – all the funnies – to help boost your returns. The book goes through all the tools you need for successful investing. If there's any question on basic derivatives you need to know the answer to, it'll be here.

The Harriman Book of Investing Rules

Collected wisdom from the world's top 150 investors. Tons of unmissable rules from the greatest traders ever. Read and learn! It's one of those books you can keep in the bathroom because you can pick it up anytime and have a great read. A brilliant book of wisdom to keep dipping into.

The Investor's Guide To Understanding Accounts by Robert Leach

This may sound like a really boring one, but Robert has turned what could be a very unexciting subject into an interesting one. Ever wondered how to look at a set of accounts and know whether it's all good or there is trouble ahead? Are they cooking the books? There's also an excellent ten point summary which will point you in the right direction.

> You can order any of these through my website, www.nakedtrader.co.uk. Delivery is usually very fast and often next day. Click on "Books".

I keep my website updated with reviews of the latest books as they are published, so do check in for those.

Quiz – What sort of investor are you?

Here's a fun quiz to test your skills as a potential investor. Answer all the questions honestly. Do not cheat and look up the answers.

Pick only one answer for each question. Note down the question number and which letter you picked. If you did badly on the quiz in the first book I hope you do better now!

Questions

1 You are new to trading and someone offers you Direct Market Access. Do you:

a- Say "That sounds cool, when can I have it?"

b- Tell them you'll think about it

c- Say "Call me back in about a year"

d- Ask for more information and a fact sheet

e- Say "I've got broadband thanks and don't want to switch so sod off"

2 Someone on a bulletin board says a share is about to double and it's time to get in quick. Do you:

a- Wait for it to move up then buy

b- Get in quick before it goes up

c- Ignore the post and move on

d- Short it

e- Research it properly then decide

3

You've been to a free seminar and now they want you to pay £3,000 for a weekend one. Do you:

a- Say thanks, but it's way too much

b- Write out the cheque immediately

c- Negotiate the price down

d- Use the £3,000 to buy an investment instead

e- Ask around to see if anyone else did the seminar and was it worthwhile for the money

4

You're new to trading. Do you:

a- Buy a "guaranteed winning system" and use it

b- Learn about the craft slowly and surely

c- Buy loads of different shares – spread the risk

d- Get stuck into spread betting using leverage

e- Buy into tips from the papers

5

When researching a share is it best to look at it from the point of view of:

a- Gordon Ramsay

b- Posh Spice

c- Mr Spock

d- Jade Goody

e- Sir Alan Sugar

6 What's the best clue a share is about to rise:

a- Good volume is coming in

b- It issued a profits warning

c- Tipped by a magazine

d- It came out with a great report

e- A director bought some shares

7 What's the best time of the year to buy shares:

a- Just before Christmas

b- Just before Easter

c- On your birthday

d- In May

e- On St Ledgers Day

8 You decide you want to short a share. What are you looking for in making the decision to short a particular company?

a- It's gone up a lot and it's time it came back a bit

b- It's a one product company

c- A profits warning

d- High debt

e- The word "challenging" in its last report

9 You want to buy a share but the spread is 7%. Do you:

a- Phone your broker and try and deal inside the spread

b- Buy it anyway

c- Wait for the spread to narrow later in the day

d- Check it's history if the spread is usually narrower

e- Forget it and move on

10 The price of your favourite share is sinking rapidly one morning. Do you:

a- Hide behind the sofa

b- Wait and see if it's a tree shake

c- Only sell if it hits your stop

d- Have a cup of tea and toast

e- Get out pronto

11 You've read *The Naked Trader 2*. Do you think the writer is:

a- An absolute genius and should be knighted

b- The best financial writer in the world

c- Too good-looking to write books on money

d- A smug git

e- A complete bullshitter

Now look at the answers and add up the numbers.

Scores

1. a-5 b-2 c-1 d-1 e-2
2. a-4 b-5 c-1 d-2 e-1
3. a-1 b-5 c-3 d-1 e-2
4. a-5 b-1 c-2 d-5 e-3
5. a-2 b-4 c-1 d-5 e-1
6. a-1 b-5 c-3 d-1 e-3
7. a-1 b-1 c-5 d-4 e-2
8. a-4 b-2 c-1 d-1 e-1
9. a-2 b-4 c-2 d-2 e-1
10. a-4 b-1 c-1 d-2 e-3

(Anyone answering d or e to question 11 is disqualified from the quiz.)

Add up all your scores for your final total.

Analysis

- **18 or below:** Master investor!
  You have every chance of success in the stock market. Your approach to shares looks to be solid and I have every confidence that you will soon be in profit.
- **19–25:** Good potential
  You have the makings of a good investor, but you must be careful not to blow it by taking too many risks. Take it easy.
- **26–35:** A lot of work to do
  You are too liable to take major risks and you're likely to make losses unless you temper your gambling instincts.
- **36–50:** Oh dear!
  Did you really read the book? You need to get right back to basics before you lose all your money!

Three little letters addendum

And finally if you just skimmed the book but don't have the concentration span to read it all (I understand, it's OK) just remember these three letters:

DBC

Don't Buy Crap!

Ta ta!